What Readers and Clients Are Saying About Danielle Brooks and GOOD DECISIONS... *most of the time:*

"*Good Decisions...Most of the Time* has a fresh approach to nutrition education. I liked being able to skim it for 'nutrition nuggets.' The recipes were helpful to get one started in eating a new way. The rationale for what food type or micronutrient being discussed was clear. This book should be helpful to health providers and patients alike."

— Janine Cooley, MD

"Like many women approaching forty, I found myself at a weight I wasn't happy with, and rather than try all the fad diets I had tried before, I reached out to Dani in 2009 and asked for help to manage my weight. But I didn't realize that the help and tools she gave me were about much more than my weight, losing weight is a benefit from eating healthy. Yes, I lost weight by following the guidelines. But more importantly, she helped me discover how important the food is that we put in our bodies and how they make us feel. To this day, both my husband and I have changed our eating habits, not for weight control but to make us feel better and hopefully live longer. Here are some of the other rewards from following Dani: energy all day (no crashes), glowing skin, healthy hair, weight loss, regularity, etc…

"Like all people, we try to make 'good decisions...most of the time,' but when we stagger too far off course, both my husband and I will gravitate right back to our 'Dani Diet' (as we called it), because we feel so good when we do. But even during those times of indulgence, we still implement changes from 2009 that will forever be a part of our eating plan. I am thrilled to dive into the book, knowing it will be filled with tips, advice, and encouragement—surely a life-changing read."

— Wendy Miller, Client

"Danielle Brooks disperses nutritional wisdom quietly and delicately. The results are powerful, long-lasting, and delicious."

— Dr. Patti Mullen, ND, LMP, Owner Panacea Natural Medicine

"Chock-full of healthy eating options for life, *Good Decisions* helps you navigate the jungle of nutritional advice, and provides sound, practical guidance and insight to make certain you choose your foods wisely."

— Susan Friedmann, CSP, international best-selling author of
Riches in Niches: How to Make it BIG in a small Market

"*Good Decisions...Most of the Time* is like an encyclopedia dedicated to healthy-eating. I encourage you to read it all the way through, but you can also use it to find info on whatever you want, whether it's how to reduce the gas effect of vegetables or which grains to eat. And best of all, it offers practical, doable advice, and author Danielle Brooks understands we're going to eat that piece of chocolate some of the time."

—Tyler R. Tichelaar, Ph.D., and award-winning author of
Narrow Lives* and *The Best Place

GOOD DECISIONS

...most of the time

Because life is too short not to eat chocolate

How to increase energy, improve mental clarity, slow aging,
boost sex drive, and lose weight in the process!

Danielle Brooks
Nutritional Therapist

Good Decisions ... most of the time

By Danielle Brooks ©2014

Editors: Jeannine Mallory and Linda Lane
Proofreader: Tyler Tichelaar
Book Indexing: Clive Pyne
Cover Design: Bonnie Wharton and Fusion Creative Works
Interior Design: Fusion Creative Works, fusioncw.com
Photography: Sarah Flotard
Food Styling: Malina Lopez and Sarah Flotard

Paperback ISBN: 978-1-938686-61-0
Hard Cover ISBN: 978-1-938686-63-4
eBook ISBN: 978-1-938686-62-7
Library of Congress Control Number: 2014912850

Published by:
Aviva Publishing
Lake Placid, NY
518-523-1320
www.avivapubs.com

Printed in the United States of America

To Todd Tzeng

It is your constant support, encouragement, and belief that anything can be achieved that made this book possible.

Acknowledgments & Gratitude

Many people helped me clarify the intention of this book and contributed toward its purpose.

I am grateful to all of my clients over the years; I have learned so much from you and am honored to be trusted with your nutritional needs.

I wish to thank the following teachers and mentors who inspired and compelled me to continue to learn and grow: Wayne Rasmussen, Rodney Bragg, Lonnie Sellers, Ken Roll, Doug Rank, and Dr. Bob Adams for their faith and trust in me when I needed it most. Gray Graham, for his enthusiastic teachings that inspired me to learn more. I am especially grateful to Mark Yamada, Ph.D., whose help and guidance were invaluable in my understanding the psychology of food and the psychology of me; without you, I would never have come to know myself.

My sincerest thank you to my editing team, Jeannine Mallory and Linda Lane, both of whom were very patient editors and guides in writing this book.

And many thanks to Patrick Snow, whose guidance and resources made writing and publishing this book a smooth process.

I would also like to thank Andrew Allshouse, N.D., for bringing clarity to the subject matter and for his guidance through several chapters.

Many thanks to Kim Swanson and everyone at the office for holding down the fort so I could have the time and freedom to write.

I'd also like to acknowledge Stacy King, Kris Curnutt, Tina Neil, and many others who have supported and encouraged me along the way.

Lastly, thank you to food stylist Malina Lopez and photographer Sarah Flotard for their help in making my healthy recipes look as delicious as they taste.

Disclaimer

Contents

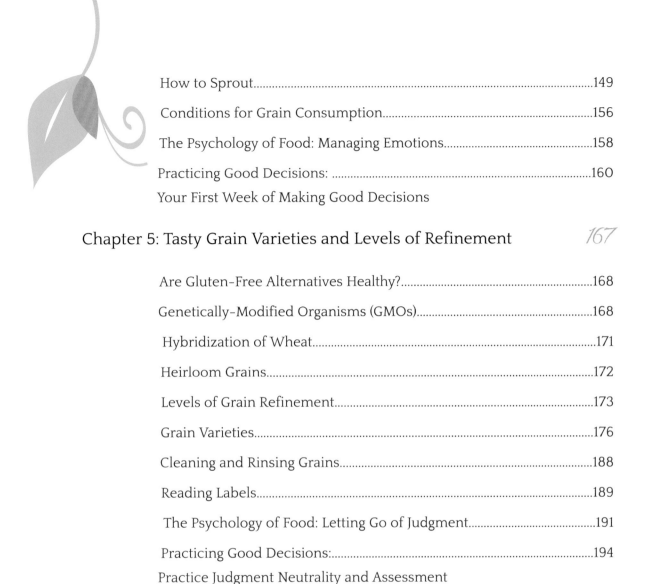

Chapter 7: Healthy Proteins for All Lifestyles   *225*

Chapter 8: Fats and Oils

Chapter 9: Cooking With Fats and Oils

Preface

When I became a nutritional therapist I was so excited to begin helping people that I could hardly restrain myself and practiced on anyone who would let me. I would sit down with my clients and customize the perfect diet just for them. We would talk about how we would improve digestion, regulate blood sugar levels, and eliminate food allergies, and how all of this would contribute toward weight loss. Then, filled with hope and excitement, my clients would leave my office revitalized and well-equipped to take on the world and embark on a healthy new lifestyle.

Then, two weeks later, they would return to my office frustrated and upset because they just couldn't do it. This was when I realized I was trained on how to create a diet, not how to help people *implement* the diet. I continued to do my best as my client's personal cheerleader, but of the many people who walked through my doors, only a small percentage were able to implement the diet and succeed at reaching their goals.

It wasn't until I was seeing a counselor for personal reasons that I stumbled onto "The Psychology of Food" and discovered the mental aspects of weight loss and behaviors around food. I learned how, by using truth and knowledge vs. emotion and other methodologies and tools, I could help my clients overcome the mental hurdles and reach their goals. Now, when I customize diets for my clients, I also give them the tools and information needed to *implement* those diets. This practice has given my clients immediate results and a "can do" spirit that has been amazing to watch.

I also began to see patterns in the diets I customized, and I discovered that many people have similar issues. I am constantly working on improving digestion and regulating blood sugar levels. I am also constantly removing the same foods from people's diets that are problematic. When I was putting together the templates for these protocols, I realized that so many people could benefit from this material. I could share what I had learned with not just one person, but with many people if I wrote a book.

This book you now hold in your hands was born from my desire to give this information and knowledge to the masses. Instead of being a cheerleader to one, I can be a cheerleader to many. Today, I believe that anyone can lose weight and reach personal goals simply by making a few simple changes in how he or she thinks about him- or herself and food.

While this book is primarily about nutrition, which foods are healthy, and which foods are best avoided, with recipes and nutritional nuggets dispersed throughout, what really sets it apart is that each chapter ends with the psychology of food and homework assignments that give the reader the psychological tools needed to overcome mental hurdles involved with any dietary changes.

By following the principles in this book, you can achieve weight loss, increased energy, mental clarity, hormonal balance, and even younger-looking skin. These results are just what happens when you bring the body back into balance and restore the foundations of nutrition by making *Good Decisions...Most of the Time*.

Author's Note

Millions of Americans are obese and in a state of ill health. Fast food and TV have become our new pastimes. As a result we are not only obese but extremely unhappy and unmotivated as well. The way we are eating now is not working; therefore, we must make a move away from processed and fast foods toward wholesome fruits, vegetables, nuts, seeds, and quality proteins so our bodies can function optimally, our minds can focus clearly, and our spirits can shine.

I have found that people have the most success with my book when they use the recipes and resources at www.gooddecisions.com. Here you will find the most recent nutritional information and tools that will make you feel great about your body, your weight, and your health. It is a supportive community of like-minded people on the same journey.

Just to say thanks for buying my book, I'd like to give you as a bonus "10 Muffin Top Melting Drink Recipes" designed to reduce that annoying muffin top doctors lovingly call the liver roll. These recipes are designed to aid digestion and decongest the liver, resulting in a flatter tummy and a happy liver. Download *10 Muffin Top Melting Drink Recipes* at www.gooddecisions.com/muffin_top

Introduction

When I see clients, I don't give them medications, and I typically don't recommend many supplements. I find that when I work with my clients to clean up their diets, improve digestion, address their sugar addictions and food sensitivities, their bodies begin to improve and heal on their own. Congested livers become happy livers; hormones come back into balance; and stressed-out adrenals have a chance to recover, which leaves clients feeling more energetic, alive, and at peace. When we address nutritional foundations, everything else just falls into place. *Good Decisions...Most of the Time* is based on these foundations. If you follow the suggestions in this book, you too have the opportunity to eliminate food allergies, experience balanced blood sugar levels, improve digestion, and as a result, any toxicity in the body will begin to decrease. This decrease in toxicity brings an amazing increase in energy and mental clarity that you may have never thought possible.

Your Hallway of Life

Unfortunately, our current health care system thrives on the basic premise of treating the symptoms, and not preventing the illness. During my nutritional training program, Gray Graham, founder of the Nutritional Therapy Association and author of *Pottenger's Prophecy: How Food Resets Genes for Wellness or Illness*, taught us about "the hallway of life." Think of your life as a hallway, along which you travel throughout your life. When you're born, your hallway is that of perfect health. As you age and consume additives, preservatives, sugar, coffee, cigarettes, alcohol, hydrogenated fats, and a myriad of other unhealthy things, you begin walking down the hallway toward poor health. When you eat this way, you're heading toward the end of the hallway, which marks an early death. If you feel sick because of what you've done to your body, you may visit your family physician, who will run some tests and most likely tell you that you're fine. You are not sick—yet. Your physician may make some recommendations that you may or may not follow. A year or so may go by, and you may visit your physician again. This time, you may test positive for "something," and you may end up on some kind of medication that masks your symptoms but does not cure the underlying problem.

You may continue on your journey down the hallway of life toward an early death. However, at some point, you may contemplate what you're doing. You may find yourself in the middle of that hallway, and then realize that you can turn around. Yes, you can turn around and walk toward improved health and wellbeing. All you have to do is leave behind the multitude of unhealthy foods and walk the other way.

Along this hallway, you'll find different levels of health and illness. You choose how far to walk in one direction or another; it's up to you. You have a choice: you can turn around and walk toward better health by drinking water instead of soda, by eating vegetables instead of pastries, and by snacking on nuts and seeds instead of candy. Or, you can continue eating unhealthy foods and walk toward illness.

Whether you're a vegetarian or omnivore, it's important to ensure that what you eat gives you the nutrients your body needs not just to function, but to thrive. I've worked with vegetarians who lived on potato chips and pasta and were exhausted all the time. I've also worked with omnivores whose diets consisted mostly of cheeseburgers, fast food, and fish sticks. Both thought their diets were moderately healthy and did not connect their physical symptoms with their nutrition (or lack thereof). Whether you are a vegetarian or a meat-eater, *Good Decisions* will enable you to look at your own diet and determine whether it's healthy or not. It will teach you the basics of how to prepare certain foods, and you will be able to differentiate clearly between healthy foods and foods that are best avoided.

Now, life is too short to skip the occasional bacon cheeseburger with French fries and an ice-cold beer…and life is definitely too short not to eat chocolate. That's why I titled this book ***Good Decisions…Most of the Time.*** When you make *Good Decisions…Most of the Time*, your body will be better able to deal with the occasional sweet treat or processed food. These indulgences won't influence your health as adversely when you don't consume them on a regular basis. In fact, the more *Good Decisions* you make, the more your cravings for unhealthy items fade.

This book will teach you all you need to know about food: Which grains are most nutritious, and how are they best prepared? Which proteins are ideal for your lifestyle and you? What is a good fat and what is an unhealthy fat? Which foods will support your sex drive? Which foods can you eat to relieve constipation? Which foods will help you look and feel younger? Which foods will give you more energy? I'll answer these questions and more. As you read *Good Decisions*, please keep in mind what works for one person may not work for another. Everyone is different, with different metabolisms, food sensitivities, ethnicities, and beliefs. We are all biochemically unique and need different things. For example, one person may not be digesting her food or absorbing her nutrients while another may have huge blood sugar fluctuations and be riding the highs and lows of sugar addiction. Some may have toxicity symptoms; others may have hormonal imbalances; still others may have food allergies.

There is no special diet or one way to eat for everyone, but there is an abundant choice of wholesome natural foods for all of us to choose from, and cook, as we desire.

This is not a diet, which is only temporary. It's a way of life. You don't have to count calories or limit your portion sizes. The primary components of the *Good Decisions* way of life teaches you to eat healthy food, learn to be in tune with your body, and honor it by eating only until you're full. The *Good Decisions* way of life is not about limiting intakes, but rather excluding unhealthy foods and incorporating nutrient-dense whole food.

While the title of this book is **Good Decisions...Most of the Time,** the word "good" is best used synonymously with "healthy." *Good Decisions* doesn't demonize any food, but simply clarifies which whole foods are nutrient-dense and increase health and wellbeing, and which foods lack nutrients or have been shown to contribute to disease.

As you read, you'll notice that I repeat myself. I do this deliberately because I've found that many people find it easier to learn when key points are mentioned more than once. It helps to ensure the important information sinks in.

Throughout this book, you will come across several **Nutritional Nuggets.** These are fun, informative facts about foods you may find helpful and enjoyable.

You'll also find many recipes to illustrate how healthy food can be delicious without using sugar or processed foods.

Each chapter ends with a section covering **The Psychology of Food**. This section may help you understand how certain behaviors and thought patterns can deter you from reaching your goals.

I also include *homework* that may help you to self-govern more effectively.

I hope you'll become excited and empowered by what I share and feel inspired to implement these changes in your own life. Allow this book, and others, to empower you to make informed decisions and motivate you to stop, glance about yourself, and ask, "Where am I in my hallway of life? Which way do I want to walk?"

Chapter One

Simple Carbohydrates and the No Sugar Challenge

In this chapter, you will learn how certain simple carbohydrates contribute to weight gain, hormonal imbalances, fatigue, mental stupor, and more. You will learn the basics of simple carbohydrates, what makes them healthy or unhealthy, and information you can refer to throughout life to guide you when making decisions about simple carbohydrates. We will delve into the first nutritional foundation, discuss why sugar is considered to be an "addictive" substance, and provide steps you can take to move away from sugar's sweet temptation. I'll touch on social and emotional issues that may come up as you begin the journey toward increased health and wellbeing, and define what "Good Decisions…Most of the Time" really means.

Our Love/Hate Relationship with Carbohydrates

With the popularity of Atkins and other low-carbohydrate diets, many of us are afraid to eat carbohydrates. Those who aren't afraid of carbohydrates are often addicted to them, and they spend much of their time riding the ups and downs of the carbohydrate roller coaster.

"Just one more pastry" or "I'll start tomorrow" are two of many justifications we use to stay on the roller coaster. And that's just what it feels like—one big ride. Instinctively, we know these foods are unhealthy for us, and even though we know they may contribute to weight gain, more cravings, and mood fluctuations, we consume them anyway. We all know someone who turns into a raging monster because she hasn't eaten in several hours. (I've heard other, not-so-nice adjectives.) Well, that raging monster may be the result of unbalanced blood sugar levels and a dependency on carbohydrates that affects mood and mental clarity.

That overweight version of you looking back at you in the mirror may be the result of a serious carbohydrate dependency. "How can this be?" you ask. You don't eat sugar, soft drinks, or candy, and only indulge your sweet tooth occasionally. What many people don't realize is that certain complex carbohydrates (such as whole grain bread, rolls, crackers, and pasta) break down rapidly in the body and are converted to glucose, which is also known as blood glucose or blood sugar. We use some of this blood sugar for energy, but most of it ends up in the blood en route for storage somewhere in the body—as fat.

Nutritional therapists earn a living trying to steer people away from carbohydrates such as grains that have been refined into flour or corn that has been refined and processed into high fructose corn syrup. Refined carbohydrates such as soft drinks, candy, crackers, cookies, and pastries are other culprits made with sugar that affect us adversely and lead to obesity. It's easy to point the finger at these refined carbohydrates. We know these are obvious culprits, but hidden or added sugars found in refined products such as bread, rolls, pasta, and even yogurt can be deceiving and equally difficult to remove from your diet. These tasty, mind-numbing, "take-your-mind-off-your-breakup" foods are just as wildly addicting as pastries or soft drinks. Once consumed, these refined flour products break down just as quickly as sugar; they go directly into your bloodstream, which prompts your pancreas to release insulin. High insulin levels then drive these sugars to your liver and other areas of your body, where they are stored as fat. These foods often offer you very little beyond the short-term comfort you need when you want to soothe yourself.

Even whole-grain breads, cereals, pasta, and some well-known health foods can turn out to be anything but healthy. Just read the long lists of ingredients or find out how they're processed and prepared to get a better understanding of how unhealthy they can be. These so-called "healthy" foods can actually rob your body of nutrients and, while they elevate your blood sugar levels and may give you some temporary energy, they will always let you down in the end, leaving you tired and fatigued.

Diabetes, a disease once found only in adults, no longer discriminates; the number of children with diabetes is on the rise. Have you ever tried to take your kids off sugar by removing or reducing their high-sugar breakfast cereals, only to give in because their resulting behavior is worse than giving in and allowing them their treat? Or have you noticed your own behavior when you've tried to remove sweets such as ice cream, bread, or even sweetened coffee from your diet—only to fall off the wagon because of mood swings, mental fog, and headaches? The sensation you get when sugar hits your tongue is similar to falling in love, and you ask yourself, "How could this be bad?"

In one study, researchers placed sugar water and cocaine water in the cages of rats. While it may seem unbelievable, the rats went to the sugar water every time—they preferred it to the cocaine water. That's how addictive sugar is. Learning the difference between healthy carbohydrates and unhealthy carbohydrates will make a big difference when it comes to regaining health, losing weight, regulating blood sugar levels, balancing mood fluctuations, improving mental clarity, and gaining more energy. Getting off the unhealthy carbohydrates is the first step toward increased health and wellbeing, and it is the first goal of *Good Decisions…Most of the Time*.

Here's the good news: now that you know these foods are addicting, you know weight loss has nothing to do with willpower! That's right; when your blood sugar levels drop and you can barely think, your body is telling you, "You need food now!" When blood sugar levels drop, your brain doesn't have the fuel (food) it needs to think clearly. This is dangerous. Shakiness, irritability, and impaired mental function can lead to loss of consciousness, seizures, and even brain damage if the body isn't given something quickly to raise blood sugar levels. If you don't have anything healthy on hand, that donut in the breakroom you would never reach for suddenly becomes your savior.

Slowly removing high sugar items, and incorporating more quality protein, fat, and vegetables that release glucose slowly, will balance blood sugar levels and get you off the roller coaster within a couple of weeks. This change will give you energy that does not fluctuate, increase your mental clarity, and help you lose weight—a delightful side effect! So, let's put aside the controversy over the high-carb vs. low-carb diets, and focus instead on which carbohydrates to avoid and which carbohydrates will balance your blood sugar levels, regulate digestion, and give you the nutrients you need—not just to make it through your day, but to thrive your way through your day.

What Are Carbohydrates?

Carbohydrates come from plant-based foods such as vegetables, fruits, legumes, and grains. While primarily considered a source of energy, some carbohydrates, such as vegetables and legumes, are much more than that. Yes, they supply energy, but they also deliver fiber, vitamins, minerals, antioxidants, and a long list of nutrients vital for optimal health. Antioxidants play a crucial role in the prevention of cell damage and protect tissues from harmful chemicals, additives, and preservatives often found in processed foods. For the rest of this chapter and the next, we will focus on simple carbohydrates: which ones to avoid and which ones pack the biggest nutritional punch. Let's start with the basics.

Molecularly, a carbohydrate is an organic compound that consists of carbon, hydrogen, and oxygen. Carbohydrates (also called saccharides) are divided into four chemical groups:

1. Monosaccharides

2. Disaccharides

3. Oligosaccharides

4. Polysaccharides

In general, monosaccharides and disaccharides are referred to as "simple" carbohydrates. Because of their small size, they break down quickly in the body and can raise blood sugar levels rapidly. Some simple carbohydrates, such as fruits and some dairy, contribute significantly to health, while others, such as refined white (table) sugar, do not. All simple carbohydrates, however, tend to elevate blood sugar levels rapidly, and can contribute to weight gain, decreased energy, hormonal imbalances, and that mental fog many of us complain about. This is very important to understand because turbulent blood sugar makes a lot of work for the body. It burns up a lot of hormones and occupies the pancreas and liver for some time after consumption, which distracts these organs from other important functions.

Here are some examples of simple carbohydrates:

- White table sugar
- High fructose corn syrup
- Agave nectar
- Honey
- Maple syrup
- All fruits
- Certain dairy products

What Makes a Carbohydrate Healthy or Unhealthy?

The nutrient content, or value, of carbohydrates is what makes them either healthy or unhealthy decisions. A nutrient is a substance, such as fiber, vitamins, and minerals, which humans need to live. The nutrients in carbohydrates build and repair tissues, regulate body processes, and are converted into energy. How these carbohydrates are refined and then prepared for a meal also plays a large role in nutrient content and whether or not they are good for us.

As a rule, the less refined or processed by man, the more vitamins, minerals, and nutrients the carbohydrate will typically provide you.

Nutrient-dense food has a high value of vitamins, minerals, fiber, antioxidants, and other nutrients that are essential to our bodies. Some carbohydrates, such as vegetables, fruits, and legumes, are nutritional powerhouses and are extremely nutrient-dense, which makes consuming them *very Good Decisions*. Others, such as white bread, pasta, sugar, soft drinks, and Twinkies® have had most nutrients processed out of them; they're nothing more than "diabetes in a box" or "osteoporosis in a can." I will often refer to those foods as "empty," which means they contain little or no nutrient value.

Understanding the difference between healthy and unhealthy carbohydrates will give you the edge when it comes to weight loss, hormonal balance, sports performance, digestive wellness, and more. When you know why a food is healthy or not, you'll have a deeper understanding—a deeper "knowing," so to speak—that will motivate you and give you the power you need to avoid certain foods and incorporate others. The emotional drive to eat certain foods can be overcome when you pull yourself out of the feeling and use your intellect instead. This will help you replace old habits that no longer serve you with new habits that bring increased health and wellbeing. When someone knows how certain foods can impact her body adversely, she is more likely to avoid them.

Making Good Simple Carbohydrate Decisions

Let's place the simple carbohydrates into categories. This process will make it easy for us to choose between healthy simple carbohydrates and simple carbohydrates that have been shown to be unhealthy or problematic. Of the simple carbohydrates, we have two groups to choose from: unrefined and refined.

Refined Simple Carbohydrates

Refined carbohydrates provide calories but lack many vitamins, minerals, and fiber—nutrients our bodies need—which were stripped away during refining and processing. Often, unhealthy chemicals are used to create a more bleached (pure-looking) product. These foods contain "empty" calories and often contain harmful substances. Refined simple carbohydrates are best avoided most of the time. These include white table sugar, agave nectar, high fructose corn syrup, brown sugar, and a host of other sweet products that line our grocery shelves.

Unrefined Simple Carbohydrates

Unrefined simple carbohydrates are healthier choices because they have not been refined or processed, which leaves many of their nutrients intact. Be aware, however, that even though they have not been refined and have many health-giving properties, these substances still break down quickly into glucose and can cause elevated blood sugar levels. Sugar in any form, if over-consumed, can create optimal conditions for disease and can cause problems in the body. However, for those occasions (not most of the time) when you need to sweeten something, it is always best to reach for a sweetener that has some healthful qualities and adds flavor as well.

Healthy Simple Carbohydrates (Use Occasionally) Unrefined Simple Carbohydrates	Unhealthy Simple Carbohydrates (Avoid) Refined Simple Carbohydrates
Organic Fruit	White Table Sugar
Dried Dates or Unrefined Date Sugar	Any Artificial Sweeteners
Raw or Organic Dairy Products*	Conventional Dairy Products
Raw Unfiltered Honey	Fruit Juice
Grade B Maple Syrup	Corn Syrup
Organic, Unrefined Coconut Sugar	Agave Nectar
Sucanat	Candy, Soft Drinks
Organic, Unrefined Whole Cane Sugar	Brown Sugar

*Due to a risk of infection, neither the FDA nor the CDC recommends consumption of raw milk.

The Downfalls of Simple Carbohydrates and Sugar

It is very important to understand just how adversely sugar and other refined simple carbohydrates can impact the body when they are over-consumed. Let's look at how simple carbohydrates impact the body in greater depth.

Sugar and Mental Health

Sugar and the insulin response affect the brain directly. When sweets are consumed regularly, insulin crosses the brain-blood barrier, where it regulates how your brain uses and stores sugar for energy needed to fuel thoughts and emotions. Consuming large amounts of sugar, especially in the form of fructose corn syrup, can interfere with insulin's ability to regulate neurological processes that control memory and learning. In short, a high fructose or sugar diet sabotages learning and memory.[1]

Nutritional Nugget

Want to lower your blood sugar levels naturally? Sulfur compounds found in onions and garlic decrease blood glucose levels and improve insulin secretion and sensitivity. These bulbous beauties are best consumed raw, or lightly cooked, and are delicious when added to salad dressings, vegetables, or marinades.

Simple Carbohydrates Stimulate Appetite and Lead to Obesity

Regardless of whether they are refined or unrefined, simple carbohydrates are converted to glucose quickly in the body, leading to blood sugar "ups" and the eventual letdowns. Most simple carbohydrates are found in processed foods, which contain few nutrients and tend to be less satisfying. They leave you wanting more, and can actually stimulate your appetite. Simple carbohydrates are fattening because they tend to be low in nutrients and high in sugar, so the body will store the sugar, but crave more nutrients.

Because simple carbohydrates, such as table sugar and even some complex carbohydrates such as bread and pasta, have very few nutrients, you will often find these products fortified with vitamins or minerals to compensate for the nutrients lost during the refining process. What's left is a very unbalanced product.

I've heard of these refined white products referred to as the "white devil," which seems very appropriate because they can alter your mood, lead to cravings, compulsive eating, sugar and/or carbohydrate dependency, and weight gain. According to the World Health Organization (WHO), sugars and other simple carbohydrates are a leading factor in the worldwide obesity epidemic.[2]

Candida and Simple Carbohydrates

When over-consumed, refined sugars, natural sweeteners such as honey and maple syrup, and the sugars found in fruits can also feed Candida infections. Candida is a yeast that normally lives in the digestive tract and vagina. Candida feeds on sugar, and in certain conditions, can grow unchecked and cause a wide range of health problems. Symptoms such as redness or itching in skin crevices, a foul odor, cottage cheese-like vaginal discharge, white coating on the tongue, and a decrease in mental function can all be attributed to Candida overgrowth. Removing sugar from the diet eliminates Candida's "food" and causes it to "die off." To help eliminate Candida, nutritional therapists may also ask their clients to remove fruits completely from their diet for a period of time. Then, when the sugar dependency has been conquered and the Candida gone, fruits may be added back to the diet in small amounts, over a period of time.

Sleep and Simple Carbohydrates

All simple carbohydrates are rapidly converted to glucose in your body. Most cells use glucose as their main fuel source. When our immediate glucose needs are met, our body signals for the release of insulin, a hormone released by the pancreas. By secreting insulin, your pancreas works to remove excess glucose (sugar) from your blood. Cortisol, a counter regulatory hormone that directs the insulin/cortisol "orchestra," also increases when too many simple carbohydrates are consumed.

This is a complicated process, but for our purposes, I've condensed it: sugar affects cortisol levels directly, causing cortisol spikes that are like little bursts of adrenaline, which are not conducive to sleeping. Removing simple carbohydrates reduces insulin and cortisol activity, easing the load off this system, making cortisol less active, and sleep much easier. This is important, as people who tend to sleep less tend to stay up later and consume more. Lack of sleep also raises blood sugar levels, can make insulin less effective, and may boost *ghrelin*, a hormone that stimulates appetite.

Sex Hormones and Simple Carbohydrates

Sex hormones are directly affected by the consumption of sugar. It turns out that "eating too much fructose and glucose can turn off the gene that regulates the levels of active testosterone and estrogen in the body."[3] I don't know about you, but as a woman, I like to keep my sex hormones as regulated as possible. It's hard enough keeping sex drive alive without the side effects of sugar on the body. Many simple carbohydrates can also make you feel bloated and gaseous, further reducing sex drive. No one feels sexy when he or she is bloated—no one!

Cardiovascular Disease and Simple Carbohydrates

Contrary to what most people think, elevated levels of triglycerides (a type of fat in your bloodstream and fat tissue) aren't always caused by consuming too much fat. Elevated triglyceride levels also result from consuming too many sweeteners or refined sugar and flour products, which end up in the body stored in the form of triglycerides.

When I have new clients with high cholesterol or elevated triglyceride levels, I strongly suggest they eliminate all simple carbohydrates and increase their vegetable and protein intake. Within two weeks, their numbers are most often back within normal levels. It is best to avoid all simple carbohydrates except fruit and certain dairy products most of the time.

Sugar Addiction

When sugar addiction comes up in a conversation, many people relate to and identify with it on a very personal level. We all know what it's like to crave something sweet, and at one time or another, we have all given into sweet cravings for that short-term sugar rush, only to be let down with fatigue shortly after. Many people laugh, joke, and connect with each other when talking about sugar's sweet addiction because we all know exactly what it feels like.

Symptoms of sugar addiction include irritability when meals are skipped or delayed, craving sugar at the same time every day, headaches, nausea, fatigue, anxiety, and moodiness when sugar is removed or cut back. If you consistently crave sweets and have trouble resisting desserts and sweet treats, it usually indicates an addiction is present.

How addicting is sugar? In 2010, *The Journal of Psychoactive Drugs* published a study that showed consumption of sugar releases euphoric endorphins in some people's brains in a manner very similar to drugs that are commonly abused. Other research shows that a high intake of carbohydrates, including sugar, releases another feel good chemical in the brain called serotonin. These are the chemicals responsible for that "rush" you feel after indulging in something sweet. In addition, a major pleasure center in the brain called the *dopamine center* is also "tickled" by sugar, further instilling a pleasurable connection to sugar that makes us want more.

Interestingly, sugar follows the same pathway in the brain as a habit-forming drug and brain imaging techniques show similarities between the brains of people who are obese and people who abuse drugs and alcohol.

This information does not bode well for overweight Americans addicted to sugar who have been told for the last thirty years that in order to lose weight, all we need to do is exercise and decrease our caloric intake. Calories in, calories out, is a mantra that has been repeated for decades. But 100 calories from vegetables function in the body completely differently than 100 calories from a sugary piece of cake. One has fiber, vitamins, and minerals that the body can use; the other is simply sugar, which triggers an enormous insulin surge that drives the sugar into storage as fat.

This calorie in, calorie out type of thinking has put an enormous psychological burden on the large percentage of Americans who are obese and restricting their calorie intake but getting nowhere when it comes to weight loss. This has left so many young obese children feeling helpless, and so many obese adults thinking there must be something wrong with them because they don't eat an enormous amount of calories but continue to gain weight. What makes it even more difficult is many people don't even know they are addicted to sugar; yet they consume it hidden in everything from ketchup and tomato sauce to canned soups.

In order to lose weight and regain health, the only foods that will pull America out of this sugar stupor are real foods such as vegetables, fruits, quality proteins, and fats. Real foods may not tickle your dopamine center like sugar or make you dependent on it, but they will regulate your blood sugar levels, increase mental clarity, and yes—promote weight loss.

If you have tried to quit sugar before but found the temptations too much to deny, you may be unknowingly stuck in the grips of addiction. The symptoms of drug addiction are the same for those addicted to sugar. For instance, sugar addicts experience cravings, an escalation of tolerance levels, and withdrawals that parallel those of "street" drugs. An escalation of tolerance levels means that users of sugar need more and more to feel the same effect. This escalation of tolerance levels is one of the symptoms of substance dependence.

The good news is that sugar cravings can be stopped within two weeks or so of avoiding sugar and sweets completely, but while "avoidance" may be the most commonly used method to treat addiction, it is not always easy or achievable, especially when you consider the vast number of food products that contain sugar.

My clients find that when food is off-limits, it takes on a strange power that makes the things they can't have more enticing. When ice cream is off-limits, it becomes so much more than just ice cream. When eaten, it can become a symbol of many things (defiance, rebellion, indifference, even freedom) and the brain can come up with many reasons why death is preferable over ice cream avoidance. This emotional or feelings part of us doesn't care for intellect or common sense; it just wants to end the discomfort of not having the ice cream and be soothed now by eating it!

So, cold turkey and complete avoidance may not always be the answer. For those of you who have tried cold turkey and it didn't work for you—it is helpful to know that just as our taste buds have been conditioned to crave sugar, they can be conditioned to crave it less and even find it distasteful. For instance, when the amount of ice cream and frequency eaten is decreased gradually over time, your taste buds will get used to less sweetness and your appetite for it will decrease. This means that it can be eaten more mindfully; the screaming emotions within us lessen and we are able to cope more from intellect versus emotion. This process demystifies ice cream and it loses its power as your appetite for it decreases.

When you repeatedly eat a food, your affinity toward it will increase. When you decrease the repetition at which you consume it, your appetite for it will decrease. It's like escalation of tolerance levels in reverse. You are essentially training your taste buds to prefer less sweetness. Notice I said "sweetness" and not "sugar." Artificial sweeteners can be sweeter than sugar and will only feed an addiction, as will unrefined sweets like honey and maple syrup.

To begin the process of eliminating sugar's hold on you, pay attention to the "sweet" things you eat daily. Then begin to decrease sweets in small increments. For instance, if you drink your morning coffee with three teaspoons of sugar, only use two and continue to enjoy it until your taste buds have adapted. You are training your palate to prefer less sweetness. Once you are used to this level of sweetness, decrease the amount of sugar again and just keep repeating the process until you have eliminated your craving for sweets altogether.

Some people prefer to go cold turkey. If you can do this, great, but not everyone is the same. We all need to go at our own pace and honor what feels right for us.

Don't Fool Yourself

Do you deny that you have an addiction but crave bread, pasta, or French fries? These highly refined starchy foods are complex carbs that the body breaks down into simple sugars. Eaten without better foods, starches can make blood sugar surge and crash just like sugar does. Chips, crackers, white rice, white flour, and potatoes also do this. So, if you eat these foods, shrink your portions over time and decrease the frequency at which they are eaten.

Scientific evidence against the unhealthy aspects of sugar usage has been building for decades. In low and middle income countries, overconsumption of refined carbohydrates, such as sugar, has been shown to cause an increase in several disease conditions in children.[4] Hypoglycemia, obesity, and dental disease, along with decreased ability of our children to perform simple learning tasks, have all been linked to sugar.

Sugar's connection to Attention Deficit Hyperactivity Disorder (ADHD) is perhaps the most well known connection between sugar and cognitive performance, yet ADHD's connection to sugar is often minimized. Because our eating habits are often passed down to our children, it is not uncommon to see entire families riding the sugar roller coaster together.

Sugar may be classified as a food, but many feel it should be classified as a drug,[5] and others feel it should be classified as a toxin. I agree with this perspective.

In the 1950s, British researcher John Yudkin published persuasive findings[6] that excessive use of sugar was associated with the following conditions:

- Increase in blood cholesterol
- Rise in triglycerides
- Increase of adhesiveness in blood platelets
- Increase in blood insulin
- Increase in blood corticosteroid
- Increase in gastric (stomach) acidity
- Shrinkage of the pancreas
- Enlargement of the liver and adrenal glands

Nutritional Nugget

Eating small amounts of protein throughout the day (every two hours) can help curb cravings for sweets. Proteins digest slowly, which keeps you feeling full for longer and stabilizes your blood sugar levels. This makes the mad rush for the cookie jar less probable.

Other studies connect sugar consumption with heart disease.[7] I could go on, but the big question here is: Why didn't sugar leave our shelves back in the '60s when these compelling studies came out?

Over the years, large food companies have become powerful enough and have had enough money and influence to push aside these studies and get their products to market. Despite the fact that sugar is not good for us, it lines our shelves anyway. When processed sugar came on the scene, the sugar industry realized huge profits. With something this tasty and addictive, how could they go wrong?

Sugar consumption has also been associated with hyperactivity, behavior problems, lack of concentration, and violent tendencies.[8] That's not surprising, considering how we feel when our blood sugar levels drop and we are forced to go without it.

Cancer, which feeds on sugar, is often found by measuring high levels of glucose metabolism in the body. Today, the entire food processing industry would lose a lot of money if sugar were acknowledged to be dangerous to health, a primary cause of heart disease and diabetes and, as researchers found at Princeton University, addicting.[9]

Sugar is extracted from naturally sweet foods such as sugar cane and beets, which contain nutrients such as B vitamins, magnesium, and chromium. These nutrients play a huge role in regulating your blood sugar levels. Unfortunately, when these foods are refined into sugar, all the nutrient rich substances are discarded. What's left does nothing more than elevate your blood sugar levels and create havoc in the body.

Recommended Amounts of Sugar

So, how much of the sweet stuff is too much? Current WHO guidelines suggest that we consume no more than 10 percent of our total daily calories from added sugar.[10] In 2009, the American Heart Association (AHA) recommended half that amount (5 percent).

To clarify, let's take the standard 2,000-calorie diet, which is based on calorie information found on food labels. Five percent of this 2,000-calorie diet is 100 calories, which is the equivalent of 25 grams of sugar. According to these recommendations, we should consume no more than 100 calories from sugar sources daily or no more than 25 grams. One can of Pepsi contains 41 grams of sugar! That's roughly 10 cubes of sugar—and more than 160 calories.

An average blueberry muffin contains 28 grams of sugar and 112 calories from sugar. As you can see, one sweet splurge is all it takes to throw you over your allotted amount.

Personally, I believe that even this recommendation (100 calories daily from sugar sources) is too much. It's just enough to keep us sugar-dependent and on the sugar roller coaster. Many people consume much more than this amount on a daily basis. We add sugar to our coffee and grab a muffin for the road. For lunch, we eat white bread and candy and chase it down with a soft drink. Then we have dinner, which consists of pasta, bread, and a glass of wine. Yes, wine and beer are simple carbohydrates too. Dinner is often followed with a sweet dessert. Is it any wonder diabetes is on the rise, and there are so many people addicted to sugar?

If the recommendations are to keep sugar intake low, why do so many people feel safe consuming it in large amounts?

Some people instinctively know that sugar is not good for them. Many passionate mothers swear that by removing sugar, they have reversed attention deficit hyperactivity disorder (ADHD) and improved behavior dramatically in their children. Studies continue to support this hypothesis,[11,12] yet other studies and even our doctors downplay the effects of sugar, negating what these mothers know instinctively. Research from the University of Alabama at Birmingham (UAB) provided the first evidence that Type 2 diabetes in children may be linked to their mothers' blood sugar during pregnancy.[13]

There is little doubt that refined simple carbohydrates are the culprits behind many conditions such as diabetes, hypoglycemia, and hormonal imbalances.[14,15]

I wonder what would happen to the sugar industry if, all of a sudden, sugar was declared "unhealthy" and "addictive"—which it most certainly is. Perhaps, like tobacco, one day sugar will have a label warning us of its health dangers.

Good Decisions recommends avoiding sugar.

Sugars You May See on Food Labels

The words sugar and saccharide come from the Greek word *sákkharon*, which means "sugar." The names of monosaccharides and disaccharides are easy to identify because they often end in the suffix *ose*, which also means sugar. The term "sugars" refers to all monosaccharides and disaccharides (simple carbohydrates) present in food.

While there is conflicting data on fruit fructose, in general, simple sugars are carbohydrates that break down quickly and are most likely to raise blood sugar levels. The impact of fruit and dairy on the body is not as dramatic because fruit and dairy contain fiber, fat, protein, and other nutrients that slow sugar's entrance into the bloodstream. While they do elevate blood sugar levels rapidly, they do not impact it as dramatically as refined and processed sugars.

Refined and processed foods typically contain simple sugars that have been refined and processed. They are the culprits most often responsible for diabetes, hypoglycemia, hyperglycemia, obesity, and hormonal imbalances. These processed sugars are separated from whole foods and, in their refined state, offer little to no nutritional value; they are among the foods to avoid, most of the time.

Glucose

Most carbohydrates we eat are converted into glucose during digestion. This is a natural process, and it is this form of glucose that gives our body the energy it needs. However, be aware of a manmade form of glucose, which is glucose syrup, a liquid form of glucose widely used in the manufacture of processed foods that is not as healthy as its natural counterpart.

Is glucose a *Good Decision*? No.

Dextrose

You'll find dextrose in many food ingredient lists. It is another word for sugar that has been extracted or isolated with solvents (refined) and transformed into other foods (processed).

Dextrose is not a *Good Decision*.

Fructose

Fructose, or fruit sugar, occurs naturally in fruits, some root vegetables, honey, and cane sugar. It is the sweetest of the sugars. It only becomes dangerous when it is refined and processed from fruits or vegetables or used to make sucrose (table sugar). It is also used to make high-fructose corn syrup, which most nutritional therapists, including myself, beg you to avoid because it can be so inflammatory and damaging to the body.

Refined and Processed Fructose is not a *Good Decision*.

Galactose

Galactose is found in dairy products, sugar beets, and seaweed. It is a component of lactose, a milk sugar you consume through dairy products. Your digestive tract breaks lactose down into galactose. Consuming dairy has many health benefits, but when these sugars are isolated and removed from the dairy product and used to create a new product, the new product lacks "synergy." This means it is not as healthy without the other components that made up the original food. You are no longer consuming fat-soluble vitamins, minerals, and immune-boosting fatty acids. Instead, you have another isolated (simple) sugar that will elevate your blood sugar levels quickly, leaving you vulnerable to health problems and weight gain.

Refined galactose is not a *Good Decision*.

Sucrose

Sucrose is a sugar found in the stems of sugar cane and the roots of sugar beets. Sucrose also occurs naturally in other plants, alongside fructose and glucose, particularly in fruits and some root vegetables. The proportions and combinations of these sugars determine the range of sweetness you experience when you eat these foods. Sucrose is also found in table sugar. When you eat anything that contains refined and processed sucrose, you will see the word "sucrose" listed among the ingredients. This means the sugar has been isolated from the cane or beet (refined), typically through the use of solvents, and then added to products to add sweetness (processed). Any food that contains refined sugar in the form of sucrose will keep you mentally reeling as your body goes through the ups and downs of sugar dependency. Obesity in the U.S. has risen dramatically in the last thirty years, primarily due to increased consumption of sugar found in processed foods.

Foods with refined sucrose are not *Good Decisions*.

Maltose

Maltose is a sugar formed during the germination of certain grains. One of the more popular grains with maltose is barley, the source of the malt used to make beer. Barley used in soups and stews is delicious, as is the occasional beer. But let's not fool ourselves, no matter how Irish I am, and no matter how much you love beer, maltose still breaks down quickly in our bodies to glucose and, when over-consumed, can cause many problems. Maltose is especially unhealthy for blood glucose control; malted milk balls (Whoppers) and malted milk shakes are the biggest offenders.

Maltose is not a *Good Decision*.

Are Dairy Products Good Decisions?

Dairy products are produced from milk and are also a source of simple carbohydrates. There are healthy dairy choices and unhealthy dairy choices. Let's learn the difference between the two.

Most milk products, organic and conventional, have the potential to create mucus and inflammation. Some people have a low tolerance for milk because they lack intestinal lactase, an enzyme that digests lactose (milk sugar). In addition, some people are allergic to a milk protein called casein, which is one of the more difficult proteins for the body to digest. If you are one of these people, dairy is an unhealthy decision for you because it may cause inflammation, diarrhea, headaches, and a whole host of other symptoms, which can lead to disease.

If you are uncertain how your body does with dairy, pay attention to your body when you consume it and ask yourself the following questions: Does your heart rate go up when you consume it? Does it make you feel gassy or bloated? Do you get pain or cramps in your lower belly? Does it cause diarrhea? Do you break out in a rash? Do you feel anxious after you have consumed it? Paying close attention to your body when you eat certain foods will give you much insight into how your body does with that food.

If you do well with dairy, you may use these healthful foods in small amounts, and they can be very *Good Decisions*.

Among nutritional therapists, there's some controversy over dairy consumption. Some say dairy is good, and some say to avoid it. The decision to include dairy in your diet is not black or white because there are many factors to consider. A primary consideration, of course, is whether you are sensitive or allergic to it.

Everyone is different—what may work for one person may not work for you. The appropriateness of dairy consumption depends on each individual. Some dairy products can be consumed in moderation if your body does well with them. Much depends on the type of milk, where it came from, how it was processed, and what has been added to it, in determining whether or not it will be problematic or mucus producing.[16,17] A visit to a naturopathic physician or other health care professional may help you rule out whether or not dairy may be appropriate for you.

The reason I say small amounts is because dairy can be a source of "hidden sugars." For instance, one small six-ounce container of yogurt can have up to 30 or more grams of simple carbohydrates. That's equivalent to 7.5 cubes of sugar! Many brands of yogurt contain artificial flavoring, coloring, and other synthetic ingredients. Read your food labels and, instead of looking at the nutrition facts, look at the ingredient list. Often you will find ingredients such as modified cornstarch, high fructose corn syrup, carrageenan, artificial colors, and so-called "natural flavors" that are anything but natural. If you see an unfamiliar ingredient on the list, or anything you can't identify, avoid the product altogether until you can do your research.

Nancy's or Stonyfield's plain yogurt brands are healthful yogurts. No sugar is added, and these yogurts contain six different strains of probiotic bacteria instead of just one. Some kefir and clabber brands offer ten or more strands of probiotic bacteria that live and grow in your intestinal system, which are very beneficial for your health. Probiotics are often used to prevent or treat intestinal disorders, stimulate your immune system, and produce antimicrobial substances.

Don't fall for the "low fat" dairy items touted over the last thirty or more years. They may be low in fat, but they are usually higher in sugar or contain artificial sugar, flavoring, and other ingredients to compensate for the flavorful fat that has been removed. You will learn in the chapter on fats that not all fats are the monsters they have been portrayed to be. Organic whole milk and plain yogurt can be used to create delicious, healthy dishes, and are full of protein, quality fat, and minerals that are good for bones and vibrant healthy skin.

Plain, whole-milk yogurt can be sweetened with fresh berries and other fruit. This yogurt is much better for you than already-sweetened, artificially-flavored, or non-fat varieties. While low-fat products tend to be higher in sugar, whole milk products tend to be higher in protein and quality fat, which provide more nutrients. An additional benefit of whole milk products is they are more satiating and taste much better. When you milk a cow, a thick layer of cream will form on the top of the milk. In this cream are fat-soluble vitamins, proteins, and fatty acids that are good for the immune system. When this layer of cream is removed to make a non-fat product, what you have left is basically sugar water.

Another factor to consider with dairy is how the cow is treated. Conventional dairy cows are fed an unnatural diet of genetically modified corn, antibiotics, growth hormones, and chicken and pig slaughter byproducts. These substances make their way into the milk and dairy products that end up on your table and in your body when you eat them. People who have penicillin allergies will sometimes react to meat or dairy products because of the amount of antibiotics in them.

If you choose to consume dairy, choose local raw milk or grass-fed organic products made from the milk of cows that have not been fed genetically-modified corn, antibiotics, or growth hormones, but rather good old-fashioned grass. These milk products tend to be richer in Omega-3 fatty acids and conjugated linoleic acid (CLA), which boost your immune system and the taste is far superior. We will talk more about genetic modification in Chapter 5, but for now, foods that have been genetically modified are not *Good Decisions*.

Raw Milk

Historically, many societies depended on the raw milk of cattle, sheep, goats, and camels for protein and fat. The practice of fermenting (souring milk) is used in all traditional groups that keep herds. The fermenting process utilizes enzymes for partially breaking down lactose and pre-digest casein. The end products, such as yogurt, kefir, and clabber, can often be tolerated by adults who cannot drink fresh milk. I am a proponent of raw milk products because they contain life-giving enzymes, probiotics, proteins, and fats that our ancestors enjoyed as nature intended, untampered with by man.

I know what you're thinking. "Really? Raw, you say?" Yes! It's very good for you, and it's delicious. In many states, you can buy raw milk on the farm and in stores. In some cases, you may have to purchase a small share in a cow to receive regular deliveries.

Thanks to the Internet, we have access to many healthy foods. Do an Internet search by typing "raw milk" and the name of the area you live in to find many options and locations for you to obtain raw milk. The Weston A. Price Foundation's (www.westonaprice.org) "Real Milk" project has made huge strides toward getting raw milk on our grocery shelves. Sally Fallon Morell, president of the foundation and author of *Nourishing Traditions: The Cookbook that Challenges Politically Correct Nutrition,* has done much to encourage and support raw milk consumption for many years. Her cookbook is a gem, filled with many delicious and extremely nutrient dense recipes utilizing raw milk.

Cardamom Spiced Milk

Serves: 2
Total Time: 30 minutes

Ingredients

- 2 cups raw or organic whole cow's milk
- 4 cardamom pods, crushed
- ¼ teaspoon fennel seeds
- 1 cinnamon stick
- 2 cloves
- 2 slices fresh ginger

Directions

1. In a small saucepan, bring the milk to a simmer. Add the remaining ingredients, cover, and reduce heat to low. Let mixture steep for 30 minutes.

2. Strain into your favorite teacup or mug and sip while still warm. You can double or even triple the recipe to have a large batch on hand. This mixture stores well in the fridge and can be sipped before bed as a comforting sleep aid. It is also delicious over ice as a yummy way to ease gas and bloating.

Opponents of raw milk feel that the risk of E. coli and other food-borne illness is still too high. I have enjoyed raw milk products since 2002 and have never been sick or had any health issues as a result of doing so. My health has only improved. I highly recommend that you try raw milk, and do your own research into this healthy food. Of course, as with every food, there is a risk. You can get E. coli from spinach, listeria from cantaloupe, and salmonella from chicken or eggs. If we live in fear, we don't live at all. You must make your own choice and follow what feels right to you. How the farm handles raw milk appears to be what determines your risk, so visiting a farm and finding out how it handles its raw milk may put your mind more at ease.

If you are hesitant to try raw milk, Organic Valley offers GrassMilk, a non-homogenized artisanal milk that has not been homogenized and is minimally pasteurized. It still has the cream on top just like the old days, and all you have to do is shake and pour. This is one of the tastiest pasteurized milk products I have tried.

Limit your consumption of milk products to organic grass-fed cultured whole milk, cultured buttermilk, whole milk yogurt, butter, cream, and raw cheese. These products are the most nutritious and contain high levels of protein, quality fat, enzymes, and probiotics.

Unfortunately, the majority of conventional dairy products come from cows on feedlots that are fed a number of unnatural things that do end up in the milk, so this is one product where I really encourage you to choose organic; this ensures that your milk is free of traces of these substances.

Butter and Cream

Contrary to what most people believe, butter and cream are not unhealthy. Organic, grass-fed cream contains nutrients such as fat-soluble vitamins A, D, E, and K, as well as protein and healthy fats that boost the immune system. The fat-soluble vitamins A and D in butter and cream are vital to health because they act as catalysts for mineral absorption and protein utilization. Adding a bit of butter, yogurt, or cream to your grains or vegetables enhances mineral absorption and delivers some phenomenal nutrients. Additionally, whole fat products are satiating and won't leave you feeling hungry.

Nutritional Nugget

For centuries, women (including Cleopatra) have used clarified butter, also known as ghee, topically for younger-looking skin. This product not only does the body good internally, but also nourishes your skin to help you look younger externally!

Butter and cream contain very little lactose and casein, and may be tolerated by those who are lactose intolerant. Fat also slows the passage of lactose through your digestive system, giving you more time to digest it. Those who are extremely intolerant of milk protein may consume ghee, a clarified butter in which the milk solids have been removed.

Dairy products are marketed for their high protein content, but it's important to know that some contain more carbohydrates than protein. For example, butter, cream, and cheese do not have high amounts of carbohydrates; they are higher in fats and proteins. Other products, like milk and yogurt, do contain significant amounts of simple carbohydrates that can raise blood sugar levels rapidly.

If you have transferred your pastry dependency to dairy, that's definitely a step in the right direction! Dairy is much better than pastries, donuts, pop, and cookies. But just as with fruits, dairy is most healthful when it is consumed in moderation and only when you are certain you are not addicted to it.

Dairy Recommendations

Good Decisions recommends dairy only for those who tolerate and do well with dairy. If you lack intestinal lactase, are allergic to casein, or experience pain, gas, mucus, inflammation, diarrhea, headaches, or other symptoms, dairy is best avoided. If you are uncertain as to how your body does with dairy, avoid it for a week or two while you are on the No Sugar Challenge and see how your body feels. Many people feel better when they do not consume dairy products, while others love it and tolerate dairy well.

All-Star dairy products include:

- Organic or raw whole fat milk or buttermilk
- Organic or raw plain whole milk yogurt, kefir, or clabber
- Organic or raw cheese
- Organic or raw half-and-half, heavy cream, and butter

When sugar and simple carbohydrates are removed from the diet completely, many symptoms such as fatigue, memory loss, and anxiety go away. All of my clients who stepped up to the "No Sugar Challenge" found a level of mental clarity they never imagined. Their energy levels balanced out, they felt better than they had in years, and most lost weight. One thing we know is that eliminating sugar from our diets will certainly cause no harm.

So, how about you? Are you ready to step up to the "No Sugar Challenge?"

The No Sugar Challenge

Building the First Nutritional Foundation

Welcome to the first of many challenges to come! The best way to get good at something is to practice. Eating is no different. If you want to lose weight, and increase vitality and mental clarity, then removing sweets from your diet is the perfect place to start.

The "No Sugar Challenge" is designed to balance your blood sugar levels. It is not too complicated and there isn't a long list of rules or special directions, other than to decrease, then eliminate simple carbohydrates, grains, dairy, and any processed foods from your diet. Rely on fruits and dairy in the beginning if they help you get started.

You may go through withdrawal symptoms, and the more hard-core or "cold turkey" your approach, the greater the withdrawal symptoms may be, but the quicker you will likely get through the withdrawal phase. Go at your own pace; everyone is different, so honor who you are, where you are in the process, and how you are feeling. Be gentle with yourself as you begin this process. Some people are able to eliminate all the simple carbohydrates and find that the dependency and cravings end in two weeks. Others may take longer.

Try not to take this too seriously, and know that while you may feel some discomfort saying no to your favorite sweet, it is not something you can't overcome. I will be here with you in spirit and walk you through it as best I can.

Grains, soy, and dairy are eliminated not only because of the potential blood-elevating effects, but also because many people are allergic or sensitive to them. It's good to give the body a break from any foods that have the potential to create inflammation.

Consume mostly vegetables, legumes, nuts, seeds, and organic animal proteins with a little quality fat for satiation. Think salmon with salad and asparagus, chicken with roasted vegetables, lentil soups, bean salads, chili, and even a steak with a baked potato. Your plate should hold mostly vegetables with a small to moderate serving of protein depending on your size.

No Sugar Challenge Guidelines

Most people will lose their cravings for unhealthy foods within one to two weeks. For others, it may take up to four weeks for cravings to disappear. Many are thrilled to experience weight loss without feeling hungry or deprived. Coffee, pop, alcohol, and refined or processed foods are not allowed.

Quality Protein

Each meal should include a minimum of 4 ounces of quality protein. Meat, poultry, fish, and eggs are unlimited, as are legumes (beans, peas, and lentils). Always choose organic grass fed animal protein sources. This choice keeps antibiotics, growth hormones, and the inflammatory effects of genetically modified foods to a minimum. Always soak legumes in water for 24 hours to optimize nutrient absorption and digestibility.

Vegetables

Eat as many as you want; you can't eat too many vegetables. Focus on the dark leafy greens and a variety of dark rich colors. Consider vegetable juicing or purchase a commercial blender to increase intake of plant foods. Eat some vegetables raw or slightly cooked every day, making sure to chew them thoroughly. Starchy vegetables such as potatoes or yams should be avoided. Always choose organic vegetables; this choice keeps cancer-causing pesticides as well as genetically-modified food items to a minimum. Add flavor and nutrients to your vegetable dishes by cooking them with onions, garlic, and ginger, and a small amount of quality fat.

Fruits

No fruits are allowed.

Grains

Consume no wheat or flour products, including bread, rolls, muffins, and pasta. The only grains allowed are whole grain brown or wild rice. Grains should be soaked before cooking. Place 1 cup dry grain in pan with 2 cups water and two tablespoons lemon. Soak for 24 hours. Drain, rinse, and then cook as normal.

Quality Fats

No artificial fats, hydrogenated fats, or refined fats such as margarine, canola oil, or vegetable oil. Eat plenty of wholesome unrefined fats and oils such as butter, ghee, coconut oil, olive oil, and walnut oil.

Nuts

Eat plenty of raw nuts, especially Brazil nuts, cashews, almonds, walnuts, pumpkin seeds, and sunflower seeds.

Dairy

Do not consume dairy.

Sweeteners

No sweeteners of any kind are allowed.

Snack every two hours

To avoid erratic blood sugar fluctuations, eat something every two hours. Only a small amount of food is necessary at one time.

Drink plenty of water

Try to drink your body weight divided by two in ounces per day.

The No Sugar Challenge is the heart of the *Good Decisions...Most of the Time* lifestyle. There are no portion restrictions or recommended amounts, only the requirement to eat only wholesome, natural, real foods. The No Sugar Challenge is hypoallergenic in nature and an elimination diet of sorts, designed to quiet inflammation, which allows the body to heal as you find your way back to whole foods and away from sugar's sweet temptation.

How will you know when you have succeeded? When you no longer crave, want, or need to have something sweet. You may be surprised to find that when you are no longer dependent on sugar, it doesn't even sound good! Once the dependency on sugar has abated, you can introduce fruits, whole grains, and dairy back into your diet, one item per week, with a heightened awareness of how you feel after you consume those foods.

Nutritional Nugget

Nuts, legumes, and hard-boiled eggs as snacks can help reduce cravings for something sweet. Brewer's yeast on salads or in smoothies is a great source of chromium, B vitamins, and amino acids, all of which can help keep cravings at bay.

In the beginning, while you are trying to kick the sugar habit, you may find yourself reaching for fruit or dairy many times during the day to ease your sugar cravings. That's okay in the beginning; moving to fruits or dairy instead of refined white sugar is an excellent way to start cleaning up your diet. However, if you consume more than two fruits per day and find that you "need" them, "want" them, and get anxious without them, don't be fooled. You are still addicted to sugar; you have just transferred your addiction from refined sugar to fruits. Don't let this dishearten you. Keep moving forward; reduce the number of fruits and dairy you eat daily until you no longer crave them. Once you've lost your cravings completely and find yourself forgetting about fruits and dairy, you are no longer addicted. It typically takes anywhere from two to four weeks for blood sugar levels to regulate and sugar cravings to dissipate and go away.

Removing simple carbohydrates is the first step in your hallway of life toward improved health and wellbeing. If you make only one small change, take one small step toward reducing sweets in your diet, you will still be making progress toward improved health.

One important effect that my clients always report after a couple of weeks on the No Sugar Challenge is an improvement in mental clarity. Another effect frequently reported is a reduction of fatigue and increased energy levels. Weight loss is just a natural side effect when you balance your blood sugar levels and begin to address the foundations of health and nutrition.

The Glycemic Index

We can't talk about simple carbohydrates without mentioning the *Glycemic Index*. The Glycemic Index (GI) measures a carbohydrate-containing food's potential to increase blood sugar levels. Food with a high GI raises blood glucose more rapidly and to higher levels than does food with a medium or low GI. A food's GI value is obtained by monitoring your blood sugar after eating the food. If there is a large blood sugar increase, the food will be labeled as having a high GI. Because we are all biochemically different, GI values can vary from person to person. Low GI carbohydrates typically cause only small fluctuations in your blood glucose and insulin levels.

Many dieticians and nutritionists recommend using the Glycemic Index to increase your mindfulness and awareness of high-sugar foods. This can be a valuable tool, as food with a low to no GI are supposed to be your best decisions. However, this isn't always true. In addition to the Glycemic Index, you'll need to understand the difference between whole foods and processed foods, nutrient dense, and nutrient poor foods. For instance, a pineapple may have a GI of 66, but it contains fiber, vitamins, minerals, antioxidants, and anti-inflammatory properties. On the other hand, a chocolate chip cookie may have a GI of 44, but that cookie may contain hydrogenated fats, additives, preservatives, and artificial colors and flavors. Don't fall into the trap of believing foods that are low on the GI Index are always good for you.

Low GI	Medium GI	High GI
55 or less	56-69	70 or more

What Does "Good Decisions...Most of the Time" Mean, Anyway?

After you have completed the "No Sugar Challenge" and your blood sugar levels have balanced out, it will be time to move into making *Good Decisions...Most of the Time*. This is the perfect transition because your blood sugar levels are regulated and you will no longer need to eat every two hours unless you wish to. Dairy and fruits may be consumed in small amounts with an awareness of how you feel after you have consumed them. If you find yourself gravitating to them frequently, you may still be experiencing cravings and in the grips of addiction. Stay alert!

If you are a coffee lover and have spent the last four weeks away from coffee, pay close attention to how you feel if you choose to bring it back into your diet. Many people love the taste of coffee, but don't like the way it makes them feel afterwards. Often they feel more tired than energized by coffee and find green tea gives them the caffeine hit without bogging them down. *Good Decisions* is not about demonizing coffee, but increasing your awareness of how you feel when you drink it. This allows you to make a conscious decision about coffee and whether or not it contributes to how you wish to feel. Beer and wine can also be approached this way. I find that I thoroughly enjoy one glass of wine, but after a few sips of the second glass, my body is done with the experience and it is not as enjoyable. When I don't listen to my body, I usually wake up the next day not feeling so great!

When defining *Good Decisions...Most of the Time*, I asked for some help from family, friends, and clients. We played around with several different scenarios to discover what would work best, which time frame was long enough for us to make gains toward our goals of feeling better and losing weight, and what "unhealthy decision" frequency was enough for us not to feel deprived.

When *Good Decisions* were made during the week and freedom given to make unhealthy decisions on weekends, we found that most of the gains made during the week were lost. When we made *Good Decisions* for longer than a week, we felt at a loss for some of our favorite foods and beverages and didn't enjoy the process; we felt deprived.

It seemed to us that the perfect combination was allowing for one "unhealthy decision" *meal* per week. This was enough to prevent us from feeling deprived, yet not so much as to negate the gains we made during the week. On the day we allowed ourselves an unhealthy decision meal, some of us splurged on bacon cheeseburgers and beer, some went for pasta and dessert, while others decided they simply wanted an additional glass of wine.

Everyone in our group chose the evening meal in which to splurge, but that doesn't mean it needs to be restricted to that time. If you have a luncheon scheduled, and you really want to enjoy a martini and dessert, choose that day. If family brunch on Sunday is a tradition and you love the coffee cake and waffles, choose that meal. Whether you tend toward sweet or savory, the meal you choose, and what "unhealthy decisions" you choose during that meal is up to you; it is your decision!

The next day, depending on the splurge, some of us didn't feel so great. Most of us, however, were excited to get back to making *Good Decisions*. Those who over-imbibed on alcohol seemed to have the toughest time getting back on track.

Overall, we found that making *Good Decisions* of lots of vegetables, legumes, nuts, seeds, and quality proteins with a little fat made us feel great. In addition, when only given one meal a week to splurge, we didn't lose most of what we had gained.

We also found that when we didn't have something for a while, we appreciated it so much more. The pasta was moaned over, the wine was savored, and the bacon cheeseburger elicited nirvana—that transcendent state in which all suffering is vanquished! Having fulfilled our desires, while retaining our sense of self and purpose, without guilt or self-flagellation, we had made *Good Decisions...Most of the Time.*

The Psychology of Food

Social Impacts and Self-Awareness

As you begin the *Good Decision* journey, you may encounter some unforeseen challenges, one of which may be how your family and friends react to your new way of eating. Change, even for the better, often presents difficulties for those close to us. They and others may see you embark on a healthier way of life and try to pull you back into old habits because it's more comfortable for *them*. They may be jealous, or they may be painfully reminded of their own poor health. Regardless, know that this will pass with time. As you stick to making **Good Decisions…Most of the Time** and maintain your new way of eating, eventually it will become the new normal, and your friends and family will adapt and accept that eating well is just a part of who you are today.

It may be uncomfortable in the beginning when you go out to dinner and, instead of ordering an appetizer, salad, main course, and dessert, you order only fish and a salad. Many wide eyes may accompany your decision not to have dessert. Again, know that this will pass. It is not easy letting go of what others think, especially if you have commiserated and bonded with them over food in the past. You may feel very disconnected and alone for a period until you discover new friendships, or your old friends, seeing you regaining health and looking radiant, decide they want to join you in feeling better.

Be aware that during this process, you may lose some friends who will find others to engage with who will share their unhealthy eating habits since some people deal with life by escaping into food. If they need to be soothed, sugar can do that, and as temporary as that solution may be, the short-term relief they get with sugar is enough. Honor where they are and honor your choices on this journey down your own hallway of life. Continue to remind yourself that any discomfort you feel when making *Good Decisions* will pass as you and your social network adapt to your new way of life.

CHAPTER ONE

Practicing Good Decisions

Experience Some Discomfort!

Your first homework assignment—should you choose to accept it—is to schedule a date to meet your friends for dinner. When you arrive, instead of ordering beer, wine, or a cocktail, order water with a slice of orange or lemon. Proceed to order fish and vegetables or a salad—and bypass dessert. Pay attention to how you feel, and pay attention to how your friends respond to your menu choices. Don't tell them what you are doing. Try to be as graceful as possible; perhaps think of a catch phrase you can use repeatedly such as, "I'm trying to make *Good Decisions...Most of the Time*." If you are uncomfortable, don't feel that you have to do or say anything to soothe yourself or your friends to make the discomfort go away, but know that the discomfort, at some point, *will* go away.

Follow-Up

Were you still able to enjoy the company, without the extra food? With practice and repetition, it will get easier and become natural. The more you practice, the sooner the discomfort will dissipate and the sooner you will be walking your hallway of life with more control and confidence.

Chapter Two

Sweet Alternatives

In this chapter, you will learn how spices can be used to aid blood sugar regulation and how they can be used instead of sugar to create mouth-watering desserts. You will learn which sweeteners to choose when a special occasion arises and which sweeteners to avoid most of the time. Are artificial sweeteners and Stevia Good Decisions? Which sweet spice will heat up your sex life? Which sweetener can be used to minimize muscle cramps, and which sweet fruit can relieve constipation naturally? These questions and more will be answered as we peel back the layers and discover new ways to tickle our dopamine centers. We will end with the psychology of food and exercises that may be helpful to you as you begin your Good Decisions journey.

Occasional use of raw honey or natural sweeteners is a part of many traditional societies and, in their unrefined form, these natural sweeteners are much better decisions than their refined counterparts. The vitamins and minerals in unrefined sweeteners add flavor and enhance the nutritional value of dishes. It's easy to replace margarine with butter; butter tastes better. However, replacing white table sugar with raw honey or grade B maple syrup isn't as exciting, but it can be just as easy.

Natural unrefined sweeteners give food certain qualities, tangible qualities that ooze deliciousness, as if the food you are eating contains life within it that will enhance your own life. And it does. There's nothing like enjoying a honey-roasted pear with a touch of cinnamon. It doesn't just feed your craving for something sweet; it feeds the body as well as your senses.

Now that you know how simple carbohydrates affect your body, you can make conscious choices, *Good Decisions*, about which of these foods you will allow into your diet. When a special occasion arises, and you're going to prepare something sweet, it's still possible to make nutrient-dense choices that won't affect your body as adversely as refined and processed sweeteners.

If you don't choose to step up to the "No Sugar Challenge," but would like to move away gradually from processed sugars or substitute more healthful sweeteners in your diet, there are many recommended alternatives to choose from.

Natural Sweeteners

Fruit

If you need to sweeten a dish, reach for a complementary fruit to mash or juice into the dish instead of sugar. Fruits, such as crushed pineapple, applesauce, strawberries, cherries, or blueberries can naturally sweeten almost any dish.

Avoid fruit juice unless it is pressed through a juicer and consumed immediately. Fruit is best when juiced with a complementary vegetable. For example, carrot, apple, and ginger make a delicious, healthful juice beverage, great for the immune system and skin. Beet, orange, and ginger juice is a nice pairing that has an affinity for the liver. Grapefruit, garlic, and lemon are also good for the liver and support immune functions. These are not only tasty but healthful as well. Leafy greens can also be combined with fruit; kale, apple, and celery are a delicious and nutritious combination.

Nutritional Nugget

The secret weapon I mentioned earlier against constipation is the mighty apple. One to two apples a day can ease even the most stubborn cases of constipation. This is because apples contain *sorbitol*, a substance that attracts water. Apples also contain fiber and pectins, which increase the volume and viscosity of the stool. If you are not a fan of raw apples, homemade applesauce works just as well.

Low glycemic fruits are useful when trying to kick the sugar habit. Think pork tenderloin with a cherry glaze, a roasted apple stuffed with nuts, butter, and cinnamon, or a broiled grapefruit dusted with cinnamon. Grains such as oatmeal really don't need brown sugar when you can mix in fresh peaches, apples, strawberries, blueberries, or pears. Even dessert can be as simple as nectarines and blackberries dusted with cinnamon, nutmeg, and mint!

Are fruits a *Good Decision*? Yes!

Vanilla Rum-Soaked Pineapple

Serves: 8

Total Time: 10 minutes, plus 2-8 hours soaking time

Ingredients

- 1 large, ripe pineapple, sliced vertically into 8 long wedges
- ¼ cup rum
- 2 tablespoons butter
- 1 teaspoon vanilla extract
- 1 teaspoon fresh minced ginger
- ¼ teaspoon allspice
- ¼ teaspoon ground cloves

Directions

1. In a large bowl, combine pineapple and rum. Let soak for 2-8 hours.

2. In a large saucepan, melt butter over medium-high heat. Add pineapple, rum marinade, vanilla, ginger, allspice, and cloves and bring to a boil. Reduce heat and simmer until liquid is reduced and pineapple is glazed. Serve warm or at room temperature.

Grade B Maple Syrup

Maple syrup, made from the sap of black or red maple trees, is a good source of manganese and zinc and, to a lesser degree, potassium and calcium. I recommend Grade B maple syrup because it contains more nutrients than Grade A and has a thicker, richer flavor.

A University of Rhode Island scientist recently discovered fifty-four beneficial new compounds in pure maple syrup, five of which have never been seen in nature. Among the five new compounds discovered is *quebecol*, a compound created when the maple sap is boiled to create syrup.[1] Quebecol is said to have antioxidant and anti-inflammatory properties. Manganese, known for its ability to maintain blood sugar levels, is the highlight of this sweetener.

Maple syrup is low on the glycemic index and can be used to sweeten salad dressing, replace honey for a different taste, or be used instead of table sugar in some baking.

One of my most popular recommendations for maple syrup is as an electrolyte mixture that combines Grade B maple syrup, lemon, and cayenne pepper. This was adapted from The Master Cleanse, a lemonade diet created by Stanley Burroughs.[2] When I was on this cleanse, I noticed that my level of flexibility improved dramatically, and the menstrual cramps I used to get went away. After a bit of research, I found that this combination is ideal for use as a sports drink/electrolyte replacement beverage. Since then, when any of my athletic clients have mineral and electrolyte deficiencies, I encourage them to make this mixture and sip on it throughout the day instead of artificially flavored "sports drinks."

Nutritional Nugget

Depression getting you down? Incorporate a few more chillies in your diet. They are one of the most effective herbs for depression. The dose must be high, so the best way to get this herb is in capsular form. Cayenne pepper is widely available in this form. Start with one capsule and increase dose as tolerated up to 6-10 capsules a day. You can also enjoy the Electrolyte Lemonade as a gentle way to stimulate yourself out of feeling down!

Maple syrup contains zinc and potassium, with calcium, magnesium, and sodium chloride electrolytes occurring in their natural ratios. The high level of manganese in this mixture is an essential cofactor in a number of enzymes important in muscle energy production and antioxidant defenses. Lemon contains potassium, and also has small amounts of calcium, magnesium, and phosphorus, not to mention a huge kick of vitamin C, which makes this drink great for your immune system as well. Cayenne pepper contributes vitamin A, and it is known for its pain-relieving effects, cardiovascular benefits, ability to help prevent ulcers, as well as its ability to break up mucus (great when you're sick). Cayenne is also a driving herb, which helps increase the absorption of these minerals. You don't need much of this mixture (as little as one cup a day) to experience positive results.

If you find yourself waking up in the middle of the night screaming because your calf muscle has cramped in on itself, this electrolyte lemonade is for you!

Is grade B maple syrup considered a *Good Decision*? Yes.

Electrolyte Lemonade

Serves: 2
Total Time: 3 minutes

Ingredients

- 2 tablespoons Grade B maple syrup
- 3 tablespoons fresh squeezed lemon juice
- Dash of cayenne pepper
- 16 ounces water

Directions

1. Combine all ingredients and pour over ice. This is also great as a hot beverage during the winter, as it is very warming and comforting when you are sick and need help breaking up mucus. To make the hot version, combine the maple syrup, lemon, and cayenne pepper in your favorite mug and pour boiling water into the mug until full. Enjoy! This recipe can be doubled or tripled and put into a sports bottle for convenience. I like lots of cayenne pepper, but others like it much milder, so I suggest starting with a little and then increase it as desired to the amount that is right for you. Many people look at this recipe and make a funny face, but once they taste it, they are often surprised at how delicious it really is!

Raw Unfiltered Honey

Honey is made when the nectar from a flower mixes with the saliva of a bee. (Sounds delicious, no?) Depending on the quality of honey, it contains anti-microbial, and antioxidant compounds, as well as probiotic bacteria. It also contains trace amounts of vitamins and minerals. Honey is usually sold over the counter in most grocery stores, and it is usually pasteurized, clarified, or filtered so it's important to read the label and know what to look for. I recommend raw honey. This is honey as it exists in the beehive or as obtained by extraction, settling, or straining without adding heat (caution: some honey that has been "minimally processed" is often labeled as "raw honey"). Raw honey contains some pollen and may contain small particles of wax.

Humans have used honey throughout history to treat a variety of ailments. Some wound gels, which contain antibacterial raw honey, have regulatory approval and are now available to help treat drug-resistant strains of bacteria. One New Zealand researcher says a particular type of honey (Manuka honey) may be useful in treating drug-resistant infections.[3] Because of its unique composition and chemical properties, honey is great for long-term storage and is easily absorbed even after long preservation. Honeys, and objects immersed in honey, have been preserved for decades and even centuries.[4]

Because of the natural presence of botulinum endospores in honey,[5] you should not give honey to children under one year of age. Adults and older children have more fully developed digestive systems, which generally destroy the spores. Infants' digestive systems have not yet developed and, therefore, they may contract botulism from honey.[6] The Glycemic Index (GI) in honey depends on the type of honey, but most brands do tend to be high, so don't go overboard with this sweetener.

Nutritional Nugget

Local raw honey is often sought after by allergy sufferers because the pollen impurities are thought to lessen susceptibility to hay fever.

Honey may be used as a substitute in many recipes that call for sugar; Asian dishes particularly do well with honey as a substitute in recipes that just don't taste the same without a hint of something sweet. I find honey does exceptionally well over fruits before roasting, in spiced rice puddings, and in herbal teas to help the medicine go down.

Is raw unfiltered honey a *Good Decision*? Yes!

Pistachio Cardamom Kulfi

Serves: 8
Total Time: 1 hour, 15 minutes, plus time to freeze

Ingredients

- 8 cups organic whole or raw milk
- 12 green cardamom pods, lightly crushed
- ½ cup raw honey
- 2 tablespoons almonds, finely chopped
- 4 tablespoons unsalted pistachio nuts, skinned and finely chopped

Directions

2. Put the milk and cardamom pods in a saucepan and bring to a boil. Reduce heat to low and simmer for 1 hour or until the milk has reduced to half of its original amount. Whenever a skin forms on top, stir it back in. Add honey and stir until it dissolves. Cool and strain into a glass bowl.

3. Add the almonds and half of the pistachios and put into the freezer. Every 15 minutes, remove the milk from the freezer and, using a whisk, stir it well to break up any ice crystals.

4. When the mixture begins to stiffen, pour into porcelain or glass ramekins and return to freezer until frozen completely. To serve, run the ramekins under hot water briefly to release the iced milk from the mold. Sprinkle with chopped pistachios.

Dried Dates

Dates are the fruit of the date palm tree. They are raw and unprocessed (but read the ingredient list just to make sure), and they have lots of nutrients such as potassium, iron, and vitamin A. It's easy to use dates to sweeten smoothies, baked goods, sauces, and more by making a paste with the dates. To make a paste, simply use dried dates and soak them in warm water overnight. Then blend the dates with some of the water used to soak them to a consistency similar to honey. (When I make my own almond milk, I add some dried dates to sweeten the batch.)

Are dates a *Good Decision*? Yes!

Date Sugar

Date sugar is the byproduct of the date palm industry; manufacturers usually use cosmetically inferior dates (which are not sold as whole fruits) to create date sugar. First, the fresh dates, which are about 60 percent sugar, are dehydrated. Then, this product is ground to be used as a sweetener. Date sugar is an excellent alternative to table sugar and contains calcium, iron, magnesium, phosphorus, zinc, copper, manganese, selenium, and potassium. It is also a moderate source of B vitamins and iron. Most often, date sugar is unrefined, unprocessed, and raw, but be sure to read the ingredient label to be certain. Look for the word "unrefined," as refined versions of this product do exist. This is an excellent choice for occasional use as a sweetener. Date sugar is also a great substitute for any recipe calling for brown sugar.

Is unrefined date sugar a *Good Decision*? Yes!

Coconut Sugar

Unrefined coconut sugar is made from the sweet sap or nectar of flower buds cut from coconut trees. It is also called palm sugar, coco sugar, coconut palm sugar, or coco sap sugar. After being harvested from the blossoms of the coconut tree, the sap is boiled down into a syrup-like substance. This is further reduced to crystal, block, or soft paste form. Be sure to read the labels to verify that you are getting organic, unrefined coconut sugar.

Coconut sugar tastes lighter than maple syrup and honey and has a hint of caramel flavor to it. I like this sugar because it won't turn certain recipes as brown as with jaggery or rapadura sugars, but will still turn a white cake into a light, caramel-colored cake.

Coconut sugar contains potassium, magnesium, iron, and zinc. Coconut sugar also contains vitamins B1, B2, B3, and B6. I often wonder why anyone would use refined white table sugar when all these nutrient-containing alternatives are available.

Coconut sugar is also rich in Inositol, a substance reported to reduce pain. Additionally, because of its beneficial effects on the central nervous system and its role in the development of healthy cells, Inositol is recommended as a treatment for anxiety, depression, bipolar mood disorder, obsessive-compulsive disorder, and panic disorders.

Keep in mind that isolated supplemental or synthetic inositol may function differently in the body than inositol in combination with other nutrients in food. Whole food sources of nutrients are always recommended over synthetic alternatives. Don't go wild with sweeteners—remember they are best used occasionally on those sweet special occasions.

Is coconut sugar a *Good Decision*? Yes!

Unrefined Organic Whole Cane Sugar

Unrefined organic whole cane sugar, also known as rapadura, is made from the sugar cane plant. A press is used to express the raw cane juice, which is then evaporated over low heat while being stirred with paddles. Then, it's sieve-ground to produce a grainy sugar. Unrefined organic whole cane sugar has not been cooked at high heat and then spun to change it into crystals as with table sugar. Also, the molasses has not been separated from the sugar using harmful chemicals. Molasses contains the majority of nutrients such as potassium, magnesium, manganese, selenium, and calcium. Once the molasses is removed, you have very few nutrients left indeed. Unrefined whole cane sugar is the closest thing to raw sugar cane that you can get; it also contains iron and

Vitamin B6. It has a mild, caramel-like flavor, which is delicious for occasional baking and infrequent use as a sweetener.

Is unrefined organic whole cane sugar a *Good Decision*? Yes!

Sucanat

Sucanat™ is a trademarked brand name that comes from the French words for "natural sugar cane." Sucanat is made from the sugar cane plant. The juice extraction processes are mechanical and, unlike typical sugar cane processing, no chemicals are added.

Sucanat is similar to unrefined organic whole cane sugar or rapadura. It used to differ from rapadura in that the sugar stream and the molasses stream were separated during processing and then re-blended to create a consistent product. This process no longer occurs.

Sucanat is currently made by mechanically extracting sugar cane juice, which is then heated and cooled *(dehydrated)* until tiny brown crystals form. It has not been cooked at high heats and spun to change it into crystals, and the molasses has not been separated from the sugar. Like unrefined organic whole cane sugar, it contains nutrients such as calcium, potassium, magnesium, manganese, copper, and iron.

Is sucanat a *Good Decision*? Yes!

Although these are all natural choices that many traditional societies have consumed for generations, they still break down rapidly into glucose in the body, which can result in blood sugar irregularities, increased cortisol production, and other hormonal imbalances, as well as mental fog and weight gain when over-consumed. Use them sparingly—not most of the time.

None of these products are used in the "No Sugar Challenge." This initial phase of elimination is building one of the foundations of your *Good Decisions* way of life. It is designed to get you off sugar and out of the addicting cycle of blood sugar fluctuations. Once you have this foundation firmly in place, your cravings will be gone completely, and you can enjoy some of these products—in small amounts—on special occasions.

You can often adapt a recipe so it doesn't use any sweetener. You'll find these recipe adaptations result in delicious meals. Please be aware; if you notice that you must have these natural sweeteners regularly, you still might be caught in that cycle of sugar addiction. Removing all sugar products for two to four weeks is the best way to get off sugar and get your blood sugar levels back to normal. Then, you can use these wonderful natural sweeteners in your not-so-most-of-the-time dishes if you wish to.

If you have chosen to step up to the No Sugar Challenge and experience withdrawal as a result of cutting out refined table sugar, you can use the following sweet spices to satisfy your sweet tooth. Spices are great to reach for when those powerful emotions arise and you need soothing or something to reach for when you experience the discomfort of not having sugar.

Using Sweet Spices

Cooking with spices and herbs is one of my favorite things to do. Discovering all the health benefits your spice cabinet may hold is quite fun and, in times of upset tummy, gas, or other uncomfortable health conditions, you can often find relief as close as your spice cabinet. Spicing up a dish with sweet spices adds distinct flavors and lessens your temptation to add sugar. They also have many health-giving properties as well. Use a sweet spice whenever possible before you turn to sweeteners.

Allspice

Allspice is the dried dark-brown berry of an evergreen shrub. It has a taste similar to a mix of nutmeg, cinnamon, and cloves. You can use allspice when preparing ham, Swedish meatballs, baked goods, and desserts to add a nice touch of spicy sweetness. Medicinally, allspice has been used throughout history in the treatment of toothaches, muscle aches, and for its blood sugar-regulating effects. This valuable spice can be used to control appetite and prevent unhealthy swings in your blood sugar levels. Like many spices, allspice is a digestive aid, and consuming allspice with meals can result in stronger digestion, reduced gas and bloating, and decreased nausea.

Is allspice a *Good Decision*? Absolutely!

Cinnamon

Cinnamon is obtained from the inner bark of tropical evergreen trees. It has a wonderful sweet flavor and can be used as a ground powder or dried stick. This spice can be used in just about anything. From sweet dishes to stews and curries, you will be pleasantly surprised to find that a small amount of cinnamon goes a long way. Two teaspoons of cinnamon can change a tart, tongue-puckering apple pie to a sweet one. It can replace brown sugar in oatmeal or sprinkled on fruit to liven up a simple dessert.

One of cinnamon's best attributes is its ability to lessen the impact of sugar on your blood sugar levels. Cinnamon also slows the rate at which your stomach empties after meals, which also reduces the rise in blood sugar after eating. Researchers measured how quickly the stomach emptied after fourteen healthy subjects ate 300 grams (1.2 cups) of rice pudding alone or seasoned with 6 grams (1.2 teaspoons) of cinnamon. Adding cinnamon to the rice pudding lowered the stomach-emptying rate and significantly lessened the rise in blood sugar levels after eating.[7]

In the December 2003 issue of **Diabetes Care**, a study found that when people with type 2 diabetes consumed as little as 1 gram of cinnamon per day, they had reduced blood sugar, triglycerides, LDL (bad) cholesterol, and total cholesterol. Researchers concluded that including cinnamon in the diet of people with type 2 diabetes would reduce risk factors associated with diabetes and cardiovascular diseases. This little spice packs a powerful punch and can be added to any dish or beverage as a substitute for, or in addition to sugar, to lessen sugar's impact.

Is cinnamon a **Good Decision**? Yes!

Cloves

Cloves are the aromatic dried flower buds from a tree in the family Myrtaceae. Cloves have a sweet or bittersweet taste and can be used when ground or dried. Cloves are great when used to sweeten dishes or in curries and stews. And who can't visualize a glorious clove-studded ham? Cloves go well with chicken, can spice up an otherwise boring cranberry sauce, or can be added to fresh applesauce or juice. I find cloves delicious when sprinkled on pears.

Medicinally, cloves are used to increase hydrochloric acid in the stomach and to improve peristalsis, so their use before meals in appetizers can be very valuable.

Are cloves a *Good Decision*? Yes!

Nutritional Nugget

Clove oil, applied to a cavity in a decayed tooth, relieves toothache, making this spice very valuable if you can't get in to see your dentist right away.

Nutmeg and Mace

Mace and nutmeg are two slightly different flavored spices, both originating from the fruit of the nutmeg tree. This "nutmeg apple" looks similar to an apricot. When the mature fruit splits open, the nutmeg (a seed surrounded by a red, slightly fleshy covering, or aril) is exposed. The dried aril alone is called mace. The nut is removed and dried to produce nutmeg. Both have a warm, sweet, spicy flavor and are best when freshly ground. They are often used in cakes, especially pound cakes, cookies, muffins, pies, ham, and sweet potatoes. Who needs sugar when you have all of these wonderful spices?

Are nutmeg and mace *Good Decisions*? Absolutely!

Cardamom

Cardamom is the papery pod and dark brown seeds of a plant of the ginger family. It can be used ground or as whole pods. Cardamom is used in Scandinavian bakeries, German and Russian pastries, and in the Middle East and India. This spice can be used instead of sugar when making baked goods and with creams to make cardamom-flavored ice cream, which is mouthwateringly delicious.

Nutritional Nugget

Studies have found that nutmeg may be useful in enhancing libido. But use caution since nutmeg can also be added to milk as a sleep aid, and the last thing you want when trying to enhance libido is to fall asleep!

Medicinally, green cardamom is frequently used in South Asia to treat infections in teeth and gums, to prevent and treat throat troubles, and to prevent and treat congestion of the lungs. You can steep the seeds in milk, water, or almond milk for use as a digestive aid to relieve gas and bloating. "Really?" you say. If you feel gassy and bloated—absolutely!

Is cardamom a *Good Decision*? Yes!

Star Anise

Star anise is a large, rust-colored, star-shaped fruit of an evergreen tree, primarily grown in China and Japan. Each point contains a seed and often the whole fruit is used. This spice has a sweet spicy flavor, and can be used whole or ground. Star anise is used in Asian dishes where meats such as poultry, lamb, beef, duck, or pork are slow-simmered, as well as in some Malaysian dishes. Vietnamese pho utilizes this wonderful spice to flavor its unique broth. It can be used to replace sugar in fruit compotes and jams, and it gives baked goods a rich, delicious uniqueness that will have your guests moaning with delight. It has become more popular recently because it combines well with fish, leeks, and pears.

In traditional Chinese medicine, star anise is prescribed as a digestive aid and to help ease colic in babies. Interestingly, shikimic acid, one of the chief ingredients in the antiviral drug Tamiflu, is extracted from star anise.

Is star anise a *Good Decision*? Yes!

Vanilla Beans

Vanilla beans are the long, greenish-yellow seed pods of a tropical orchid plant. More of a fruit than a spice, one inch of vanilla bean is roughly equal to one teaspoon of pure vanilla extract. Sweet and fragrant, vanilla is best when used from whole or dried beans. Vanilla is a great sugar substitute and can be added to breakfast grains, coffee, and desserts such as ice cream, pudding, and cake.

The active compound in vanilla is vanillin. Vanillin is a polyphenol with strong antioxidant activity. Some neurological diseases such as Alzheimer's and Parkinson's disease are associated with formation of a chemical called peroxynitrite, which causes damage to brain cells. Because vanillin has such strong antioxidant activity, it may offset some of this oxidative damage, keeping brain cells healthy and preventing the devastating effects of diseases such as Alzheimer's.[8]

Is vanilla a *Good Decision*? Yes!

Using Sweet Herbs

You can also use the following sweet herbs to sweeten and add flavor to a dish. Vegetables are especially good with herbs added. If you're trying to make vegetables taste better, reach for an herb or spice to take your mind off the fact that you're eating vegetables.

Anise Seed

Anise seed is often confused with star anise, but the plants are not alike. Star anise is the fruit of a tree, and anise seed is an herb that is a member of the parsley family. Anethole is the oil that accounts for the distinctive, sweet, licorice taste of both anise seed and star anise, but star anise is bitterer than anise seed.

Anise seed smells like black licorice and can be used whole or ground. These delicious seeds are often used as a flavoring in some cookies, candies, pastries, and even in poultry dishes.

I love it with pork and have a sweet anise seed pork recipe that is to die for! Look for it on my website at www.gooddecisions.com. Anise extract is also used to flavor the Greek liquor ouzo.

Is anise seed a *Good Decision*? Yes!

Nutritional Nugget

Chewing on ½ teaspoon of anise seeds after a meal can relieve uncomfortable gas and bloating. Also, one teaspoon of the seeds can be steeped in one cup of boiling water as a tea for similar results.

Sweet Basil

This herb is somewhat pungent and sweet. It's a bit odd to think of this herb for use as a sweetener, but you'll be hooked after you try it. Use fresh basil to get the best results. Add it to dishes at the last moment, as cooking quickly destroys the flavor. Use sweet basil with eggplant, tomato dishes, pesto, Vietnamese and Thai dishes, and salads, as well as when cooking vegetables to make them more interesting. Corn, tomato, peppers, and eggplant are divine when served with a dusting of fresh basil.

Scientific studies have established that compounds in basil oil have potent antioxidant, antiviral, and antimicrobial properties and potential for use in treating cancer.[9,10,11,12] In India, it is traditionally used for supplementary treatment of stress, asthma, and diabetes.[13]

Is sweet basil a *Good Decision*? Yes!

Sweet Basil Gelato

Serves: 8

Total Time: 10 minutes plus chilling and freezing time

Ingredients

- 1 cup firmly packed basil leaves
- 2 cups raw or organic milk
- 1 cup raw or organic cream
- ½ cup unrefined organic whole cane sugar
- 1 tablespoon lemon zest
- ¼ teaspoon salt
- 2 egg yolks

Directions

1. Combine basil, milk, cream, cane sugar, zest, salt, and yolks in a blender and puree until smooth. Chill in the refrigerator.

2. Pour into an ice cream maker and freeze according to manufacturer's instructions. Serve garnished with fresh basil leaves.

Caraway Seed

Caraway, also known as "meridian fennel," is an herb seed of the parsley family. Because caraway and anise seed are from the same family, caraway also has an anise-like flavor and aroma that comes from essential oils. It has a sweet, nutty flavor and is best when used whole. It is often used in rye bread and with cabbage as a sauerkraut favorite. It also makes wonderful applesauce, cakes, cookies, herbal vinegars, and Hungarian goulash. Caraway helps stimulate gastric secretions and, therefore, plays an important role in stimulating appetite and digestion. It also regulates stomach function and has anti-inflammatory properties for the intestines, which make this an ideal herb for those with irritable bowel syndrome. Additionally, it strengthens the body's immune system and helps ease cold symptoms. In the Middle East, it is used in a dessert that's traditionally served in celebration of a new baby, and it's thought to help increase the milk supply for nursing women. All of this—from your spice cabinet! I often steep caraway seeds in water to sip on as a tea during the winter months.

Is caraway seed a *Good Decision*? Yes!

Coriander and Cilantro

Coriander is not the same as cilantro, although they are products of the same plant. The fruits (seeds) are generally referred to as coriander, and the leaves are referred to as cilantro. Ground coriander seed is wonderful in desserts and sweet pastries, as well as in curries, meat, and seafood dishes. It can also be used in cakes, breads, cookies, or when pickling.

Coriander seeds have a health-supporting reputation that is high on the list of the healing spices. In parts of Europe, coriander is often referred to as an "anti-diabetic" plant. In parts of India, it has been used traditionally for its anti-inflammatory properties. In the United States, coriander has been studied recently for its cholesterol-lowering effects. I love coriander and cilantro with seafood, especially when I have menstrual cramps, or when I've worked out very hard and feel inflammation coming on. The Omega-3 fatty acids from fish combined with the anti-inflammatory properties of coriander are an anti-inflammatory dream meal come true.

Is coriander a *Good Decision*? Yes!

Fennel Seeds

Fennel seeds are small, yellowish-brown, seeds from a plant related to the celery and parsley families. In its plant form, fennel looks similar to celery with a bulbous white base. The seed can be used whole or ground and has a flavor similar to anise seed. Its distinct flavor is identified often in Italian sausages, but it can also add flavor to seafood and chicken dishes as well. The aromatic seeds have a licorice-like taste. In Asia and South America, fennel seeds are offered at the end of a meal to sweeten the breath and aid digestion.

Fennel is helpful in colic, protects the liver from harmful substances, and has a slight pain-reducing potential. Chewing on slices of raw fennel or dried fennel seeds after a meal aids digestion and relieves gas.

Is fennel a *Good Decision*? Yes!

Wine as a Sweetener

Wine and alcoholic beverages can add sweetness to many dishes, desserts, and main courses. They can bring depth and flavor to a sauce or broth, character to a dessert, and even replace fat when something needs a quick sauté. Wine is used in marinades to tenderize and bring extra flavor to proteins.

- White wine is great for sautéing vegetables or chicken.
- Red wine is often used in lamb, beef, or veal dishes.
- Madeira wine is often used in French cooking to bring flavor to a sauce or as a marinade for pork or chicken.
- Marsala wine is a vegetarian favorite that brings an earthy, rich flavor to mushrooms and anything else it comes in contact with.
- Rice wine is becoming more popular and can bring a light, fresh flavor to seafood and vegetables.
- Sweet dessert wines are exceptional for replacing sugar in dessert recipes, and a little goes a long way in creating a thick, syrupy sauce that you can pour over roasted fruit.

Wine has many health benefits; even the Bible instructs us to drink wine regularly. "Drink no longer water, but use a little wine for thy stomach's sake" (1 Timothy 5:23). It turns out that wine contains constituents that stimulate gastric juice secretions, which aid digestion. These constituents are produced when wine goes through the process of fermentation.

Wine and 100 percent dark chocolate (cacao) have many healthful properties; both stimulate digestion and are a delicious pairing! Yet, while even the Bible heralds wine for the stomach, it is still high in simple carbohydrates, as is chocolate. These are best reserved for those not-so-most-of-the-time special occasions.

Fennel and Muscat Orange Compote

Serves: 6
Total Time: 20 minutes, plus two hours to chill.

Ingredients

- 1½ cup Muscat wine
- ½ teaspoon fennel seeds
- 1 star anise
- 4 navel oranges
- 1 teaspoon fresh squeezed lime juice
- ½ cup thinly sliced fennel bulb
- Fennel fronds and star anise to garnish

Directions

1. In a small saucepan, bring wine, fennel seeds, and star anise to a boil. Reduce heat and simmer until liquid is reduced to ¼ cup. Set aside.

2. Segment oranges: Cut off the navel and stem ends of the oranges. This gives you a stable cutting surface and makes it easier to trim away the rest of the peel. Start at the top and slice downward following the curve of the fruit to trim away the skin and the pith. Use a paring knife to cut the orange segments away from the membranes (do this over a bowl to catch the juices). Slip the knife between one of the segments and the connective membrane. Cut until you reach the middle of the orange, but don't cut through any of the membrane. Do this again to create a wedge between membranes. Scoop out the segment using a scooping motion with the knife under the bottom edge of the citrus segment, and gently pry it away. The side still attached to a membrane will peel away, leaving you with a perfect wedge. Repeat with all the other segments.

3. Strain fennel wine mixture over orange segments and captured juices. Add lime juice and fennel slices; gently toss to coat fennel and oranges. Refrigerate for two hours or overnight. Serve chilled, and garnish with fennel fronds and star anise.

Other Sweeteners for Occasional Use

While better than white table sugar, the following sweeteners are recommended only for occasional consumption.

Jaggery

Jaggery, also known as gur, is an unrefined sugar made from sugar cane or the sap of date palms. The molasses and crystals have not been separated and, in its unrefined state, jaggery retains many of its vitamins and minerals, as well as some fiber. It is made without the use of chemical agents. Jaggery is part of many Indian recipes; its wonderful flavor is similar to brown sugar. Because it is heated to as high as 392F, it loses some of its nutritional strength. Still, it is a better choice than white table sugar.

Jaggery plays an important role in Indian culture, both in food and religion, where it is considered worthy of being offered to the gods. Many devotees prepare Paramannam—"Food of the Gods"—which consists of rice cooked in milk and flavored with jaggery and cardamom. Fresh jaggery is pale golden yellow, and it often can be mixed with crushed cardamom.

You need to check jaggery for freshness. Put a piece of jaggery in your mouth. If you notice a dominant salty taste, then it is not fresh. The older it gets, the saltier it tastes, which is important to keep in mind when you use jaggery in a dish. Old jaggery, however, should not be avoided.

In medicine, fresh jaggery can increase ailments such as cold and cough, as well as cause digestive disorders if consumed in excess. Old jaggery doesn't seem to have these side effects. The medicinal properties of jaggery are supposed to diminish in about three years' time.

In Ayurvedic medicine (a system of healing that originated in ancient India), jaggery is considered beneficial in the treatment of throat and lung infections.[14] The glycemic index of jaggery, however, is high and it is sweeter than table sugar. Use it sparingly, in authentic Indian dishes made to please the gods—and the spirit!

Is jaggery a *Good Decision*? Yes!

CHAPTER TWO

Sweeteners to Avoid

Molasses

Molasses is a byproduct of the process of refining sugar cane, grapes, or sugar beets into sugar. Blackstrap molasses is a byproduct of sugar cane. "First" molasses is left over when sugar cane juice is boiled, cooled, and has its crystals removed. If this product is boiled again, the result is called "second" molasses. Blackstrap molasses is made during the sugar syrup's third boiling. It contains substantial amounts of calcium, magnesium, potassium, and iron, but considering all molasses is a waste product of the sugar industry, we never really know what chemicals are used in the extraction process. Although one tablespoon of unsulphured molasses provides 15 percent of the daily value of manganese, some magnesium, potassium, and iron, it is not an ideal source of these nutrients.

There are three grades of molasses: sulphured, unsulphured, and blackstrap. Sulphur is used to process unripe green sugar cane. This chemical sulphur is not good for most human consumption. Sun-ripened sugar cane is processed without sulphur. Molasses is composed of 50 percent sucrose, has been refined, and is not a healthy decision. If you do choose to use molasses, choose organic, unsulphured blackstrap molasses and use it sparingly, only in those few dishes that just wouldn't taste the same without it.

Is molasses a *Good Decision*? No.

Muscavado, Turbinado, Demarara, and "Organic Raw Sugar"

These are all refined sugars, although not as refined as white sugar. These sugars go through a process called clarification, which typically involves unhealthy chemicals, although it's sometimes done through pressure filtration. After clarification, the product then goes through filtration, where it is treated with activated carbon. It then goes to a boiler, where it's heated in a vacuum, and fine "seed crystals" are added to aid in the formation of sugar crystals. Crystallization leaves behind a substance called "mother liquor," which will ultimately be made into molasses. To separate the mother liquor from the sugar crystals, they are put into a centrifuge. The final product is raw sugar, which is ready to be refined further into white sugar. Crystals are then reunited with some of the molasses in artificial proportions to make muscavado, turbinado, and demerara sugars.

In reality, "raw" sugar is not raw; it has been cooked and a lot of the minerals and vitamins are gone. Still, it's better than refined sugar because a little of the molasses, which contains nutrients, still clings to it. Because many of the valuable nutrients have been refined out of this product, often by chemical means, these are best avoided completely.

Are muscavado, turbinado, demarara, and "organic raw sugar" *Good Decisions*? No.

White Table Sugar

White table sugar is refined much more than the sugars just discussed, beginning with a process called affination. This is where the raw sugar crystals are melted into syrup and any remaining molasses is removed. Then the sugar is washed. From there, the sugar is clarified and bleached (decolored), either with phosphoric acid and calcium hydroxide or with calcium dioxide. Finally, the solution is boiled one last time to concentrate it into white granulated sugar crystals. Crystallized refined sugar is pure sucrose and contains no vitamins or minerals, just calories. Crystallized refined sugar is a "pure" industrial product, and can hardly be considered a food. Studies are beginning to show that it is closer to a drug—a drug that affects our bodies adversely and is very addictive.

Is white table sugar a *Good Decision*? No!

Brown Sugar

Brown sugar is simply white sugar mixed with molasses.

Is brown sugar a *Good Decision*? No.

Agave Nectar

Agave nectar can be found in most grocery stores. The main component of agave is starch, the same starch that is found in corn or rice. The process in which agave starch is converted into refined fructose, and then sold as the sweetener agave nectar, is similar to the refining process for high fructose corn syrup. It goes through a conversion process that refines, clarifies, heats, chemically alters, centrifuges, and filters the non-sweet starch into a highly refined sweetener: fructose.

Because fructose is not converted to blood glucose, refined fructose doesn't raise or crash blood sugar levels, hence the claim that it is safe for people with diabetes. Unfortunately, the downfalls of how this sweetener is processed far outweigh any perceived benefit.

Agave nectar is 90 percent fructose. High fructose corn syrup is 55 percent fructose. Once eaten, refined fructose appears as triglycerides in the bloodstream or as stored body fat. Elevated triglyceride levels, caused by consuming refined fructose, are building blocks for atherosclerosis, also known as "hardening of the arteries."

Studies have proven the relationship between refined fructose and obesity.[15] Additionally, fructose has been shown to cause mineral depletion, insulin resistance (which leads to diabetes), heart disease, liver inflammation, and obesity. In addition, it may be toxic if used during pregnancy.[16] Agave nectar is no better than high fructose corn syrup, and as more studies are done, it may end up being much worse.

Is agave nectar a *Good Decision*? No!

Stevia

Stevia (*Stevia rebaudiana*) is an herbal plant grown for its sweet leaves. It is up to 300 times sweeter than table sugar! It's considered a low glycemic, carbohydrate-free, calorie-free sweetener, and has been used in its natural form for centuries. It has quickly become popular in the U.S. and in many other countries.

In its whole leaf form, stevia has been shown to help stabilize blood pressure, normalize blood sugar levels in diabetics, and decrease the risk of osteoporosis by enhancing calcium absorption. In its natural form, stevia is a *Good Decision*.

As an herb, the sweet qualities can be removed from the leaf the same way you would make a tea. This liquid can then be boiled down or "concentrated" into a sweet liquid. The leaves can even be dried to form a powder. These methods have been used for centuries, and are safe methods for extracting and utilizing the sweet properties of this herb.

The sweetness of the stevia plant is due to the production of sweet constituents in the plant's leaves. These constituents, also known as steviol glycosides, are 50-450 times sweeter than sucrose. There are at least ten known steviol glycosides in the stevia leaf, with stevioside and rebaudioside A the most prevalent.[17]

Steviol glycoside extracts taken from stevia leaves are used to make sweeteners such as Truvia® and PureVia™. Truvia is a blend of rebiana and erythritol (developed jointly by Cargill and The Coca-Cola Company). PureVia was developed by PepsiCo and the Whole Earth Sweetener Company, a subsidiary of Merisant.

Both products use rebaudioside A, an extract derived from the stevia plant. Truvia and PureVia are not made from whole stevia, just two of its sweetest compounds, which raises important questions. Are these sweet constituents safe once you remove them from the original plant? How are these constituents removed and refined? Our bodies react differently to the two compounds; each compound is metabolized differently and remains in your body for different lengths of time. Although refined stevia is considered safe in small amounts, side effects are still possible. Documented side effects include gastrointestinal upset, myalgia (muscle pain), and asthenia (weakness).[18]

Instead of helping in weight loss, stevia, whether in extract or whole leaf form, may lead to obesity because it is up to 300 times sweeter than sugar, which tricks your body to overeat, since you are not getting any calories from stevia itself.

Many companies are jumping on the stevia bandwagon, extracting the sweet components and processing it in different ways, so it has become difficult to know how these components have been altered, what chemicals may be used in extraction, and whether these chemicals may still cling to the product. How the extracts are refined, and which products can be trusted, is a research paper waiting to be written.

Stevia comes in many forms. Powdered stevia is a white, powdered extract, produced in bulk or in packets, and blended with a filler. This is the most processed form of stevia. Some powdered forms of stevia extract can contain maltodextrin, a food additive derived from cornstarch that may contain MSG and "natural" flavors that are in no way natural. Once again, it is important to read the labels, particularly the list of ingredients.

Because compounds from the stevia plant can be legally used as a "natural" sweetener, the Coca-Cola and Pepsi companies plan to introduce a new beverage made with rebiana, an extract of stevia leaves, which is 200 times sweeter than sugar. But according to a report by toxicologists at the University of California, Los Angeles, several, though not all, laboratory tests show that the sweetener causes DNA damage, which raises the prospect that it might cause cancer. In a letter to the FDA, the Center for Science in the Public Interest said the agency should require additional tests, including a key animal study, before accepting rebiana for Generally Regarded as Safe (GRAS) status.

Many health practitioners say the extract made from the leaves of the stevia plant is the safest sweetener on the market. And unlike aspartame and other artificial sweeteners that have been cited for dangerous toxicities, these practitioners consider stevia to be a natural alternative that's ideal if you're watching your weight or if you're maintaining your health by avoiding sugar. Until more studies come out, I will continue to avoid the refined extracts made from this sweetener and will not recommend them to my clients, if solely for the reason that they may stimulate appetite and leave you hungry for more.

Some dark stevia concentrates are made by boiling stevia leaves in water and cooking them without any chemicals or alcohol until the liquid reduces and the proper concentration is reached. Dark stevia concentrate is a thick, dark-brown liquid that makes a good substitute for brown sugar and is a form of stevia that has not been refined or processed.

Green stevia is the dried leaves of the stevia plant. If you do choose to consume it, be sure to find green stevia powder, which is the unrefined whole stevia leaf. It is different from the processed white stevia powders and stevia liquids that are popular in health food stores. When looking into stevia for your own use, be sure to read the ingredient lists to be sure nothing else was added to it. You will either see stevia extracts listed as the main ingredient or unrefined whole leaf stevia listed as the main ingredient.

Are unrefined whole leaf green stevia powder and liquids *Good Decisions*? Yes.

Are refined and processed white stevia powders and liquids *Good Decisions*? No.

Evaporated Cane Juice

Evaporated cane juice is a loosely defined term. The FDA defines evaporated cane juice as any sweetener derived from sugar cane syrup.[19] Demerara, muscovado, and turbinado could all be considered evaporated cane juices and are heavily refined.

Is evaporated cane juice a *Good Decision*? No.

Brown Rice Syrup

Brown rice syrup is made when cooked rice is cultured with enzymes, which break down the starch in the rice. The resulting liquid is cooked down to a thick syrup, which is about half as sweet as white sugar and has a mild butterscotch flavor. It is composed of about 50 percent complex carbohydrates, which break down more slowly in the bloodstream than simple carbohydrates, resulting in a less dramatic spike in blood sugar levels. It is worth noting that the name "brown rice syrup" describes the color of the syrup, not the rice it's made from. It's made from white rice and contains few nutrients.

Is brown rice syrup a *Good Decision*? No.

High Fructose Corn Syrup

High fructose corn syrup goes through a conversion that refines, clarifies, heats, treats with chemicals, centrifuges, and filters the non-sweet starch from corn into a highly refined sweetener called fructose. There are many reasons to avoid this sweetener—its link to obesity being number one. It is made mostly from genetically modified corn, and many unhealthy chemicals are used in the refinement process. There is little nutrition in high fructose corn syrup—this we know for sure.

When I think about sweeteners, I think about how they are harvested. Would I eat raw honey straight from the hive? Absolutely. Would I suck on raw sugar cane? Sure. But I don't see myself walking into a cornfield and sucking on a corncob as a way to get high fructose corn syrup.

Is high fructose corn syrup a *Good Decision*? No!

Artificial Sweeteners

We've talked about how natural sugars are processed and refined to create a more consistent product with a longer shelf life. Now let's talk about manmade attempts to mimic nature.

Artificial sugars are created in labs, not in nature, and the process involves many different molecules and isolated amino acids. For instance, Splenda® is made from sugar through a process of chlorination. Adding chlorine to the sugar changes its structure and makes it unusable by the body, which is what makes it low calorie.

NutraSweet® is a totally artificial product.

Sweet'N Low® products are artificial products with a complex chemical structure of dextrose and saccharin. Dextrose is a natural carbohydrate used to dilute saccharin, which is the actual sweetener. Sweet'N Low is an artificial product, with a complex chemical structure.

Many studies show a convincing connection between artificial sweeteners and cancer.[20] One study, funded by the European Union and published in the *American Journal of Clinical Nutrition*, found that regular consumption of artificial sweeteners by pregnant women may increase their risk of premature birth.[21]

Another study conducted by researchers from Purdue University and published in the journal *Behavioral Neuroscience* determined that regular consumption of artificial, low-calorie sweeteners might actually cause people to gain more weight than similar consumption of white table sugar.[22] That's right—more weight. Researchers supplemented the diet of rats with either the artificial sweetener saccharin or with sugar. They found that the rats in the saccharin group actually gained more weight than the rats in the sugar group. This seemed to occur because the saccharin-consuming rats came to associate a sweet taste with the absence of calories and began to overeat as a consequence.

It seems that artificial sweeteners do not usually satisfy our craving for sweets or carbohydrates. In fact, artificial sweeteners may cause your taste buds to become accustomed to sweet flavors, which will cause you to want more sugar, not less.[23] The more sweets you eat, the more you get used to the sweet taste, and the more you'll require additional sweetness to satisfy your cravings. This is ironic, since originally, artificial sweeteners were developed as a sugar substitute for people with diabetes. Then, manufacturers discovered a huge market in a calorie-conscious society. Artificial sweeteners are synthetic food additives, and the side effects of these products do not look promising.

There is much to be uncertain about when it comes to these products, and while there are many studies attesting to the problems associated with these sweeteners, few studies have attested to any health benefits of artificial sweeteners.

Some scientists are concerned about the biochemical quirks of artificial sweeteners. For instance, the sweetener aspartame (NutraSweet®) is essentially a combination of two amino acids: aspartic acid and phenylalanine. Amino acids affect the brain differently than sugars. In natural foods, these amino acids enter the brain in conjunction with other naturally occurring nutrients. On their own, however, these isolated amino acids may have an unnatural effect and affect the brain in ways we may not know about for years to come.

While many artificial sweeteners have been approved for use in the United States, there are as many studies that indicate their safety as there are that warn of their dangers. Following are the top artificial sweeteners in the U.S. market:

- Aspartame, e.g., NutraSweet and Equal®
- Sucralose, e.g., Splenda®
- Neotame
- Acesulfame Potassium Acesulfame, e.g., SweetOne® and Sunnett®
- Saccharin, e.g., Sweet'N Low

While many of these may be listed as "safe," their nutrient content is nonexistent. There is no manganese, potassium, iron, or magnesium. They do not contain fiber, antioxidants, or any other health-supporting properties.

These products are not found in nature (which is why they are called artificial), and we do not know what the consequences of long-term consumption may be. Researchers have studied these artificial sweeteners as isolated products, so no one knows what happens when they're combined with other substances. When we consume artificial sweeteners, we don't just open a pack and swallow it; we consume them most often with other manufactured ingredients in processed foods.

Good Decisions recommends avoiding all artificial sweeteners.

Sugar Alcohols

Sugar alcohols are also known as sorbitol, xylitol, mannitol, maltitol, lactitol, isomalt, erythritol, and hydrogenated starch hydrolysates. These sugar alcohols are often made by adding hydrogen atoms to sugars. For example, adding hydrogen to glucose makes sorbitol. Xylitol in its natural form is found in the fibers of fruits and vegetables, as well as fibrous material from sugar cane, birch wood, or corn. When it goes through industrial production, however, Xylitol is derived from hardwoods or corncobs; it is then processed through a series of chemical reactions that involve the use of sulfuric acid, calcium oxide, phosphoric acid, and active charcoal. This results in a bleached, powdery blend of sugar alcohols that are not absorbed by the body but taste sweet. The problem with these substances, other than the fact that they have few nutrients, is that too much unabsorbed sugar alcohol traveling through the intestinal tract can cause bloating, gas, and diarrhea. Just what you need from a sweetener, right? A hydrogen gut bomb!

The FDA only requires a "laxative effect" warning notice on labels if consumers ingest 50 grams of sorbitol or 20 grams of mannitol from the food in a day. However, just 10 grams of sorbitol can cause stomach distress. Sugar alcohols are used as sweeteners and bulking agents. They are found in many processed foods labeled "sugar-free," including hard candies, cookies, chewing gum, soft drinks, and throat lozenges. They are also used in toothpaste and mouthwash.

Are sugar alcohols *Good Decisions*? No.

The Bottom Line on Sweeteners

Refined white table sugar, artificial sugars, and sugar alcohols come with many risks and few nutrients. Sugar alcohols and artificial sugars do not contain vitamins, minerals, antioxidants, or any other nutrients that will feed the human body. Some of them don't even satiate our sweet tooth and can actually stimulate appetite!

Honey, maple syrup, coconut sugar, fruit, spices, and herbs all offer something nutritionally valuable in the form of vitamins, minerals, antioxidants, fiber, and more.

When it comes to something sweet, *Good Decisions* recommends sticking with natural sweeteners for those not-so-most-of-the-time occasions.

I do realize that life is too short not to have chocolate and other sweet treats occasionally, which is why I include many dessert recipes on my website. These recipes have been adapted—I took what I'd call an unhealthy decision and made it better. Contrary to what many people think, honey, maple syrup, wine, spices, herbs, and unrefined cane and coconut sugar can be used as substitutes in any recipe and often improve the taste and nutrient value of the dish. Healthy choices don't have to taste bad. With a little ingenuity and creativity, you will be surprised to find how many ways there are to sweeten a dish without harming the body.

If you have chosen to step up to the "No Sugar Challenge," your sugar cravings will soon be a thing of the past and you'll enjoy the way you feel. It may seem challenging at first, but the more you use natural sweeteners, the easier it will get. Soon, you'll be confident in your ability to use herbs and spices to sweeten dishes, and on the special occasion when you choose to utilize honey, maple syrup, or unrefined coconut sugar, you will thoroughly enjoy it—without the addiction, without the guilt, and without adverse effects on your body.

CHAPTER TWO

The Psychology of Food
Truth and Knowledge vs. Emotion

Many of us ask the questions: Why, when we want to lose weight, do we know we should eat vegetables, legumes, and nuts, but falter and end up eating fast food, potato chips, or candy bars? Why, when it comes to things that we really want to do or achieve, do we start out with the best of intentions only to fall short?

The answers to these questions often involve methodology. How we go about providing for ourselves in healthy ways—whether we use emotions or truth and knowledge as the driving force behind our actions—is actually what determines how likely we are to succeed.

For example, say you decide to eat nuts as an evening snack. Then, out of nowhere, arises a powerful "desire" to eat the chocolate cake in the fridge; a difficult tug of war ensues. Nuts or chocolate cake...nuts or chocolate cake...? It can make for a very uncomfortable situation and can often drive you crazy!

If the decision is made based on truth and knowledge, you know that the protein and cholesterol in the nuts will likely aid sleep and help regulate your blood sugar levels throughout the night, helping you sleep better. If, however, you make the decision based on a strong "urge" (emotion), you will eat the chocolate cake to soothe yourself and to avoid the discomfort that arises from not having it. Even though you know that this behavior may result in weight gain and increased blood sugar levels, which can adversely affect sleep. It may also trigger guilt later on, especially if you overindulge!

Eating the nuts may not seem as appealing or tasty as the chocolate cake and feelings of rebellion may arise. You may tell yourself that it doesn't matter; you don't care if you are overweight, you deserve to have a treat; and you can likely come up with a number of other excuses. The excuses you come up with to choose the chocolate cake often arise from uncomfortable emotions that have not been acknowledged or managed. In short, you may not have been taught how to delay gratification for a greater cause.

The behavior that results from emotion is generally intended to soothe us, but those good feelings are short-lived and usually last only long enough to eat the chocolate cake, after which you may berate yourself for not having the willpower to make the healthy choice. But willpower really has nothing to do with it; however, learning how to handle your emotions does.

When a decision is made using knowledge and truth, you believe and trust in the knowledge that if you eat chocolate cake, it may not be conducive to weight loss. The challenge arises when you are in the heat of the moment and everyone at the table is eating chocolate cake but you. The emotions can be so strong, and sitting with the discomfort can be very uncomfortable. Learning to "abide" and let the emotions pass can be challenging. This experience is something I personally know very well. I love food, particularly chocolate cake, and I have fought the battle many times over whether or not to have the chocolate cake. This process makes *Good Decisions…Most of the Time* easier. Practice, it turns out, may not make perfect, but the more we practice, the better we become at being able to withstand the temptation.

The decision to lose weight or eat healthier can be made from intellect, but sticking with knowledge means you may have to bypass dessert. Just because you make the decision based on intellect doesn't mean you won't shift into feelings when you don't feel like behaving in a way that will bring you your desired results. When you operate from feelings and then falter, it is understandable because emotions can be so much more powerful than intellect, and the human body is naturally wired to operate based on emotions, i.e. seek pleasure; avoid pain.

To overcome this emotional-based eating involves increasing your awareness of the battle going on within you. It involves practice—practice being aware of your emotions and making a conscious effort toward doing the behavior that will bring you the effect you want. In this case, it would mean sitting with the discomfort of not having chocolate cake, learning to abide. This would be considered acting according to knowledge and truth, not feelings.

The ironic thing is that when you practice, you will find that your goal of losing weight is not the goal. The real goal is managing your emotions. We are driven to make an uncomfortable emotion feel better or make it feel less bad. The discomfort of not having chocolate cake is often so strong we give in to soothe ourselves and avoid the discomfort of not having what we want. In this day and age, where instant gratification is the American theme, we are not taught to delay gratification. In fact, we are often taught the opposite, and are encouraged to seek gratification.

There comes a point when you are sitting in the restaurant that another person orders dessert and then practically pushes it onto your plate. The emotion involved in saying "No" to someone and/or the emotion involved with the desire to have the dessert, can be so strong that it can be difficult to operate from truth and knowledge. This is what I refer to as the heat of the battle. And, the only way to win this battle is to sit through it—to allow the emotions to well up, but not act from them. When you do this, the emotion passes and you have won the battle, you have learned to abide. The more you do this, the more you "practice" abiding, the easier it becomes.

Whether it is weight loss, eating better, getting up earlier, or exercising that you would like to achieve, it is vital to realize that by using truth and knowledge, we can achieve our goals. That vision of your best self can become a reality by allowing your discomfort to be present, knowing it will pass.

Practicing Good Decisions

Awareness

Your homework today involves an awareness exercise. When you sit down for an evening meal, leave some food on your plate. Do not finish the whole portion on purpose. And don't over-serve yourself, knowing you must leave some behind! A good example meal for this exercise is to prepare an oversized chicken breast or piece of fish, and a large amount of salad greens or vegetables. When you sit down to eat, check in with your thoughts and emotions, and observe them like you're a third party on the sideline. Try to eat with a heightened awareness of when your body tells you it is beginning to feel full. When you receive the first inkling of a satiation signal indicating you have eaten enough, stop eating. Sit back and pay attention to your emotions and thoughts. You may find that the good angel on one shoulder and the little devil on the other may really go at it!

See if you can laugh at this and other thoughts that dance around in your mind. Then, after you are done laughing, and sitting in some discomfort, take action based on truth and knowledge and put your leftovers in a container for lunch tomorrow.

Chapter Three

Complex Carbohydrates and Digestive Wellness

In this chapter, you will learn about complex carbohydrates, which starches and gums to avoid and how to thicken a sauce naturally. How much fiber do you need? Which complex carbohydrates are most nutritious? Which should you avoid? These questions and others will be answered in this chapter. You will also learn how to improve digestion in order to achieve the perfect poop. You will discover which vegetable supports the liver and eliminates the nasty itch and burn of hemorrhoids, and which vegetable combination increases sexual function, immunity, and decreases inflammation. We will touch on nuts and seeds, and continue practicing the art of delaying gratification to gain confidence in our ability to reach our goals.

Complex Carbohydrate Basics

Remember from Chapter 1 that carbohydrates are organic compounds consisting only of carbon, hydrogen, and oxygen. We divided the carbohydrates into four chemical groups:

1. Monosaccharides

2. Disaccharides

3. Oligosaccharides

4. Polysaccharides

The monosaccharides and the disaccharides are the simple carbohydrates we discussed in chapters one and two. Oligosaccharides and polysaccharides are more complex and consist of many monosaccharides (simple carbohydrates) linked together, which is why they are known as "complex" carbohydrates.

Because polysaccharides consist of longer and more complex molecules, it requires time for the body to break them down, which means blood sugar levels don't elevate or drop as quickly as with simple carbs. Because of this, it's more likely your body will use this energy as opposed to storing it as fat.

Complex carbs contain nutrients in the form of fiber, vitamins, and minerals. They are a good source of antioxidants, which boost immunity and protect the body from the many unhealthy chemicals we encounter daily—from auto exhaust and industrial pollution to the chemicals in our shampoo—that can burden our livers and cause disease.

Examples of complex carbohydrates are:

·   Vegetables
·   Legumes
·   Whole grains

These foods have many healthful qualities. For instance, fructo-oligosaccharides (FOS) are found in many vegetables and serve as food for your intestinal microflora.[1] Microflora are those health-building probiotic organisms that live and grow in your intestinal system that were mentioned earlier. FOS can be found in leeks, onions, asparagus, burdock, chicory, and Jerusalem artichokes.

Complex carbohydrates such as vegetables, legumes, and whole grains are very nutrient-dense and contribute significantly to health and vitality. Unfortunately, they can also be refined into unhealthy versions of complex carbohydrates, which can be deceiving.

Complex carbohydrates, like simple carbohydrates, fall into two groups: unrefined and refined. As with simple carbohydrates, refining takes away many of the nutrients, vitamins, minerals, and fiber found in complex carbohydrates, which result in a much less nutrient-dense choice.

Unrefined Complex Carbohydrates: *Healthy Decisions*	Refined Complex Carbohydrates: *Unhealthy Decisions*
Organic Vegetables	Potato chips, French fries, Corn chips, Crackers
Organic Legumes (peas, beans, and lentils)	Processed soy products
100% Organic whole grains	Refined grain/flour products, Bread, Cereal, Pasta, White rice
Nuts and seeds	Biscuits, Cakes, Cookies

I can hear you screaming now! "What?! No pasta? No bread?" Remember, the name of this book is *Good Decisions...Most of the Time*. Pasta in small amounts may be consumed on those not-most-of-the-time special occasions. On those occasions, when you do consume pasta, try to eat it with high-fiber vegetables, legumes, protein, and a little healthy fat to slow the entrance of sugar into your bloodstream.

You will soon find that when you don't eat pasta regularly, it won't impact your health as dramatically when you do have pasta, but it may still put you on the couch wanting a nap!

Complex carbohydrates from whole grains provide sustained energy for athletic events and can help manage blood sugar irregularities. When I say whole grains, I mean those that have not been refined into flour. This refinement increases the surface area of the grain dramatically. Instead of having to work to break the grain down, your body hardly has to do a thing, as your blood sugar levels elevate quickly. The refined flour used to make whole grain bread and pasta breaks down sometimes just as quickly as white bread and cookies! This does not bode well for the athlete depending on complex carbohydrates as a sustainable energy source while training.

Starches

Starches are polysaccharides (complex carbohydrates) found in certain plants. This is the story of how healthy complex carbs can turn unhealthy. Refined starches are the most common carbohydrates in the human diet and include wheat, corn, rice, and root vegetables.

Starches are used to make bread, cereals, pancakes, pasta, French fries, and tortillas. Pure starch is processed away from the plant and refined to form a white, tasteless, and odorless powder that is often used in recipes as a thickening or binding agent. Starch in its raw form does not digest easily; in fact, up until the time humans started soaking and fermenting grains, and utilizing fire, eating raw grain was not a great way to get energy. Chewing on a raw whole grain like a wheat berry straight from the field, you have to admit, just wouldn't be very satisfying.

There are healthy starches (unprocessed and unrefined), and there are unhealthy starches (processed and refined). Unprocessed, "healthy" starches include brown rice, potatoes, organic corn, whole grains, and root vegetables. When properly prepared, these have many nutrients to support good health.

Often, people connect starchy foods with weight gain because starch breaks down relatively quickly into simple sugars, which can contribute to weight gain and elevated blood sugar levels. These days, it seems that anything that may cause weight gain is suspicious and many people believe they should be avoided. It's this misunderstanding about the nutritional value of these complex carbs that makes people avoid them.

Unrefined starches do have value in a balanced food plan, and you can consume them from time to time without a huge amount of guilt. However, if you find yourself gravitating toward potatoes, corn, and rice with every meal, you may want to take a break. Strong food cravings are the clues from your body that you may need to take a break from starchy carbs or at least reduce your intake of them for a while. It may be that you're still on the blood sugar roller coaster and aren't getting the most nutrient-dense foods nature has to offer.

It's always interesting when someone says, "I can't eat potatoes because of the starch and sugar," yet they have no problem reaching for a piece of pie. Reaching for a baked potato is a much healthier decision than eating a piece of pie, no matter how you slice it!

In their whole, unrefined form, these complex carbohydrates are nutritious, and they may be consumed in moderation. In their refined forms, however, these starches are highly processed, and chemicals such as sulfur dioxide, a potent asthma trigger that can affect the lungs and respiratory tract adversely,[2] are often used during the extraction process. Highly processed carbohydrates such as flours are also often bleached to make them appear more appetizing. They are not as nutritious as their whole food counterparts.

Today, the main commercial refined starches are cornstarch, wheat flour, and potato starch, but new starches and gums, such as arrowroot, locust bean gum/carob gum, guar gum, and tapioca starch are making their way to our grocery store shelves. These foods often go through the same extraction process, utilizing chemicals such as the sulfur dioxide mentioned before.

Refined starches contain few nutrients, break down much quicker than do their whole food counterparts, and elevate blood sugar levels more quickly and are best avoided most of the time.

Soon, you'll learn about some much healthier alternatives that can be used to thicken your favorite soup, sauce, or gravy!

Chilean Sea Bass with an Orange Dijon Reduction Sauce

Serves: 4

Total Time: 20 minutes

Ingredients

- Four 4-ounce Sea Bass filets, about 1-inch thick, washed and patted dry
- 1 teaspoon ghee
- 1 cup fresh squeezed orange juice with pulp
- 1 teaspoon Dijon mustard
- 1 tablespoon fresh chopped rosemary
- 2 tablespoons organic butter

Directions

1. Preheat oven to 425°F. Melt ghee in an oven safe skillet over medium-high heat coating the pan well. Using a paper towel, wipe the pan if needed to absorb any excess ghee. Place filets in pan presentation side down (skin side up); they will sizzle and make you feel like a professional chef. Sear until nicely browned. Flip the filets so the skin side is down and place in preheated oven for 10 minutes. Remove fish from pan and cover with foil.

2. While fish rests, drain any excess fat from the pan, leaving any bits and pieces in the pan to add flavor to the sauce. Whisk the orange juice, Dijon mustard, and rosemary together in a bowl. Pour into the saucepan and bring to a boil. Reduce heat to medium and continue to simmer gently until the sauce is reduced by half. Remove pan from heat and add 1 tablespoon butter, stirring until the butter is completely melted before adding the second tablespoon. Pour sauce over fish, garnish with a rosemary sprig, and serve. (The more pulp you extract from the orange when you juice it, the thicker the sauce.)

Gums

Gums are polysaccharides (complex carbohydrates) of natural origin that, when refined even in small amounts, can cause an increase in the thickness or stickiness of a solution. For instance, guar gum has eight times the thickening power of cornstarch and is used in many recipes that call for cornstarch. Locust bean gum, guar gum, and xanthum gums are often used to thicken dairy products. It would not be unusual to see one of these gums in the ingredient list on the back of a milk carton you thought was just good old-fashioned milk and nothing else.

You will also see gums used to thicken almond milk, coconut milk, hemp milk, and hazelnut milk. Because they can also thicken sauces, soups, and stews, gums are frequently used in the food industry and are processed and refined for use as thickening agents, jelling agents, emulsifying agents, and stabilizers. The key words to pay attention to are "processed" and "refined." If the gum used as a thickener is white and pretty, chances are high that it has been processed and refined.

Natural gums are classified according to their origin, and there are many gums used by the food industry. The following are just a few:

- Agar: taken from the cell walls of red algae
- Carageenan: extracted from red seaweed
- Chicle gum: comes from the chicle tree and is an older base used to make chewing gum
- Gellan gum: produced through fermentation of an algae
- Guar gum: derived from guar beans
- Locust bean gum: from the seeds of the carob tree
- Mastic gum: a gum from the mastic tree used as chewing gum in ancient Greece
- Spruce gum: a gum taken from the spruce tree and used by American Indians
- Xanthum gum: derived from the coat of a bacteria called *Xanthomonas campestris*

While some of these gums, like mastic gum, may be obtained in their raw unrefined form, most have been processed and/or refined. These gums may go through a process of cleaning, drying, bleaching, and extraction for uses in more than just the food industry. Gums are used in many different industries such as pharmaceutical, textile, tobacco, and paper industries or for use as a gel material in Petri dishes. Alcohol, preservatives, and chemicals are often used in processing, and the resulting product is practically void of nutrients.

Good Decisions recommends avoiding the processed and refined versions of these gums because of the lack of nutritional value and the high level of refinement with chemical agents.

Your decision to consume certain foods should depend on how much they have been processed and refined. Processed foods wreak havoc in the body, create inflammation, increase blood sugar levels, and lack nutrients, which makes the body crave more, which contributes to obesity.

I, like many other people, love a nice thick French sauce or a mouth-watering dessert but not at the expense of my health. Fortunately, I also love discovering ingenious ways to use nutrient-dense, whole, unrefined foods in recipes as a thickening agent that won't sacrifice taste and texture. Here are some methods you can use to thicken sauces, soups, and stews healthfully, without the use of refined starches or gums.

Natural Thickeners & Thickening Techniques in Cooking

If you love to cook and are reluctant to give up your refined flour or cornstarch, the following suggestions will help. These natural, nutritious choices and techniques can be used to thicken dishes and add texture and consistency, depending on the dish.

Reduction

This technique works great for sauces and makes amazing pan or reduction gravy. Simply simmering the sauce until enough water evaporates will thicken it nicely. This technique also concentrates and intensifies the flavor and is often used when making bone broths or stews. It also increases what I like to call the "yum factor."

Pan or reduction gravy is easy to make. It uses the pan drippings after cooking meat, seafood, or poultry to add flavor to the gravy or sauce.

Brazilian Fish Stew

Serves: 8
Total Time: 50 minutes

Ingredients

- 1/3 cup fresh lime juice
- ½ teaspoon salt
- ½ teaspoon fresh-ground black pepper
- 3 garlic cloves, minced
- 1½ pounds halibut, cut into 1-inch cubes
- 1½ pounds large shrimp, peeled and deveined
- 1 tablespoon coconut oil
- 2 cups chopped yellow onion
- 1 cup chopped green bell pepper
- 1 cup chopped red bell pepper
- 1 bunch minced green onions
- 5 cloves garlic, minced
- 1 bay leaf
- 2 cups chopped tomato
- ½ cup minced fresh cilantro, divided
- Two 8-ounce bottles of clam juice
- One 14.5-ounce can chicken broth
- One 13.66-ounce can coconut milk

Directions

1. Combine first 6 ingredients in a large bowl and toss to coat. Marinate in refrigerator 30 minutes.

2. Heat oil in a large Dutch oven over medium heat. Add onion, bell peppers, green onion, garlic, and bay leaf. Cook 6 minutes, stirring occasionally until soft. Increase heat to medium-high and add tomato, ¼ cup cilantro, clam juice, and broth. Bring to a boil, then reduce heat, and simmer 10 minutes. Discard bay leaf.

3. Puree hot vegetable mixture in a blender until smooth and return to pan. Add coconut milk and bring to a boil over medium-high heat. Cook 5 minutes. Add fish mixture; cook 3-5 minutes or until fish is done. Ladle stew into bowls, sprinkle with cilantro, and serve.

Pureed Vegetables

Pureed vegetables work great for soups such as butternut squash, cream of broccoli, mushroom, or a creamy tomato soup. If you have a recipe that needs thickening, think of a vegetable that will blend in with, or enhance the flavor of, the dish.

I often use pureed tomatoes, mushrooms, red peppers, and onions in soups, stews, and sauces. Almost any cooked vegetable can be pureed for use as a thickener. Zucchini or other squash, cauliflower, potatoes, sweet potatoes, yams, or carrots are excellent choices when you don't want the vegetable to add too much flavor. Simply steam a potato, mash it into your dish, and voila!—Consistency and thickness!

Organic Cream

Cream will thicken as it reduces. So if your body does well with dairy, add organic cream to a sauce and then simmer it. The sauce will thicken more when cream is used than reducing alone. Using both reduction and adding cream is also very tasty and really increases the "yum factor"!

Organic Yogurt

Yogurt is a popular soup thickener in Eastern Europe and the Middle East. You can use yogurt in many dishes where it will provide not only texture, but flavor as well. In Greek cuisine, yogurt is used in many sauces.

Organic Butter

Adding cold butter when you finish cooking a sauce will create a thickening effect. Be sure to reduce the heat to low and incorporate the butter slowly, a little at a time, to prevent separation.

Lamb Chops with Minted Yogurt Sauce

Serves: 4
Total Time: 35 minutes

Ingredients

- 1 cup fresh mint leaves, finely chopped
- 1 cup plain whole-fat yogurt
- 2 small cloves garlic, minced
- 2 teaspoons fresh lemon juice
- Eight 1-inch thick lamb loin chops
- 1 tablespoon ghee

Directions

1. In a small bowl combine mint, yogurt, garlic, lemon juice, and add salt and pepper to taste.

2. Pat the lamb chops dry and season with salt and pepper. Heat ghee in a skillet over medium-high heat until hot. Sear chops for 3 minutes or until nicely browned. Turn chops over and cook for an additional 3 minutes for medium-rare. Transfer chops to a plate and keep warm, covered with foil. Let chops rest for 5 minutes. Serve with yogurt-mint sauce. Garnish with fresh mint.

Seared Scallops Beurre Blanc

Serves: 4
Total Time: 20 minutes

Ingredients

- 12 medium scallops, washed and dried
- 1 tablespoon ghee
- 2 tablespoons white wine vinegar
- 1/3 cup white wine
- 2 tablespoons chopped shallots
- ½ teaspoon salt
- Pinch of white pepper
- 4 tablespoons organic butter
- Green pea sprouts (to garnish)

Directions

1. Melt ghee in a skillet over medium-high heat, coating the pan well. Using a paper towel, wipe the pan if needed to absorb any excess oil. Place scallops in pan and sear until nicely browned. Flip the scallops and cook until desired doneness, 3-5 minutes for medium rare. Remove from pan, cover loosely, and set aside.

2. In the same pan, combine vinegar, wine, shallots, salt, and pepper. Simmer to reduce the mixture to ¼ cup. Remove from heat and whisk in butter, 1 tablespoon at a time. Spoon sauce over scallops and garnish with sprouts. These can also be served on a bed of pea sprouts, whichever you prefer.

Almost Eggs Benedict

Serves: 4

Total Time: 25 minutes
Ingredients

For the Hollandaise Sauce:

- 4 egg yolks
- ¼ teaspoon Dijon mustard
- 1 tablespoon lemon juice
- 1/8 teaspoon Worcestershire sauce
- Pinch cayenne
- Pinch salt
- ½ cup butter

For The Benedict:

- 4 cups sliced yellow onions
- 3 cups hash browns
- 4 medium slices pre-cooked Black Forest ham
- 4 poached eggs
- 2 tablespoons sliced green onions for garnish

Directions

1. In a blender or food processor, combine the egg yolks, mustard, lemon juice, Worcestershire sauce, cayenne pepper, and salt. Blend for about 5 seconds. Melt the butter slowly in a small pot. Do not let it boil. Set the blender on high speed, and pour the butter into the egg yolk mixture in a thin stream. It should thicken almost immediately.

2. Sauté onions over medium heat until soft and onions begin to caramelize and turn brown. Set aside and cover to keep warm.

3. Cook hash browns until crisp and nicely browned. Salt and pepper to taste.

4. While onions and hash browns are cooking, poach four eggs and sear ham until warm and ham begins to brown. You will have many pans cooking at the same time! You're a professional now!

5. Place ½ cup hash browns on a plate, top with sautéed onions, 1 ham slice, and 1 poached egg. Top with Hollandaise sauce, and garnish with sliced green onions.

Notice: Consumption of raw or undercooked eggs may increase your risk of food borne illness.

Eggs

Did you ever think you would consider mayonnaise healthy? At its heart, mayonnaise is nothing more than oil and egg whites. What about Hollandaise sauce? Yes! An egg yolk can create a delicious thick sauce or dressing, especially if the sauce contains oil or fat. Don't add the yolk directly to a hot sauce, or the yolk will cook like scrambled eggs. Instead, "temper" the yolk(s) by combining a small amount of the sauce with the eggs to bring them up to temperature gradually. Then add the tempered eggs to the sauce.

No double boiler is needed for this recipe, using the blender to emulsify the ingredients means no chance of the sauce separating! Yay! Finally! An easy Hollandaise sauce that is healthy too! This is what I call making a poor decision better.

Grains

You may also wish to use pre-soaked whole grains to thicken soups and stews. Some of the most healthful grains that can be used to thicken a soup, stew, or sauce are: red, black, or wild rice, quinoa, amaranth, buckwheat, hato mugi, and teff.

Meat and Fish Glacés

While a glaze can be any sauce spread over desserts and hams to make it shine and give it a sweet or savory flavor, a glacé is similar to a reduction sauce, but often the two terms are used interchangeably. Glacés are an old-school way of thickening and enriching sauces made by reducing broth and other flavorful ingredients, until the sauce is thick and gelatinous. The resulting sauce is then added to a meat or vegetable to increase flavor and nutrients.

Glacés can be time-consuming to prepare and expensive if you buy them ready-made. However, using them is a phenomenal way to increase flavor and add valuable minerals and nutrients to a dish. I drool whenever I make these because they are so flavorful and delicious.

This technique is by far one of my favorites, but it does require patience. I have an excellent recipe for a meat glacé on my website at www.gooddecisions.com. Store-bought versions are just as tasty and more convenient, so don't let the time required to makes these stop you from enjoying them!

Duck Breast with Cumin Demi Glacé

Serves: 4

Total Time: 30 minutes

Ingredients

- Four 4-6-ounce duck breasts
- 1 teaspoon ghee
- 1 cup demi glacé
  (your own preparation or purchased)
- 1 tablespoon cumin seeds,
  toasted and ground
- 2 cups carrots, diced
- 1 cup red potato, diced
- ½ cup sugar snap peas
- 2 tablespoons chopped parsley to garnish

Directions

1. Preheat oven to 425°F. Score the duck breast by using a small knife to cut four diagonal lines across the skin and through the fat layer. Be careful not to pierce the meat. Heat ghee in an oven safe skillet over medium-high heat, using a paper towel to soak up any excess ghee. The pan should be only lightly coated. Place the duck into the pan skin-side down and sear until nicely browned. Flip duck over and transfer to preheated oven for 5-7 minutes. Remove duck from oven and cover loosely with foil. (Save the fat dripping for sautéing vegetables later!)

2. While the duck is cooking, simmer the demi glacé with the cumin seeds for 5 minutes and set aside.

3. Steam the carrots and potatoes until almost tender. Add snap peas to the steamer, and steam 3-5 minutes. Remove from heat. Place the vegetables onto four plates. Slice the duck and place over the vegetables. Spoon the demi glacé over the duck and vegetables, season with salt and pepper, and garnish with parsley.

Roasted Chicken with Green Pipian Sauce

Serves: 6

Total Time: 50 minutes

Ingredients

- 6 small chicken hindquarters
- 1-2 tablespoons melted ghee
- ½ cup hulled untoasted pumpkin seeds
- ½ pound tomatillos, husked, rinsed, and coarsely chopped
- ½ jalapeño stemmed, seeded, and roughly chopped
- 3 romaine lettuce leaves, torn into pieces
- ½ small white onion, coarsely chopped
- 3 small garlic cloves
- ¼ cup loosely packed chopped cilantro
- 1½ cups chicken broth
- 1 tablespoon olive oil
- Unrefined sea salt to taste

Directions

1. Preheat oven to 425°F. Wash and pat dry chicken. Coat chicken lightly with ghee and season with salt and pepper. Bake for 25-30 minutes. Remove from oven and cover lightly with foil. Let rest for 10 minutes.

2. While chicken is baking, heat a small saucepan over medium heat and add the pumpkin seeds. Wait until you hear one pop, then stir constantly until the seeds have puffed, popped, and smell toasty. Transfer to a bowl and allow to cool. Place cooled pumpkin seeds in a blender, and add the tomatillos, jalapeno, lettuce,

onion, garlic, cilantro, and ½ cup of the chicken broth. Cover the blender and blend the mixture until smooth.

3. Heat the olive oil in a small saucepan over medium heat. Drizzle in the pumpkin seed mixture and cook, stirring, until the mixture darkens and thickens, 8 to 10 minutes. Add the remaining chicken broth and bring to a simmer, reduce the heat to medium-low, and simmer uncovered, stirring often, until the sauce is thick and creamy, about 15 minutes. Season to taste with salt.

4. Place chicken on a plate. Spoon sauce over chicken and garnish with chopped cilantro and toasted pumpkin seeds. Serve.

Nuts and Nut Butters

Nuts make good, flavorful thickeners for stews and sauces. Just grind them down into a flour or butter and add them to the dish. Nut butters (sesame, almond, cashew, etc.) work also. I use these often in Asian recipes, salad dressings, and sauces.

Fruit

Choose a fruit that complements the sauce, then puree it, and add it to the sauce for a thicker consistency. Apples, oranges, plums, guava, apricots, cherries, gooseberries, and quinces are all good sources of fiber and pectin that add nutrients, flavor, and consistency to sauces. Why would you want to use refined flour or genetically modified cornstarch with all of these tasty, nutritious alternatives around?

Nutritional Nugget

Are you tired of spending money on berries, just to have them grow mold? Washing fruits and vegetables in vinegar water before storing them kills mold spores and bacteria on the surface of the fruit, preventing mold, and saving you money!

Seared Prawns with Apricot Habanero Sauce

Serves: 6

Total Time: 30 minutes

Ingredients

- 1 small onion, coarsely chopped
- 3 small cloves garlic, chopped
- 1 tablespoon extra virgin olive oil
- 1 yellow bell pepper
- 1 cup water
- ¾ cup dried apricots
- 2 tablespoons raw honey
- 5 tablespoons apple cider vinegar
- 1 tablespoon Dijon mustard
- 2 teaspoons habanero pepper sauce (more if you like extra spice)
- 18 large prawns
- 1 teaspoon olive oil
- 2 cups loosely packed Bibb lettuce
- Salt to taste
- White or black sesame seeds to garnish

Directions

1. In a large skillet over medium heat, sauté onion and garlic in oil until fragrant. Add bell pepper, water, apricots, honey, and apple cider vinegar. Stir together and simmer until apricots are soft, about 15 minutes. Combine mixture with mustard, hot sauce, and salt in a food processor. Blend until smooth. Makes about 2½ cups.

2. In a large skillet, sauté prawns in one teaspoon olive oil over medium heat for three minutes, salt to taste. Place prawns on a bed of Bibb lettuce and spoon sauce over. Garnish with sesame seeds and serve.

Legumes

Legumes are a class of vegetables that includes beans, peas, and lentils. They are a very good source of fiber in the form of cellulose. Cellulose provides structure and strength to the cell walls of nearly all plants. It also provides fiber in our diets. This fiber can also thicken a sauce when you mash it into a dish. Cellulose is a polysaccharide (complex carbohydrate), and it is the most common organic compound on earth. About 33 percent of all plant matter is cellulose.

Some animals, particularly ruminants (animals that chew their cud), can digest cellulose with the help of microorganisms that live in their guts. Humans don't digest cellulose as well, which is why we refer to it as "dietary fiber" or "roughage." When we eat it, it passes right through us. Legumes, along with vegetables and fruits, are abundant in cellulose and are *Good Decisions* when it comes to thickening sauces, soups, and stews. Pureed garbanzo beans, for example, have a mild taste that works well as a thickening agent, and they are an excellent source of cellulose and fiber. Let's talk more about fiber.

What Is Fiber and Why Is It Important?

Dietary fiber is the edible portion of plant cell walls that are resistant to digestion. Because of this, it takes longer for your system to process dietary fiber. As a result, you'll have an increased feeling of fullness and satiety, which means your hunger level will decrease, and you will feel fuller, longer. This is a huge boon for weight loss, as it reduces food intake at meals. In addition, fiber slows the entrance of sugar into the bloodstream, thereby preventing large spikes in blood glucose and insulin. Legumes, fruits, vegetables, and particularly green plants are great sources of cellulose. Kale, spinach, collard greens, beet greens, and lettuce are All-Star Foods that contain plenty of cellulose as well as an abundance of other nutrients.

Nutritional Nugget

A surefire way to convert those who do not like dark leafy green vegetables is to add fresh squeezed lemon after a light sauté. This addition cuts the bitterness and changes the taste of the greens dramatically. Be sure not to overcook dark leafy greens. They are best cooked until just wilted but not soggy.

Recommended Fiber Intakes

The recommended fiber intake is 38 grams per day for men and 25 grams per day for women. Use these amounts as guidelines, but not exact numbers. Depending on your size and other factors, the amount of fiber any individual needs varies.

Paying attention to your body and bowel movements when you eat fiber will tell you whether you are getting enough. When your bowel movements become full and easy to evacuate, you have reached your goal. If you are not one to be "in tune" with your body, don't worry about it. I will teach you how to become in tune with your body in the following chapters when I discuss the psychology of food. High-fiber foods will naturally bulk up diarrhea and soften constipation.

The best food sources of fiber are vegetables, peas, lentils, beans, nuts, seeds, and fruits. One hundred grams of sunflower seeds provides 10.6 grams of fiber, 100 grams of beans will roughly give you 10.5 grams of fiber, and one cup of acorn squash will give you 9 grams of fiber. So when you eat a healthy diet, it isn't as difficult as you might think to incorporate fiber. This makes for a very happy digestive tract and helps with weight management.

Incorporating fiber-rich foods can eliminate many cases of constipation or diarrhea. Grams are the standard measurements used to label the amount of carbohydrates, proteins, fats, and fiber on all labels throughout the U.S. If you have a hard time visualizing how much 100 grams is, imagine a shot glass. The typical shot glass holds 1½ ounces, which is roughly 42.5 grams, so, 100 grams would equal almost 2.5 shot glasses.

You may have seen fiber on a label listed as soluble or insoluble. What is the difference? The body absorbs neither soluble nor insoluble fiber, and they are equally beneficial; they just have different properties when mixed with water.

Soluble Fiber

Soluble fiber is "soluble" in water. When mixed with water, soluble fiber forms a gel-like substance and swells. In the body, it binds with fatty acids. This, combined with the swelling effect, prolongs stomach-emptying time. As a result, glucose is released and absorbed more slowly. The benefits of soluble fiber include moderating blood glucose levels, lowering cholesterol, triglyceride levels, and giving you that "I'm full" sensation, which can decrease your appetite.

The biggest role of fiber is to encourage elimination, which prevents liver toxicity and promotes healthy gastrointestinal function. Sometimes the liver can be overburdened, from dealing with chemicals in our environment, pesticides on our foods, additives, preservatives, and more. By consuming adequate fiber, you generate healthy bowel movements; this aids the elimination of these dangerous, non-nutritive substances, which in turn decreases the burden on the liver. Scientific names for soluble fibers include pectins, gums, mucilages, and some hemicelluloses.

Good sources of soluble fiber include:

- Oats and oatmeal
- Legumes (peas, beans, lentils)
- Barley
- Fruits such as oranges and apples
- Vegetables such as carrots

Insoluble Fiber

Insoluble fiber does not absorb or dissolve in water, and it offers many benefits to intestinal health. It passes through your digestive system with very little change in form. Because it plays a key role in moving bulk through the intestines, it prevents constipation and reduces the risk and occurrence of colorectal cancer and hemorrhoids. It also controls and balances the acidity (pH) in the intestines, which is important because acidity is your first line of defense against microorganisms like bacteria and viruses that can cause disease after they enter your digestive system.

One of the reasons probiotics are effective in treating Candida is that they produce small amounts of acid. This helps rebalance the pH in your intestine, creating a favorable pH environment for the good bacteria to grow, and an unfavorable pH environment for Candida to grow. This makes fiber and probiotic-rich foods essential for optimum intestinal health.

Sources of insoluble fiber include:

- Green beans and dark leafy vegetables
- Fruit skins and root vegetable skins
- Whole grain products
- Seeds and nuts

Fiber's Role in Weight Loss

Every day, microbiotic organisms wage war in your body. Some of these organisms are conducive to leanness, and some obesity.[3] Eating a high fiber diet encourages organisms conducive to leanness to take up residence in the gut. This appears to happen because the lean bacteria digest more fiber, which results in an increase in short chain fatty acids. These fatty acids may increase calorie burning, and thus, decrease the potential for fat to accumulate in fat cells. They also have been shown to increase satiety hormones.

High-fiber dishes abound, and they're delicious! Some say that pooping is one of the great joys in life, and I agree. There's nothing better than the perfect poop (one which you don't have to wipe!).

Nutritional Nugget

Drinking a glass of fresh beet juice or eating beets daily for two weeks can eliminate the discomfort of hemorrhoids. It will not cure the underlying problem, which is a congested liver, but it is a fantastic way to eliminate the symptoms while you give your liver a chance to recover.

Since dietary fiber is found only in plant products (i.e., nuts, seeds, whole grains, legumes, fruits, and vegetables), these foods are essential to a healthy diet. The average American falls terribly short of the recommended daily amount of fiber, consuming on average only 12 to 17 grams per day.

Most people are unfamiliar with how many grams of fiber are available in food. The only way to get a feel for this is to take a few days and look up the number of grams of fiber on the labels of the food you consume daily. Reading about this is not enough. If you want to experience the perfect poop and get your digestion moving to the rhythm of healthy bowels, then you must know which foods are high in fiber and which are not. Once you experience what enough fiber in your diet feels like and what foods you need to consume to reach your fiber goals, you will have mastered one of the biggest nutritional challenges people face. I can tell you what high fiber foods to eat, but until you become aware of what enough fiber in your diet feels like, you may never know the joy of healthy bowel movements.

The second goal of *Good Decisions…Most of the Time* is to improve digestion. Along with regulated blood sugar levels, optimum digestion is essential to health and wellbeing. If digestion isn't working, nutrients cannot be absorbed and wastes cannot be removed. So what do you say? Shall we improve your digestion?

Improving Digestion
Building the Second Nutritional Foundation

Digestion is one of the five nutritional foundations. Your entire body depends on nutrients digested and absorbed by your digestive system to function. If this foundation is weak, your entire body can be affected, and even the healthiest food can become a toxic mal-digested mess. Digestion is so critical to nutrient absorption that some nutritionists specialize in digestive health only and limit their practice to digestive issues.

So how do we strengthen our digestive systems?

Increase Fiber Intake

Keep the 25-38 grams of fiber guideline in mind, but honor your body; you will know when you have reached your fiber goals by the toilet paper you save!

Consuming fiber from whole foods daily is the best way to get an idea of how much fiber is in certain foods, where you may be falling short, and which foods you need to add to reach your goal. Be sure to drink lots of water to help the fiber move through your intestines.

Legumes, vegetables, whole grains, fruits, nuts, and seeds will be your top fiber foods (especially legumes). Because these don't have labels, you will have to look up the amount of fiber in them. This may seem inconvenient at first, but you will get a good feel for the amount of fiber within them in only a few days. If you have been dealing with constipation or diarrhea, you may be happy to find that increasing fiber in your diet is all that is needed to bring your digestion back to normal. The more processed the food, typically the lower its fiber content will be.

Here are some ways to increase dietary fiber in your diet:

- Choose whole fruits and vegetables, with peels when possible.
- Incorporate more beans, peas, and lentils in meals.

- Incorporate nuts and seeds as snacks or part of meals.
- Choose 100 percent whole grains such as rice, quinoa, teff, amaranth, and oatmeal in place of their refined counterparts (cereal, bread, and pasta).
- Replace white rice with red, black, or brown rice. These retain the bran layer, which is rich in minerals, vitamins, and fiber.
- When cooking, replace white flour and sugar with mashed fruits and vegetables.

If you are not accustomed to a high-fiber diet, increasing your fiber intake slowly may cause an initial increase in gas or bloating. This should eventually decrease, and gas and bloating should disappear. If not, you may need to look at how well you are digesting your food and take the following steps to ensure these healthy foods are not only digested, but also absorbed.

Remove Substances that Inhibit Digestion

The stomach relies heavily on stomach acid, more specifically hydrochloric acid (HCL), to break down food. Excessive simple carbohydrate consumption, alcohol consumption, and stress can all inhibit HCL production, leaving food to rot in your belly. Addressing stress and reducing alcohol and sugar consumption will do much to aid digestion.

Eliminate Food Allergies and Sensitivities

Tuning into your body and eliminating any foods you may be sensitive to can decrease inflammation in the intestines and allow them to heal. This change may correct some cases of diarrhea, constipation, cramping, and other intestinal issues. The most prevalent food sensitivities are to wheat and other gluten-containing grains, soy, dairy, corn, and sugar. If you are unsure, eliminate these foods while you are on the No Sugar Challenge. After four weeks, bring one food item back in per week, and pay close attention to how you feel when you bring it back in. If your pulse escalates, or you experience joint pain, brain fog, headaches, skin problems, eczema, or gas, it indicates a sensitivity may be present. You may also feel bloated, fatigued, or get cramping, diarrhea, and have an increase in mucus or sinusitis. These symptoms are telling you that a certain food should be avoided.

Stimulate Gastric Secretions

Some minerals, such as calcium, require an acid environment to be absorbed and utilized. If you are stressed and production of HCL is shut down in order for you to "fight" or take "flight," mineral absorption and bone health take a back seat. Stimulating digestion with bitters and waiting until your stomach "growls" with hunger before you eat will ensure your food is digested. When you haven't eaten for a while, a message is sent to your stomach and intestines, which triggers contractions and the release of acids and other digestive fluids—which cause the rumbling, grumbling sounds you hear. Staying in tune with your body and only eating when you are hungry is an excellent way to support a healthy digestive system.

Don't Overeat

While overeating may cause your stomach to feel like it's about to rupture, the stomach is almost always capable of handling the large amounts of food we put into it. It will, however, take steps to release this pressure and the path of least resistance is usually up. This means acid reflux, indigestion, and heartburn are usually not too far behind an overindulgence. Eating large amounts of food taxes the body and overwhelms the digestive system so overeating is best reserved for Thanksgiving only.

Be Relaxed When You Eat

Digestion shuts down when you are stressed and in "flight or fight" mode. Relaxing and waiting until your stomach growls ensures digestive juices are being secreted.

Chew your Food Well

Large chunks of food are harder for the stomach and small intestine to break down, making it difficult for the body to absorb the nutrients. Chewing food really well increases the surface area of the food and helps the stomach to digest what you eat.

Regulate Blood Sugar Imbalances

If the pancreas is working hard to secrete insulin because of blood sugar irregularities, it may push aside digestive responsibilities and prioritize blood sugar regulation. This means mal-digested foods may be passed into your intestines where they can create inflammation. If you are well hydrated, your body may try to flush these mal-digested foods out of your body in the form of diarrhea. If you are dehydrated, the body will try and wring every last bit of water from these foods and constipation may occur. The body will also try to eliminate excess sugar in the urine, which may contribute to dehydration and sluggish digestion.

Drink Lots of Water

Water is one of the most helpful aids to digestion. Drinking eight to ten glasses of water each day keeps the body hydrated and the digestive tract well-lubricated. Hydration enables poop to slide effortlessly from the body, resulting in the "perfect" no-wipe "poop."

Other Helpful Hints

- *Limit water with meals.* Fluids dilute your gastric juices, making it harder for them to break down your food. Consume most of your water between meals.
- *Begin meals with a small bitter green salad.* Bitter greens stimulate digestive juices and provide valuable minerals. Endive, dandelion greens, escarole, and mustard greens are some examples of bitter greens.
- *Top bitter green salads with vinegar dressings.* Vinegar is also a digestive aid.
- *Add ginger or cloves to your foods or drink ginger tea.* They are great digestive stimulants.
- *Utilize liquid bitters.* For an extra digestive boost, utilize liquid bitters to stimulate your digestive system before meals. These can be found in most grocery stores in the mixer section.

- *Digestive aids may be indicated.* Supplemental hydrochloric acid and/or digestive enzymes can be helpful in some cases. These are available online and in some nutritional supplement stores.

Things that may help with cramps, gas, and bloating are:

- Utilize caraway, cumin, and fennel in your dishes. They ease indigestion, bloating, and gas.
- Mint tea soothes an upset stomach.
- Chewing on peppermint leaves can ease cramps and intestinal spasms.

It is important to understand digestion's role in optimal health; if digestion is compromised, it can burden the liver, throw off hormonal balance, and create toxicity, which can manifest as acne, bad breath, gas, bloating, foul-smelling bowel movements, and more.

Nutritional Nugget

To decrease gas and bloating, chew on ¼ to ½ teaspoon of fennel seeds (member of the same family as anise seeds) found in your spice cabinet. These are natural flatulence fighters (carminatives) used by the herbal community as a powerful way to decrease the discomfort of gas and bloating.

Poor digestion also compromises our immune system and makes it more difficult for us to ward of pathogens that we come into contact with.

The "Big Four" All-Star Complex Carbohydrates

Unrefined complex carbohydrates are phenomenal because they take time to break down. Therefore, the energy they release goes into your bloodstream gradually. This gradual release helps keep blood sugar levels regulated so you will not have to suffer through blood sugar ups and downs. Therefore, you'll bypass the simple carbohydrate roller coaster. Your mood will improve, mental clarity will increase, and you will be on an even keel of energy throughout the day. Complex carbohydrates support our first nutritional foundation: blood sugar regulation.

Unprocessed, unrefined complex carbohydrates provide your body with fiber, vitamins, minerals, enzymes, and other wonderful substances your digestive system needs to function optimally. They leave your body clean and running like a finely tuned biological machine! Complex carbohydrates also support our second nutritional foundation: digestion.

Weight loss is an additional benefit of consuming a diet rich in unrefined complex carbohydrates. In addition, complex carbohydrates contain antioxidants and other nutrients that help prevent cancer, diabetes, immune disorders, and more. I can't think of any better foods to accompany you on your journey down the hallway of life than complex carbohydrates. Consume these All-Star foods daily.

Let's look at the "Big Four" complex carbohydrate *Good Decisions* in a little more depth. We will start with vegetables, then legumes, and end with nuts, seeds, and grains.

1. Vegetables

Vegetables are the All-Star complex carbohydrate and *Good Decisions* encourages you to eat as many of them as you like. That's right, absolutely no restrictions with vegetable consumption. "Even potatoes?" you ask. Yes, potatoes are fine. Some sixty different phytochemicals and vitamins have been found in the skins and flesh of 100 wild- and commercially-grown potatoes. Some varieties even rival the phenolic (antioxidant) content in broccoli.[4] But this doesn't mean you should consume potatoes every day.

It's important to eat a variety of vegetables, because nutritionally, each vegetable offers something different. Bright-orange vegetables are rich in beta-carotene, a powerful antioxidant substance that helps protect cells from the damaging effects of oxidation. The deep blue-red pigments of beets and eggplant have anti-cancer properties. Cooked cabbage can lower cholesterol, and sauerkraut and sunchokes feed the good bacteria within us. For men, tomatoes are powerful in preventing prostate cancer. Mushrooms eaten in conjunction with chemotherapy have been shown to increase its efficacy.[5] I could go on and on!

Each bright color gives your body something different, so don't rely on potatoes and carrots as your staples. While both have healthful qualities, it's much better to eat a variety of vegetables.

Incorporating abundant vegetables in your diet will do much to keep your body healthy and your energy levels high. For more information on individual vegetables and how they can be used to support the body, visit my website at www.gooddecisions.com.

Can't afford to buy organic, but still want to avoid pesticides and other unhealthy substances? No problem. Visit the Environmental Working Group's website (http://www.ewg.org/foodnews/) for a list of the "dirty dozen" fruits and vegetables to avoid and the "clean fifteen" to look for.

Nutritional Nugget

Onions, garlic, and ginger! These bulbous beauties, when combined, can increase sexual function, boost your immune system, and decrease inflammation—all in one meal! This combination is so "potent" that monks avoid it completely. I suppose when you're meditating and on a search for enlightenment, the last thing you need is a little movement down there! Who said food isn't powerful?

The important thing to remember about vegetables is that you must eat them! *Good Decisions* recommends incorporating vegetables into every meal and as snacks between meals. Some people say you should only eat raw vegetables. Others say cooking increases their digestibility. I say just eat them—any way you can! The more vegetables you eat, the better.

Best Beet and Red Onion Salad

Serves: 6
Total Time: 25 minutes

Ingredients

- 2 pounds small organic beets
- 3 tablespoons red wine vinegar
- 2 tablespoons extra virgin olive oil
- 1½ cups thinly sliced red onion
- 6 cups frisée bitter greens
- Unrefined sea salt and freshly ground pepper to taste

Directions

1. Remove the root and stems of the beets and discard; clean beets with a brush or sponge and cut beets into wedges. Steam beets until easily pierced with a fork. Remove from pan and let cool.

2. Combine vinegar, oil, salt, and pepper in a large bowl, stirring with a whisk. Add beets and onion; toss gently to coat. Place on a bed of frisée lettuce and serve.

2. Legumes

Legumes are a class of vegetables that includes beans, peas, and lentils. They are often forgotten, yet they are among the most versatile and nutritious foods available. Legumes are high in folate (a B vitamin), potassium, iron, and magnesium. They also contain beneficial soluble and insoluble fiber. For a good source of protein, vegetarians often use legumes as a substitute for meat.

All legumes contain phytic acid, called phytate in its salt form, which is found in the outer layer or seed coat. Untreated phytic acid can bind to calcium, magnesium, copper, iron, and zinc in the intestinal tract and block their absorption.[6,7] This is why a diet high in unfermented legumes may not only cause gas and bloating, but lead to mineral deficiencies and bone loss, making your meal nutrient-depleting, not nutrient-giving.[8] Legumes are famous for their gas-producing effects. This happens when they have not been properly soaked. Unsoaked legumes not only produce gas, but are harder to digest.

Phytic acid also inhibits enzymes we need to digest our food. One enzyme is pepsin, needed for the breakdown of proteins in the stomach. Another is amylase, needed for the breakdown of starch into sugar. Trypsin, needed for protein digestion in the small intestine, is also inhibited by phytates.[9]

This doesn't mean legumes should be avoided; all you need to do to unlock the nutrients found within legumes is to soak them. Soaking/fermenting legumes in warm water allows enzymes, lactobacilli, and other helpful organisms to break down and neutralize phytic acid and partially break down proteins into simpler components that make them easier to digest and absorb. But don't feel overwhelmed; soaking legumes is easy.

The simple practice of soaking legumes overnight will vastly improve their nutrient availability and increase your body's ability to absorb them. Almost all pre-industrialized cultures fermented or soaked their legumes before consuming them.

The Japanese ferment soybeans to produce miso, tempeh, and natto. In fact, soybeans are best consumed only after they have been fermented.

In India, lentils are soaked in water and sprouted to make dals. Throughout history, many cultures have soaked or sprouted legumes before use in traditional dishes. How these cultures knew that soaking increases a food's nutrient availability is unknown, but perhaps, as with grains, it is just not as pleasurable chewing on raw legumes.

Nutritional Nugget

After your legumes have soaked, if you cook them using some of the flatulence fighters mentioned earlier (anise seed, fennel seeds, and raw fennel), it will decrease the gas and bloating you may experience when first increasing consumption of legumes.

Preparation of Legumes

When legumes are eaten daily, special attention needs to be paid to how they are prepared. This means soaking them for twenty-four hours. This is the minimum preparation that needs to be done before the legume is cooked.

Germinating and sprouting are also effective methods of reducing phytic acid in beans. This is done by soaking the legume for twelve hours, then draining and rinsing the beans twice daily for 12-24 hours or until the beans begins to sprout. They can then be cooked as normal. We will move deeper into soaking your own legumes at home in Chapter 4.

Sprouted Black Beluga Lentil Salad

Serves: 6
Total Time: 25 minutes (plus 36-48 hours soaking and germination time)

Ingredients

- 1 cup black beluga lentils
- 3 tablespoons extra virgin olive oil
- 2 tablespoons lime juice
- 2 tablespoons red wine vinegar
- 2 tablespoons white wine vinegar
- 1 teaspoon unrefined sea salt
- Pepper to taste
- 1 diced red pepper
- 4 tablespoons chopped cilantro
- 2 tablespoons sliced green onions, plus a bit for garnish
- Fresh salad greens

Directions

1. Rinse lentils several times until the water is clear. Place lentils in a bowl and cover well with warm water. Cover the bowl with a towel and let soak 12-24 hours.

2. Pour lentils into a strainer and rinse well. Set the strainer over a bowl to drain (out of direct sunlight). Cover with a clean dishtowel. Rinse lentils twice a day; be sure they drain well. After 24 to 48 hours, small sprouts will appear.

3. Rinse the lentils and place them in a pot of four cups of boiling water. Simmer for 15 minutes or until tender. Drain immediately through a fine strainer and rinse briefly with cool water. Drain again, set aside, and allow to cool.

4. In a large bowl, combine the cooled lentils with the olive oil, lime juice, vinegars, salt, and pepper. Add the red pepper, cilantro, and green onions and mix well. Arrange a small amount of salad greens on each plate and mound ¼ cup of the lentil mixture on top of the greens. Garnish with a few sliced green onions and serve.

3. Nuts and Seeds

Eating nuts, pumpkin seeds, sunflower seeds, flax seeds, and sesame seeds are all *Good Decisions*. Soaking or sprouting them before consumption makes them even better. You can toss seeds into a salad at the last minute or add them to a breakfast grain to add flavor and nutrients. The good news is that sprouted nuts and seeds are now more available in grocery stores and, as demand increases, so will their availability. Living Nutz is a great resource for sprouted and raw nuts and seeds. Visit its website at http://www.livingnutz.com

Nut Preparation

If you want to prepare your own sprouted nuts at home, you will find step-by-step instructions in Chapter 6. Sprouting makes nuts easier to digest and less likely to cause intestinal discomfort. Roasting them further removes phytic acid and makes very tasty nuts!

4. Whole Grains

Whole grains undergo the least amount of processing because only the outer hull is removed and the bran, germ, and endosperm remain intact. When they are soaked and cooked properly, whole grains are the most nutritious form of grain because the amount of fiber, protein, vitamins, and minerals is at its highest.

Whole grains are also referred to as hulled grains. The hull is the hard, indigestible outer shell of the grain, which is removed before it can be used for human consumption. Whole grains are important sources of antioxidant nutrients, including vitamin E and selenium. Antioxidant nutrients help protect against diseases such as cancer, heart disease, cataracts, and reduce some of the effects of aging. Who would have thought of whole grains as the fountain of youth? Whole grains, when properly prepared, also supply minerals such as iron, zinc, copper, and vitamins A, B6, and E.

When I say "properly prepared," I am referring to the soaking and fermenting of grains. As I mentioned before, chewing on raw grains isn't that pleasant, but when they're soaked, they're quite delicious and can be used in soup, pilaf, salads, and as a main dish for everything from stew to stir-fry. When cooked in broth and other nutrient-rich fluids, they are fantastic at absorbing flavors as well as nutrients.

There is so much to learn about grains that the next two chapters are dedicated solely to all the wonderful grain varieties and how to prepare them properly so they are easy to digest and all of the nutrients easy to absorb.

Sprouted Toasty Nuts

Yield: 3 cups
Total Time: 45 minutes

Ingredients

- 1 egg white
- 2 tablespoons Grade B maple syrup
- ¼ teaspoon cayenne pepper
- 1 teaspoon sea salt
- ½ cup sprouted almonds
- ½ cup sprouted cashews
- ½ cup sprouted pumpkin seeds
- ½ sprouted sunflower seeds
- ½ cup sprouted Brazil nuts
- ½ cup sprouted walnuts
- 1 tablespoon finely chopped fresh rosemary

Directions

1. Preheat oven to 300°F. Line a rimmed baking sheet with parchment paper.

2. In a large mixing bowl, whisk the egg white until frothy. Whisk in the maple syrup, cayenne, and salt. Stir in the nuts and rosemary, making sure the nuts are coated completely.

3. Spread the nuts on the prepared baking sheet in an even layer. Bake until the nuts are browned and fragrant, about 25 to 30 minutes. Remove from the oven and let cool before serving. Add more cayenne if you like spicy foods and want more of a kick from your nuts.

The Psychology of Food

Find Your Own Pace

When embarking on any new program, it is helpful not to take an all or nothing attitude. Studies show that people are more inclined to succeed when they make only one small change, but stick with it over time.

For instance, if your goal is to lose weight and you do nothing more than decrease the size of your evening meal, you will get used to this smaller portion and your body will adapt over time. Weight loss then becomes something that doesn't happen overnight, but rather something that happens gradually over time.

You don't have to increase exercise (although it will help!) or go on any dramatic cleanses or fasts. Simply making one small change and sticking with it over time, until it becomes second nature, is the key to success for many people.

If your goal is to increase energy, and you know you are hooked on sugar, trying to eliminate sweet foods all at once may be overwhelming. Cravings, mood fluctuations, and negative thought patterns may be more likely to get the best of you. But if you begin slowly to decrease the amount of sugar and sweet foods in your diet, it won't be such a shock, and you may be more likely to succeed in the long run.

The all-or-nothing approach works for some people, and weight can be lost in a very short period of time using this approach. The only problem with this approach is that if you eliminate or avoid everything and don't incorporate a few unhealthy decisions here and there, then you won't have the opportunity to practice the art of managing your emotions. The more you can expose yourself to situations in which you have to master not overeating, saying no to certain foods, and facing the heat of the battle, the better you will get at delaying gratification for the greater cause of reaching your goal. When you succeed at delaying gratification once or twice, the victory of managing emotions can be very empowering! You may then look forward to opportunities to practice delaying gratification. And when you do allow yourself a treat, it can be savored and enjoyed thoroughly without the guilt.

Good Decisions is not about eliminating all unhealthy foods forever. When you tell someone she can never have another hamburger, glass of wine, or donut, the first thing she feels compelled to do is to run out and consume those items like crazy. So in the beginning, don't put too much pressure on yourself. Make one small change and stick with it until it becomes a part of your way of life.

You will have many opportunities to practice avoiding temptations, so for now, pick something small and easy that you feel you can easily do. Perhaps it is something as simple as decreasing the amount of sugar in your coffee. When you have adapted and don't think about it anymore, savor this victory! Then, make another small change. If you get frustrated because you don't see results right away, be gentle with yourself, be patient, and know that through practice, truth, and knowledge, results will come.

A Short Story

Two people are paddling canoes across the lake; one person is moving very fast and paddling very hard. The other person is moving slowly and paddling at a softer pace. While the first paddler may get there first—they will both ultimately arrive at the same destination.

Practicing Good Decisions

Do One Thing

Your homework for this chapter includes finding something you feel you can easily cut back on or eliminate from your diet. This should be something you feel may not be contributing to your optimal health.

If you have dessert every night, perhaps instead of eating a high-sugar dessert, you may transition to fresh fruit instead. If you normally have two glasses of wine with dinner, consider cutting back to one. If you eat fast food on a regular basis, pick one day to cook a healthy meal at home. Don't feel compelled to make any more changes until you have adapted and are comfortable with the change you have made.

The goal of this exercise is to start with something easy, so you may experience the thrill of victory and gain confidence in your ability to delay gratification for a greater cause.

Be aware of your self-talk as you go through this process. If you find yourself wallowing in the role of a victim, or come up with excuses not to make any changes, look at these thought patterns and ask yourself whether this type of thinking still serves you. Be gentle, no matter what excuses your mind comes up with; simply be conscious that this is your mind's way of avoiding discomfort—nothing more, nothing less.

You will be thrilled to learn that often simply observing your thoughts is all that is needed to dissipate their power.

Chapter Four

The Ease of Preparing Grains

In this chapter, we will review how grains have been prepared in the past, and determine whether soaking grains is really a necessary step in grain preparation. Looking at the anatomy of a grain will give us insight into why grains are refined and processed the way they are today. You will learn how to prepare grains properly at home, and discover whether or not grains may be right for you. We will end with some exercises on awareness that will teach you how emotions can drive your thoughts and either serve you well or hinder your growth.

Historical Methods of Preparing Grains

Soaking grains in water for days was not uncommon for our ancestors. Throughout history and all over the world, many cultures traditionally fermented grains. In Africa, the natives ferment corn millet for several days to produce a porridge called ogi. In India, rice and lentils are fermented for at least two days before they are prepared as idli and dosas. In some Asian countries, rice receives a long fermentation before it is prepared. The Welsh soak oats. For injera bread, Ethiopians inoculate the dough with leftover liquid from the last injera dough. This inoculation is made by fermenting a grain called teff for several days.

American pioneers fermented grains to make sourdough breads, pancakes, and biscuits. This method is still used today, and many companies pride themselves on the quality of their sourdough starters. Before the onset of industrial agriculture, farmers, using wisdom passed down for generations, soaked grain in warm water before feeding it to poultry and hogs. Some Asian fermenters used a culture from mold grown on raw or cooked grains, while others chewed on a grain and then spit it into the pot.

While I'm not suggesting we go this far, I do recommend looking into why our ancestors did this, and asking the question, "Should we do this today?"

Today, many claim that soaking isn't necessary; they say it's an inconvenient step in grain preparation. Others won't eat grains without soaking them first. In a world where all we want are answers and quickly, there appears to be much uncertainty on this issue. Why? What is the best way to cook and prepare grains? Do we really need to soak them? Let's look at the anatomy of a grain to see whether we can make sense of it all.

CHAPTER FOUR

Anatomy of a Grain

Bran

While legumes' outer layer is called a seed coat, grains' outer layer is called bran. It protects the grain until conditions are right for sprouting. Bran contains protein, B vitamins, fiber, and phytic acid. Phytic acid is the main form of stored phosphorus, a mineral vital for bone health. Phytic acid needs to be broken down in order for the stored phosphorus (phytic acid) to be converted into phosphorus for utilization and absorption in our bodies. If the phytic acid is not broken down, humans cannot digest it.

In this indigestible form, phytic acid has a molecular affinity for certain minerals. This means it can bind to important minerals, such as calcium, magnesium, iron, and zinc and prevent their absorption.[1] When bound to phytic acid, these minerals become insoluble and are unable to be absorbed in the intestines.

In addition, phytate (phytic acid in salt form) acts as an acid and causes changes in vitamin B3 (niacin), which can contribute to a disease known as pellagra. Because of this, phytic acid is often called an "anti-nutrient" because it takes away nutrients from the body instead of giving them.

Thus, it makes sense that phytic acid isn't ideal for human consumption. Yet, phytic acid is found within the hull of all grains, nuts, seeds, and legumes.[2] Unfortunately, it is also found in cocoa and coffee beans (some things you really don't want to know!). So, why do we still consume these foods today? Is this why osteoporosis, tooth decay, and bone disease are on the rise? What can we do? Well, it turns out that simply cooking grains reduces phytic acid to some degree, but not enough to prevent it from robbing our bodies of nutrients.

Ruminant animals, such as cows, sheep, and goats, have no trouble with phytic acid. This is because the enzyme that breaks down phytic acid, phytase, is produced within their bellies. Mice produce thirty times more phytase than do humans[3] so they do very well eating a raw, whole grain diet.

Humans produce some phytase—some humans more than others, depending on digestive health—which means we can neutralize some of the phytic acid we consume. However, more effective methods of breaking down phytic acid include soaking the grain to promote lactic acid fermentation (the process used to produce yogurt and sauerkraut), and sprouting.[4] These methods activate the enzyme phytase, which is dormant until conditions are right for the grain to sprout. When this happens, phytase breaks down phytic acid and frees the stored phosphorus for our bodies to absorb. This also frees calcium, zinc, iron, and magnesium for absorption and utilization within our bodies.

So it appears that soaking is essential if we are to enjoy and utilize the nutrients that grains offer.

The instructions on the back of the oatmeal box used to tell you to soak the oats overnight. It turns out those instructions were there for a reason. Osteoporosis, iron deficiency, and digestive disorders are very common today, and our consumption of unsoaked grains is greater than ever. Without a doubt, eating unsoaked grains can contribute to mineral deficiencies.

Germ

While bran is the hard outer layer of the grain that protects the grain until conditions are right for sprouting, the germ is the embryo of a kernel of grain. It is the oily part of a kernel or seed from which a new plant sprouts. The germ is loaded with B vitamins, minerals, beneficial fats, and is highly nutritious.

Wheat germ is a common supplement and a good example of how crazy we have become with our eating habits. For instance, people have sprinkled wheat germ or bran on their processed cereals for years, with the intent of adding nutrients to their breakfast, when they could just consume the whole grain. It would be easier and more nutritious than ripping apart the grain, processing it into a cereal loaded with additives, preservatives, and artificial flavors, and then adding the parts removed back in. Crazy!

Extraction of the germ began during the industrial revolution when preserving flour was an issue. Transportation distances and a relatively slow distribution system collided with the shelf life of flour. Flour had a limited shelf life because when the grain is milled, the fat found within the germ is exposed to oxygen. This increases flour's potential to oxidize and become rancid. Because vitamins, micronutrients, and amino acids were relatively unknown in the late nineteenth century, removing the germ seemed like a good solution. Without the germ, flour cannot become rancid.

Today, transportation, distribution, packaging, and our ability to grind our own grains at home make removing the germ unnecessary, yet we still do. The cereal aisle of your grocery store is a sea of de-germed grains.

Endosperm

Endosperm is the tissue produced inside the seeds. It surrounds the germ and provides nutrition in the form of starch. Wheat endosperm is ground into flour for bread (all of the grain is included in whole-wheat flour), while barley endosperm is mainly used for beer production. Another example of endosperm is corn, for use as popcorn, or rice endosperm that is popped to make rice cakes. As you may guess, these are not nutrient-dense *Good Decisions* as they consist of only refined starch, which elevates blood sugar levels and offers few nutrients.

Can Phytates Be Useful?

The wonderful thing about science is that for almost every substance that has detrimental effects, there's often a beneficial use as well. The book *Food Phytates*, published in 2001, builds a case for phytates' potential ability to lower blood sugar, reduce cholesterol, and reduce the risks of cancer and heart disease.[5]

Oatmeal has always been touted as the "heart-friendly" grain because of its fiber content. The ability of phytates, the salt form of phytic acid, to bind to unwanted substances and prevent absorption could be another reason. One theory maintains that phytates bind to extra iron or toxic minerals and removes them from the body, thus assisting in their removal and promoting detoxification.

Researchers also state that phytic acid may help prevent colon cancer,[6] and it is one of few therapies used for uranium removal.[7] Uranium is naturally present in water, air, and food, but with all of the nuclear detonations on our planet since Hiroshima, uranium has made its way into our atmosphere and environment, where toxicity can occur. Phytic acid's ability to bind to substances can be an asset in some cases. For instance, it may help prevent, inhibit, or even cure some cancers by taking away some of the minerals that cancer cells need to reproduce.[8]

So yes, phytates do have their uses and can be beneficial, but along with the substances phytates pull from your body, nutrients go out as well.

So how do we enjoy grains when preparation methods can make the difference between whether a grain is nutrient giving or nutrient depleting? Several methods effectively reduce phytic acid and increase nutrient availability, and they are all easy!

How to Prepare Grains Properly

Soaking

When you soak a grain in warm water, you initiate the sprouting process. This activates phytase, the enzymes within the seed that break down phytic acid. Phytase also partially breaks down proteins, such as gluten, into simpler components. This breakdown makes them easier to digest and the nutrients more likely to be absorbed by the body.

Soaking also pulls out certain chemicals like tannins from the grain into the soaking liquid and, at a certain point, the grain begins to ferment. (This is a good thing!)

There are three methods for activating phytase and cultivating microorganisms, which break down phytic acid and increase the digestibility of grains. The first method involves soaking in water without any added ingredient. The second method involves adding an acid medium to the soaking liquid, and the third method involves sprouting.

You can use the following instructions with any grain, legume, seed, or nut. Some people recommend a tightly closed Mason jar, which allows the grain to retain the heat it generates during the sprouting process. I find a simple glass bowl in a warm location works just as well. Use warm, non-chlorinated water for soaking and keep the mixture at room temperature while it is soaking. Use the same amount of water you would normally use to cook the grain. Here is an example of how to soak brown rice without adding anything to the soaking liquid.

Soaking in Water Alone

Soaking grains in water alone will break down roughly 50 percent of the phytic acid and increase the absorption of iron by up to 53 percent.[9] These results explain why so many cultures soaked their grains for days and saved some of the soaking medium, rich in enzymes, to jump-start the next batch. Sourdough bread starter is made this way. If you enjoy making rye bread, then this is the method for you.

Brown Rice

Serves: 6
Total Time: 35 minutes, plus 24 hours soaking time

Ingredients:

- 1 cup brown rice
- 2 cups warm water

Directions:

1. Soak one cup of brown rice in two cups of warm water for 24 hours. Keep the rice covered and at room temperature without changing the water. After 24 hours, set aside 10 percent of the soaking liquid, which will keep, refrigerated, for about a month. Discard the rest of the soaking liquid and rinse the rice.

2. Cook the rice as you would normally in water or mineral-rich bone broth and butter for 35 minutes. Serve.

The next time you make brown rice or any grain, use the same procedure, but add the soaking liquid you reserved from the last batch to the new soaking water. Repeat the cycle. The process will gradually improve until 96 percent or more of the phytic acid is reduced at 24 hours.

Note: Bone broths are typically made utilizing bones instead of meat and are very similar to stocks in everything except that they are simmered for a very long period (often in excess of 24 hours). Simmering pulls nutrients from the bones into the liquid, increasing the nutrient content of the broth dramatically. The way the bones crumble between your fingers when the broth is done and the thick gelatinous quality of the broth make it worth its weight in gold. The absorbable calcium from bone broths, cultured dairy products, and vitamin D from certain animal fats can also compensate for any adverse effects of phytic acid if some still remains after soaking. These are a great way to add flavor and bone-building nutrients to any grain dish.

Soaking With an Acid Medium

If saving some of the soaking liquid is not your cup of tea, this next method is for you. I love this method and use it on a regular basis.

When you add an acid medium to the soaking liquid, not only do you initiate the sprouting process, but you're adding cultured yogurt, buttermilk, vinegar, lemon, or even a starter culture to the soaking liquid to cultivate lactobacilli and other helpful organisms that secrete phytase to aid in the breakdown of phytic acid and predigest gluten. Acidic ingredients encourage the ideal pH for phytase to do its work.

Methods of soaking whole grains in an acid medium, such as lemon or yogurt, significantly improves protein digestibility and in some cases almost doubles it.[10] It's exciting to learn how much you can improve your health by simply taking the time to soak your grains. Soaking is not as difficult or as mysterious as many make it out to be. You don't have to chant or perform any rituals (unless you wish to) in order to get great results. Soaking is especially useful for anyone with a history of digestive problems, such as gluten intolerance or irritable bowel syndrome. Here is an example of how to soak brown rice with an acid medium.

Again, you can use these instructions with any grain or legume. The only thing that may change is the soaking medium. Corn is an exception, as you will soon see.

The great thing about soaking grains is they cook faster, are tastier, and tenderer than when they have not been soaked.

Brown Rice

Serves: 6
Total Time: 35 minutes plus 24 hours soaking time

Ingredients:

- 1 cup brown rice
- 2 cups warm water
- 2 tablespoons of one of the following: cultured buttermilk, yogurt, kefir, lemon, or vinegar

Directions:

1. Combine brown rice and warm water. Add 2 tablespoons of one of the culture mediums of your choice. (Contrary to what others have experienced, I find that using lemon does not result in a sour-tasting grain. Lemon can also be used by those who have problems with dairy.) Cover and soak for 24 hours. Drain and rinse.

2. Cook the rice as you would normally in water or mineral-rich bone broth and butter for 35 minutes. Serve.

None of the medium need be saved.

Fluffy Lime and Cilantro Brown Rice

Serves: 6
Total Time: 45 minutes

Ingredients

- 1 cup pre-soaked long-grain brown rice, rinsed and drained
- 10 cups water
- 3 tablespoons fresh squeezed lime juice
- ½ cup chopped fresh cilantro
- Salt to taste

Directions

1. Bring 10 cups of water to a boil over high heat in a large pot with a tight-fitting lid. Add the rice and boil, uncovered, for 30 minutes. Pour the rice into a strainer over the sink. Let the rice drain for 10 seconds, then return it to the pot. Turn off the heat, cover the pot, and set it aside to allow the rice to steam for 10 minutes. Uncover the rice and add lime juice, cilantro, and season with salt. Lightly fluff to combine ingredients and serve.

Soaking Mediums

There are many different mediums (substances) in which to soak your grains.

Lemon and Apple Cider Vinegar

Fresh-squeezed lemon juice (don't use the stuff in yellow bottles) and organic raw apple cider vinegar will work well at encouraging the ideal pH for phytase to do its work. Ascorbic acid (vitamin C) can also reduce phytic acid's effects on iron.[11] Adding a little bit of lemon to your soaking medium can have big payoffs. I use this often when I am creating recipes for my clients who have sensitivities to dairy.

Cultured Products

Probiotic lactobacilli and other microflora found in cultured buttermilk, kefir, and yogurt also encourage ideal pH and are great soaking mediums. They secrete and are an important source of phytase, which speeds the release of phosphate from phytic acid, rendering it more soluble and thus improving and facilitating intestinal absorption.[12]

Sourdough Cultures

If you are sensitive to dairy, you can use a sourdough culture to get the same, if not better, results. These cultures are often made from rye, a grain known for its higher level of phytase. Sourdough cultures are best used when soaking low phytase grains such as oats, brown rice, and millet.

Buckwheat

Whole grains, such as rye and buckwheat, are powerful sources of phytase. When these grains are ground and added to other low-phytase grains, complete degradation of phytates occurs in a shorter time, which changes your soaking time from days to hours. To do this, add freshly ground whole grain rye flour or buckwheat flour to your low-phytase grains; then soak as usual in a warm place. Rye contains gluten; buckwheat does not.

Take heart! This may sound complex, but don't be intimidated. It's not an exact science. All you really have to do is put some grain in warm water and let it soak! Even getting the exact amount of the acid medium is not necessary. The beautiful thing about soaking grains is that it is easy. The fact that it makes grains more flavorful and nutritious is an added bonus!

Soaking Liquid Temperatures

The soaking water temperature should technically be between 113°F and 131°F, and the grains placed in a warm location to soak. Again, this is not an exact science, and your grains won't retain phytic acid because your water temperature wasn't just right. In fact, most of the time your grain will be soaking at room temperature anyway. The only thing you need to be cautious about is not using water that is too hot, as phytase is destroyed at 131°F to 149°F.[13]

How Long to Soak Specific Grains

Rice

White rice and its products are low in phytates because the outer bran has been stripped away along with all of its nutrients. Brown rice, black rice, red rice, and wild rice are much better choices, but are high in phytates. In fact, as a percentage of dry weight, brown rice can contain between 0.84 to 0.99 percent phytic acid.[14] For best results, always soak whole grain rice varieties for 24 hours.

Gluten Grains

Gluten grains (barley, durum, kamut, oats, rye, farro, spelt, triticale, wheat, etc.) are most healthful when soaked for 12 to 24 hours, ideally. The gluten in these grains is particularly difficult to digest, and these grains have a relatively high amount of phytates. As a percentage of dry weight, these can contain anywhere from 0.39 to 1.35 percent phytic acid.[15] Some of these grains have a lower phytic content than others, but between the gluten and phytic acid, it just makes sense to give them a good soaking before consumption.

The amount of phytic acid in grains, nuts, legumes, and seeds varies. Grains that contain the most phytic acid are typically fermented for 24 hours; those with less can be fermented for as little as six hours. It does no harm to soak grains for longer than 24 hours. If you can't consume the grain right away, simply store the grains in the refrigerator for up to a week after they have been soaked.

CHAPTER FOUR

Seed Grains

Amaranth, quinoa, buckwheat, hato mugi (Job's tears), and millet are considered seed grains; they do not contain gluten and have lower amounts of phytates. Teff, which is from the grass family, also does not contain gluten and has low amounts of phytates, so it does not need to be soaked as long.

I've provided the following table as a quick reference guide when soaking grains and seeds:

A Quick Guide for Soaking Grains				
Grain/Seed	Dry Amount	Filtered Water	Acid Medium*	Soak Time
Rice (brown, red, black, wild)	1 Cup	2 Cups	2 Tbsp.	24 Hours
Amaranth	1 Cup	2 Cups	2 Tbsp.	6-12 Hours
Quinoa	1 Cup	2 Cups	2 Tbsp.	6-12 Hours
Buckwheat	1 Cup	2 Cups	2 Tbsp.	6-12 Hours
Hato Mugi (Job's Tears)	1 Cup	2 Cups	2 Tbsp.	6-12 Hours
Millet	1 Cup	2 Cups	2 Tbsp.	6-12 Hours
Teff	1 Cup	2 Cups	2 Tbsp.	6-12 Hours
Unhulled Barley	1 Cup	2 Cups	2 Tbsp.	12-24 Hours
Durum	1 Cup	2 Cups	2 Tbsp.	12-24 Hours
Kamut	1 Cup	2 Cups	2 Tbsp.	12-24 Hours
Rye	1 Cup	2 Cups	2 Tbsp.	12-24 Hours
Farro	1 Cup	2 Cups	2 Tbsp.	12-24 Hours
Spelt	1 Cup	2 Cups	2 Tbsp.	12-24 Hours
Triticale	1 Cup	2 Cups	2 Tbsp.	12-24 Hours
Wheat	1 Cup	2 Cups	2 Tbsp.	12-24 Hours
Oats	1 Cup	2 Cups	2 Tbsp.	24 Hours
Corn	1 Cup	2 C. pre-soaked lime juice		24 Hours

Soaking Corn Products

An ear of corn contains seeds called kernels. When corn kernels are dried and ground, they can be used to make polenta, cornbread, tortillas, and many other corn products. Because most corn produced in the U.S. is genetically engineered, which has been shown to be controversial, it's best to choose organic whenever possible.

Dried corn or corn meal must be handled differently than other grains. Traditional recipes call for soaking the dried corn in lime water. Not the juice from a lime, but pickling lime (this can be purchased online and in some grocery stores). The soaking process enhances the absorption of certain B vitamins and improves the protein quality of the corn.

Corn or Corn Meal

Total Time: 36 hours

Ingredients:

- ½ cup pickling lime
- 2-quart Mason jar
- 6 cups warm water
- 2 cups dried corn or corn meal

Directions:

1. Place pickling lime in Mason jar and fill it with water. (If you are not using a Mason jar, the ratio is one cup corn to 2 cups limewater). Shake well, cover tightly, and let stand overnight. The powder will settle and result in a clear liquid that is limewater.

2. Carefully pour the clear limewater into another jar without disturbing any powder at the bottom. Discard the white powder. Combine 2 cups corn or cornmeal with 4 cups limewater and soak for 24 hours. Strain and lightly rinse.

3. Use corn as directed in your recipe.

The leftover clear limewater can be stored in your refrigerator for up to two weeks and used whenever you need to soak corn or cornmeal.

Today, science can answer the question of whether or not it is ideal to soak grains. I love soaking grains like my ancestors did years ago; my countertops are constantly covered with soaking grains, sprouting beans, and roasted sprouted nuts.

The soaking process for grains is easy and fun to learn. It may seem a little unfamiliar at first, so experiment with just a few dishes to allow yourself time to adapt to this new way of cooking. Once you've tried it, though, you'll see that soaking grains is not only easy but will enhance the flavor of your grains as well. I have served several cornmeal dishes to friends and family members who usually do not like cornmeal and they all loved it when it was soaked!

How to Sprout

Sprouting, like soaking is easy, and it can be extremely fun for children. If you wish to sprout your own grains and seeds at home, there are many fun ways of going about it. I love my sprouting jar with the green mesh top. It is simple, inexpensive, and very easy to use. It doesn't take up too much counter space and always yields wonderful delicious sprouts.

In nature, when the conditions are right, the seed has enough moisture for it to germinate and grow into a plant. Soaking seeds encourages them to release toxic inhibitors and sprout into life. Soaking also encourages the production of beneficial enzymes that increase the amounts of vitamins, especially the B vitamins that your body can absorb. Sprouting is also done to activate phytase within the seed, thus reducing phytic acid.[16]

Almost any grain or seed can be sprouted, including barley, dried beans, chia seeds, alfalfa, mustard, onion, mung beans, broccoli, clover, chick peas, almonds, pumpkin, sunflower, and lentils. A good resource when looking for seeds to sprout is www. mountainroseherbs.com. I recommend starting with red clover, red lentils, and brown mustard seeds to give you a variety and build your confidence.

Polenta with Mushrooms and a Sherry Broth

Serves: 8
Total Time: 1 hour, 10 minutes

Ingredients

For Polenta

- 2 cups presoaked coarsely ground corn meal (polenta)
- 1 onion finely chopped
- 1 tablespoon butter
- 10 cups chicken broth

For the Sherry Broth

- 1½ ounce package dried porcini mushrooms
- 3 cups boiling water
- 4 tablespoons extra-virgin olive oil, divided

- 1 carrot, thinly sliced
- 1 small onion, thinly sliced crosswise
- 1 medium celery rib, thinly sliced crosswise
- 4 medium garlic cloves, lightly smashed
- 8 oz white mushrooms, thickly sliced
- ½ teaspoon fennel seeds
- ¼ teaspoon black peppercorns
- 2 bay leaves
- 1 fresh sage leaf
- 1 tablespoon chopped thyme
- 1½ cups dry red wine
- 1½ cups dry sherry
- Freshly ground pepper
- 1¼ lb fresh shiitake mushrooms, thickly sliced
- ½ cup green onions, thinly sliced

Directions

1. In a large pot, sauté finely chopped onions in butter until tender. Add the 10 cups broth, salt to taste, and bring to a boil. When the broth is boiling, add the polenta and bring back to a boil. Lower the heat and keep the polenta at a low simmer, stirring every few minutes as you would a risotto to prevent it from sticking. Cook about 45 minutes or until polenta is thick and creamy.

2. In a heatproof bowl, combine dried porcini mushrooms and 3 cups boiling water and let soak until the porcini are softened. Drain the porcini and reserve 2 cups of the soaking liquid. Finely chop the porcini mushrooms. In a large saucepan, heat 2 tablespoons of olive oil. Add the porcinis, carrot, onion, celery, and garlic; cook over moderate heat until the vegetables are softened. Add the white mushrooms and cook until the mushrooms begin to brown. Add the fennel seeds, peppercorns, bay leaves, sage, and thyme. Stir in the wine, sherry, and 2 cups of porcini soaking liquid and boil until reduced to 2 cups. Strain the sherry broth into a small saucepan, pressing hard on the solids with a ladle or wooden spoon. Season the sherry broth with salt and pepper.

3. In a large, deep skillet, heat the remaining 2 tablespoons of olive oil. Add the fresh shitake mushrooms and cook over medium heat until the mushrooms are golden brown. Season with salt and pepper. Spoon the polenta into warmed shallow bowls. Top the polenta with the sautéed shitake mushrooms and spoon the sherry broth all around. Garnish with chives and serve.

Sprouted Brown Rice

Serves 6

Total Time: 24-48 hours

Ingredients:

- 1 cup brown rice
- Water

Directions:

1. Rinse 1 cup (or more if desired) of brown rice several times until the water is clear. Place the rice in a bowl and cover well with warm water. Cover the bowl with a towel and let stand 12 hours or overnight. Pour rice into a strainer and rinse well. Set the strainer over a bowl to drain (out of direct sunlight). Cover with a clean dishtowel and place in a warm location. Rinse rice twice a day; be sure it drains well. After 24 to 48 hours, small sprouts will appear.

2. At this point, you can cook the rice as normal, using slightly less water and cooking it for a shorter period of time, or you can continue to sprout it to increase its nutritional value. If you choose to continue to sprout, be sure to rinse and drain the sprouts twice daily. In one to four days, depending on what you are sprouting, the sprouts will be ready.

3. To harvest your sprouts, rinse them well and shake out any excess moisture. Remove the sprouts carefully by gently pulling ripe ones from the rest. Removing only the ripe sprouts allows less-developed sprouts to continue to grow so you'll get several harvests of delicious sprouts. Store them in a plastic bag with a moist paper towel in the fridge and rinse them every two to three days. Most sprouts will keep at least a week like this and often longer. Eat the sprouts at any time. (The longer the sprouts, the more bitter the taste.) Some larger seeds require more time before you begin to see them sprout. Do not leave the sprouts in standing water, as this causes the sprouts to rot.

If you don't want to sprout your own, and all this sprouting business is not for you, simply buy them already sprouted! One brand I love is TruRoots®. Pre-sprouted products are delicious, and handy to have on hand if you have forgotten to sprout your own grains or legumes and need something quick in a pinch. Their products can be found online and in some markets.

Sprouted Mung Bean Salad

Serves: 8
Total Time: 25 minutes

Ingredients

- 1 cup dried organic Sprouted Mung Beans
- 1 can organic corn rinsed and drained
- 1 diced red bell pepper
- 1 small diced red onion
- 2 cloves minced garlic
- ¼ cup red wine vinegar
- ¼ cup white wine vinegar
- 3 tablespoons olive oil
- ½ teaspoon dried ground cumin
- ½ cup chopped fresh cilantro
- Salt and pepper to taste

Directions

1. Cook mung beans according to package. Once drained and cooled, add remaining ingredients and mix well. This salad can be served at room temperature or chilled.

There are many ways to sprout. Like soaking, it is not an exact science. Nature does most of the work for you! If you want to take sprouting past the simple glass bowl and fine sieve strainer, you can choose several other fun methods in which to grow delicious sprouts.

Sprouting Methods

Sprouting Jars

One method is to use a Mason jar with a lid that has a screen on the top (my favorite). You can find sprouting jars online and in some organic food stores. To use this method:

- Simply fill the Mason jar one-third full with any grain or seed.
- Add filtered water to the top of the jar and screw on the top.
- Allow the seeds or grain to soak overnight, for one night only.
- Pour off the water and rinse well. You can do this without removing the top of the jar.
- Be sure all water has drained.
- Set jar upside down at an angle to ensure all the water drains.
- Rinse the seeds or grains at least twice a day.
- In one to four days, depending on what you are sprouting, the sprouts will be ready.
- Rinse well, shake out any excess moisture, and store in the refrigerator.

Sprouting Bags

Another method utilizes a sprouting bag. Sprouting bags have good ventilation and can prevent mold, which may happen with sprout jars if they are not drained enough or rinsed frequently. Most sprouting bags are made of hemp. They're easily sterilized with boiling water and can last a long time. To use:

- Simply soak your seeds in non-chlorinated water overnight.
- Moisten the bag; then pour the soaked seeds inside.
- Rinse and let any excess water drain.
- Hang the bag somewhere in your kitchen or put it on a dish.
- Rinse sprouts twice daily by dipping the bag in water for 30 seconds.
- Harvest!

Basket Sprouters

You can also use basket sprouters. Just make sure the spaces between the weaves are nice and tight so your seeds don't slip through. Also, make sure unhealthy chemicals weren't used in making the baskets. Unshellacked bamboo with a breadbasket-style weave can be found at any Asian food or supply store. These are beautiful additions to any countertop and need to be sterilized between uses. To use basket sprouters:

- Wash all your baskets by soaking them for three minutes in boiling water.
- Soak your seeds overnight in non-chlorinated water.
- After soaking, pour the seeds directly onto the floor of the basket.
- Rinse them clean and let the spray of the water spread the seeds evenly on the floor of the basket.
- Insert the basket into a plastic bag to be used as a greenhouse tent.
- Remove it from the plastic bag twice each day for rinsing.
- When sprouts are ready, rinse well, shake out any excess moisture, and store in the refrigerator.

Vertical Sprouters

Vertical or tray sprouters can also be used as follows:

- Soak your seeds in non-chlorinated water overnight.
- Pour the soaked seeds onto the sprouting tray. If the tray does not have a lid, cover the sprouter with a plastic bag so the enclosure provides a greenhouse effect.
- Rinse the seeds with the shower of your faucet twice a day. Try not to dislodge the seeds with the force of the rinse water; you want the seeds to root themselves into the small holes of the growing tray. Once firmly anchored, they grow straight and stand tall.
- Harvest!

Some people are very passionate about sprouting and prefer to use the vertical sprouters that can sprout three kinds of sprouts at once. I find that a Mason jar and fine sieve strainer work just as well. Whether you use a jar, bag, basket, or a tray, all produce nutrient-dense tasty sprouts. The process of sprouting produces vitamin C and enzymes that help digestion, and it increases carotene and vitamin B content, especially B2, B5, and B6.

From fighting cancer to helping women through menopause, sprouts are touted as having many health-giving properties. Sprouts are a super food for a reason; they contain within them life!

Conditions for Grain Consumption

Because grains can be inflammatory, they are best consumed only under the following conditions:

- You are not sensitive or allergic to the grain.
- Your digestion is working well.
- The grain is not genetically-engineered or overly hybridized.
- The grain has been properly prepared.

Grains can contribute significantly to inflammation when they are not properly prepared. Even when they are properly prepared, many people are allergic, sensitive to, or have problems digesting grains. Inflammation plays a huge role in so many diseases, from joint disease and irritable bowel syndrome to heart disease. The fire of inflammation can often be squelched by simply removing grains, refined carbohydrates, refined sugar, and processed foods from your diet. Because of this, many people avoid grains altogether and find they thrive on a mostly vegetable and protein diet.

My body does well with whole non-gluten grains, but it becomes inflamed, irritated, and full of mucus when I consume gluten containing grains so I am selective about which grains I consume. Pay attention to your body when you consume grains to determine which grains are best for you. Symptoms that you may be sensitive to grains, particularly gluten grains, include joint pain, brain fog, headaches, skin problems, eczema, or gas. You may also feel bloated, fatigued, or get cramping, diarrhea, and have an increase in mucus or sinusitis. If you experience any of these symptoms, it may be wise to take a break from grains for a while and see how you feel. If you improve and feel great not eating grains, you have your answer. Anxiety is a symptom that is reduced, sometimes completely, with the elimination of wheat and wheat products.

After you have completed the No Sugar Challenge, try bringing grains back into your diet one at a time to see how your body tolerates each grain. If you think your body does well with a grain, consume only that grain for a week just to be certain none of your symptoms return. Only incorporate one grain a week. If you incorporate too many grains at once, you won't know which one may be causing your symptoms. You may find that you tolerate brown rice and quinoa fine but spelt or barley may make you anxious, bloated, or cause intestinal irritation. Grains are a tricky bunch so when I work with clients, it is usually on a case by case basis, and I always put the All-Star Foods of *Good Decisions*: vegetables, fruits, legumes, proteins, and quality fats first.

The Psychology of Food
Managing Emotions

While whole grains are considered *Good Decisions*, most people consume more grains than their bodies need. Because grains tend to be sweet and starchy in nature, they may be addicting for some people and make up the majority of their diet.

If you find you are consuming refined grain products such as pasta, bread, or cereal on a regular basis, try eliminating these and incorporate whole unrefined grains instead. When you do this, your mind may decide it doesn't like the change and try to sabotage you. This is what can happen when you do something new that makes you uncomfortable. Continue to pay close attention to the emotions that come up and the thoughts that come into your head. It can be quite entertaining!

You may go through some uncomfortable withdrawals, and you may find yourself back in the heat of the battle. You may want to avoid those uncomfortable feelings and be emotionally driven to eat something you know is not conducive to you reaching your goal. Know that this is a coping mechanism you have learned to ease the discomfort, nothing more and nothing less.

Remember, it may seem like the goal is to manage food intake so you can feel healthier or lose weight, but the goal is really about managing emotions.

Sometimes it may feel like you are possessed by a strange emotional entity that just wants to end the suffering with a bowl of white pasta. Remember the good angel and the little devil? Try to laugh at your mind when it tries to convince you that life is not worth living without that piece of bread. Then sit in the discomfort of not having it, until the discomfort passes and you have delayed gratification.

The more you practice managing your emotions and sitting in the discomfort of not having what you want, the more small victories you will have, the more psychologically hardy you become.

Practice paying attention to your thoughts regularly—anytime you feel discomfort or feel your emotions driving you to something sweet or unhealthy, practice listening to the voice in your head like you are a third-party observer. In the beginning, you may hear your mind saying things like, "Who are you to do this?" or "Who are you kidding? You will always be fat," or "This is too hard; screw it." Don't judge your thoughts or emotions; simply notice them—you will find that the simple act of observing those thoughts is often enough to take away their power, which makes managing emotions easier.

Don't take your inner voice too seriously. Gently and non-judgmentally smile at it, feel the emotion, and wait for it to pass. If emotions become very strong and you feel unworthy or guilty, bring your awareness to the feeling and acknowledge that while you may be having a very strong emotion, it does not define you. Just because you feel unworthy doesn't mean you are unworthy. Just because you think it doesn't mean it is true.

The voice in your head may bring up many emotions, fear being a big one. Fear of what might happen if you succeed. You may become thinner and prettier, mentally sharper, sexier, and more alive than you ever dreamt. This change may be threatening to the ego, which sees it as threatening to its own version of "self." Paying attention to your thoughts and practicing awareness decreases the inner voice's power over you, and instead of being driven by your thoughts, you find you can let go of thoughts that have not served you well.

Be present and alert so that when emotion arises, you feel it, yet it won't drive your actions. With practice, you will get better and you may find yourself walking more confidently down the hallway of life toward a slimmer figure, increased energy, and mental clarity. Eventually you will become skilled at paying attention to your thoughts, and you will be more likely to laugh at them than take them seriously and they will begin to diminish.

Unfortunately, we are not taught about the psychology of food and how learned behaviors that don't suit us can play such a dominant role in our lives. Changing our inner dialogue starts with awareness of how emotions can drive our thoughts and behaviors and either serve us well or hinder our growth.

Practicing Good Decisions

Your First Week of Making Good Decisions

In Chapter 1, we talked about social impacts and practiced delaying gratification when we had dinner with friends. In Chapter 2, we talked about truth and knowledge vs. emotion and practiced observing our thoughts and emotions while only finishing half of our meal. In Chapter 3, we emphasized going at your own pace and chose one small change that we felt we could stick with over a long period of time. All of these exercises are designed to make you uncomfortable. While you may want to throw darts at my picture for causing you this discomfort, it is with the utmost love that I guide you in your practice of self-governing!

When you expose yourself to situations in which you have to master not overeating, saying no to certain foods, and facing the heat of the battle, you will get better at delaying gratification for the greater cause of reaching your goal. When you move into the discomfort instead of shying away from it, you gain strength and confidence in your ability to say no to certain foods; this strength and confidence can bring an immense sense of joy and freedom!

Your homework for this chapter is to continue to move into the discomfort, knowing the discomfort will eventually pass. If you are on the No Sugar Challenge, forge ahead! If not, try to move into the *Good Decisions* lifestyle and go the whole week before you have a meal of whatever you desire. Eat mostly vegetables, fruits, legumes, nuts, and quality proteins and fats. Cook at home as much as possible because foods you prepare are often healthier than restaurant fare.

Here is an example menu to help you through. This menu uses some of the recipes in this book:

Day 1

First thing in the morning, drink 2 glasses water with lemon. Lemon supports the liver and gallbladder and can help reduce that annoying fat roll that peaks out above your jeans.

Breakfast: Green Smoothie. Combine in a blender: 2 green apples, quartered, 3 stalks celery, leaves removed, 1 cucumber, 5 leaves kale, ½ lemon, peeled, one 1 inch piece fresh ginger. Add 2 cups coconut water. Blend until smooth. The fiber in this breakfast will contribute toward the perfect poop!

Snack: Kalamata olives and cucumber slices dipped in hummus, 2 glasses of lemon water

Lunch: Harvest Salad with Creamy Maple Walnut Dressing

Snack: Handful of mixed nuts, 2 glasses water

Dinner: Seared Halibut on Navy Beans with Lemon and Tarragon. Make enough so that you have leftovers for lunch the next day.

Dessert: Handful of fresh blueberries. Blueberries are rich in antioxidants and have been shown to play a preventative role in cancer.

Consider making the Tangerine, Thyme, and Fennel Comfort Cooler flavored water to drink tomorrow.

Day 2

First thing in the morning, drink 2 glasses of the Comfort Cooler flavored water. Flavored water is often tastier than plain water, making it easier to drink more of it. Try to drink your body weight divided by two in ounces of water. (A 140lb woman would drink 70 ounces.)

Breakfast: Leftover navy beans from dinner, with an egg cooked over easy on top! Legumes make amazing breakfasts; all it takes is a little creativity and lots of leftovers!

Snack: Roasted Garbanzo Beans, 2 glasses flavored water

Lunch: Leftover halibut and navy beans from yesterday's dinner

Snack: Sliced tomato and avocado, 2 glasses flavored water or herbal tea

Dinner: Organic Liver and Onions (Liver is an All-Star food!) Are you frowning? This is a carnivore's carnival! Okay, if not liver, try the Peppercorn Beef with Balsamic Reduction Sauce and/or the Beet and Red Onion Salad. Make enough for lunch leftovers. Cook once, eat twice!

Day 3

First thing in the morning: 2 glasses lemon water

Breakfast: Smoked salmon omelet with asparagus and green onions (no cheese). A little protein for breakfast can help blood sugar regulation into the afternoon. Pay attention to how you feel after you eat. Notice on the days you have a smoothie for breakfast you feel lighter, but become hungry earlier for lunch. Also notice how protein for breakfast keeps you sated into the afternoon. Knowing this helps you plan ahead for a busy day when it might be a while until you eat again. It can also help you plan for a day when you have an early lunch date and only need a light breakfast.

Snack: Handful of grapes, 2 glasses water

Lunch: Steak and salad leftovers (Always consume more salad than protein.)

Snack: Fresh juicy orange or an apple, 2 glasses water with lemon

Dinner: Black Beluga Lentil Salad (If this makes you gassy, chew on a ¼ teaspoon of fennel seeds.) Beluga lentils contain anthocyanins, pigments capable of forcing cancer cells to commit suicide. They are also very rich in fiber!

Dessert: Fresh strawberries

Consider making the Pineapple Ginger Elixir Flavored water to drink tomorrow

Day 4

First thing in the morning: two glasses Ginger Elixir flavored water.

Breakfast: Beet and Ginger Smoothie. Combine in a blender; 3 oranges, quartered, 1 medium beet, chopped, 1 piece of ginger about the size of your thumbnail, and 2 cups coconut juice. Blend until smooth. (You may need a commercial blender for this recipe!) This is your liver's dream breakfast! Enjoy a cup of green tea and a half of a grapefruit, roasted and dusted with cinnamon if you desire.

ALERT! Beets will turn urine and feces red/purple...this is not blood and is very normal. Beets are often used to determine transit time (mouth to anus digestion time) for this reason. Normal transit time is between 10 and 14 hours.

Soak 1 cup brown rice in 2 cups warm water with 2 tablespoons lemon for breakfast tomorrow.

Snack: Handful of Sprouted Toasty Nuts, 2 glasses of flavored water

Lunch: Black Beluga Salad Leftovers

Snack: Celery stick with cashew nut butter

Dinner: Seared Salmon with Lemon Caper Butter Sauce and a Caesar salad. (No croutons; use a lemon dressing.) I find cashews are a great substitute for croutons. Salmon is rich in Omega-3 fatty acids and can contribute toward younger looking skin.

Snack: Ripe pear and fresh peppermint leaves

Day 5

First thing in the morning: Two glasses lemon water

Breakfast: Brown rice, rinsed, drained, and cooked as normal in 2 cups water. When almost done add a chopped apple, butter, cinnamon, and raisins. Cook until apples are tender before serving. This is a vegetarian's delight, designed to regulate blood sugar levels. Adding a touch of cloves will stimulate digestion!

Snack: Handful of Sprouted Toasty Nuts, 2 glasses water

Lunch: Caesar salad with anchovies, herring, or sardines. These are All-Star foods, really, really good for you! I find I can incorporate these little fishes best blended up into a paste and added to the lemon dressing, or even sometimes right on top! If you are not in the mood for a salad, try some split pea soup.

Snack: One hard-boiled egg, 2 glasses water

Dinner: Pigeon Peas and Pork Rib Stew

Snack: Mixed fresh berries

Day 6

2 glasses lemon water first thing. Keep variety in your morning and try a cup of parsley tea, a natural diuretic if the lack of coffee is slowing things down.

Breakfast: No Crust Mushroom Quiche with Baby Greens

Snack: Roasted Garbanzo Beans, 2 glasses water

Lunch: Leftover Stew

Snack: An apple, 2 glasses water. Remember, an apple a day keeps constipation away and diarrhea at bay!

Dinner: Bitter green salad and Mussels in Spicy Coconut Broth

Dessert: Sliced mango

Consider making the Cucumber Mint Medley flavored water for tomorrow!

Day 7

First thing in the morning: Two glasses flavored cucumber water

Breakfast: Scrambled Eggs with Tarragon. Substitute butter with coconut oil. I find a little coconut oil for breakfast brings me mental clarity until noon!

Snack: Jicama, peeled and sliced into sticks, 2 glasses flavored water

Lunch: Mango Macadamia Nut Poppy Seed Salad or a bowl of chili

Snack: Orange, 2 glasses water

Dinner: Whatever you desire! You've made *Good Decisions* all week, so enjoy this meal without any guilt or self-deprecation.

This menu doesn't need to be followed exactly; it is more to give you an idea of all the foods you can enjoy. This menu contains an abundant amount of protein to help regulate blood sugar levels and ease any withdrawals or cravings you may have as you move into *Good Decisions*. It also may contain more quality fat than you may be used to. I've incorporated fats on purpose to increase the satiation of the menu and to take your mind off of the fact that you are avoiding sweets and processed foods.

Eggs, fruit, legumes, and whole grains make wonderful breakfasts. Soups, salads, and leftovers make great lunches, and your perfect dinner is lots of veggies with a moderate amount of protein. Fat is the magical ingredient that makes it all taste better!

If you slip once or twice, don't worry about it. Remember, the point of this exercise is to practice getting comfortable with discomfort. (Now that was an oxymoron, wasn't it?) Be gentle with yourself and know that it will come. When you succeed at managing your emotions and delaying gratification a few times, really revel in the feeling of achievement. The more you succeed, the easier it will become, and the victory of managing emotions will send you skipping down your hallway of life!

My sister loves to say to her temptation foods, "I've had you before; I will have you again. I'm just not going to have you right now." This is her way of paying attention to her thoughts, managing her emotions, and making *Good Decisions...Most of the Time.*

Chapter Five

Tasty Grain Varieties and Levels of Refinement

With so many grain products lining our grocery shelves, and gluten intolerance on the rise, how can we identify a healthy grain from an unhealthy one? Are gluten-free alternatives healthy? What role do genetically-modified grains play in today's diet, and why are they not Good Decisions? Which grains contain gluten, and which ones do not? What level of refinement and processing of whole grains is acceptable? Most importantly, how can I use grains? We will answer these questions and end with more on the psychology of food.

Are Gluten-Free Alternatives Healthy?

Many people who are gluten-intolerant think they are eating healthy when they consume refined and processed gluten-free foods such as crackers, bread, pasta, and cereal. These foods usually contain sugar, flour, soy, additives, sweeteners, and artificial flavorings to make them more palatable. These foods may be gluten-free, but that doesn't mean they are healthy. Gluten-free breads, cakes, muffins, pastries, and a sea of other refined and processed food items contain few nutrients and are best avoided most of the time.

Other gluten-free alternatives such as whole grain quinoa, teff, amaranth, and brown rice are very nutritious and great gluten-free alternatives for someone who loves grains but doesn't tolerate gluten.

When it comes to grains, the best grain is an unrefined whole grain, properly prepared.

Genetically-Modified Organisms (GMO)

The middle shelves of a typical grocery store are filled with foods that have little to no nutritional value. Much of the corn, soy, canola, and cottonseed oil used to make these products are made from genetically-modified (GM) plants. These plants have been engineered with bacterial genes that help the plant survive otherwise deadly doses of herbicides. Crops that tolerate potent herbicides comprise approximately 80 percent of all GM plants.

More than 81 percent of U.S. corn is genetically-modified, more than 88 percent of soybeans are genetically-engineered, and more than 81 percent of cotton, used to make cottonseed oil for frying food and making potato chips is genetically-engineered. In the U.S., 70 percent of the GM grain grown is to feed animals on feedlots. The rest feeds us. Genetically-modified foods play a large role in feeding the world's population and each year more genetically-modified plants make their way to our grocery store shelves and into our homes. The question being asked by so many is, "Is this a good thing?" Some say, "Yes," some say, "No."

GM plants are modified by shooting genes from a "gene gun" into a plate of cells, or by using bacteria to infect the cell with foreign DNA. This creates mutations in and around the insertion site and elsewhere. Genes can be inserted, deleted, or mutated to bring about desired traits in a plant.

Opponents of genetic modification do not feel that GM foods go through enough testing, and the testing that is done is not done by a neutral third party, but by the company that performs the genetic modification. While genetic modification may have potential, opponents feel it is not being done responsibly.

The largest issue being debated is whether or not these genes transfer into the DNA of bacteria inside the human digestive tract when the GM food is eaten. If a gene can be transferred into a plant cell, what is to stop it from being transferred into a human cell?

Let's look at an example of how this could occur. Bt corn, for instance, received a gene from soil bacterium *Bacillus Thuringiensis* (Bt). This gene produces a protein that kills the European corn borer, an insect fond of grains. This protein is called the Bt delta endotoxin. "To kill a susceptible insect, a part of the plant that contains the Bt protein (not all parts of the plant necessarily contain the protein in equal concentrations) must be ingested. Within minutes, the protein binds to the gut wall and the insect stops feeding. Within hours, the gut wall breaks down and normal gut bacteria invade the body cavity. The insect dies of septicaemia as bacteria multiply in the blood."[1]

This raises the question: "If Bt protein binds to the gut wall of an insect when it eats the corn, what is to stop it from binding to the gut wall of humans when we eat it?" Theoretically, this could provoke leaky gut, digestive disorders, food allergies, autoimmune disorders, or worse. When this concern was assessed, the herbicide tolerant genetic material in soybeans did show evidence of gene transfer into the DNA of human gut bacteria.[2] The UK Joint Food Safety and Standards Group warned that gene transfer may also be possible from inhaled pollen that might transfer into the DNA of bacteria in our respiratory system.[3]

Authorities have acknowledged "people with compromised immune systems or pre-existing allergies may be particularly susceptible to the effects of Bt."[4] And researchers at the York Laboratory reported that after genetically-modified soy was introduced into the British diet, allergies to soy increased by 50 percent in a single year.[5]

Proponents argue that the only way to feed the world is with GM crops; opponents say this claim isn't holding up to scrutiny, nor is the claim that GM crops have higher yields.[6] Another problem being faced is the increase of herbicide resistant weeds, which are the result of the overuse of the herbicides used on GM crops. If a crop is resistant to herbicides, more can be used without harming the plant, hence, the higher levels of herbicides that may linger on the food when you purchase it.

Proponents of GM foods are very passionate about how GM foods can be used to feed the world. For instance, in Africa, corn resistant to the African endemic maize streak virus (MSV) and tolerant to drought is being developed. Golden rice, a genetically modified crop designed to produce beta carotene, a precursor to vitamin A holds potential to help millions of people deficient in vitamin A around the globe. Salmon, tilapia, and trout have been genetically engineered to grow big fast to reduce fishing pressure on wild stocks. From malaria-resistant mosquitoes to human gene therapy, in which genetically-modified viruses are used to deliver genes that can cure disease, for every study that indicates a potential problem with genetic modification, there is another study heralding its benefits.

It can be very difficult to know on which side of the GM fence to stand. Personally, I would just like to know whether a food I choose to eat contains GM ingredients. Advocates of both sides of the GM issue would do well to get together to discuss a meaningful system in which GM skeptics could have their labels, GM proponents could have the freedom to advance the technology, and an unbiased third party would test it.

Currently, labeling laws do not require genetically-modified foods to be labeled, so if you wish to avoid GMOs, the best way is to purchase organic or products labeled GMO-free. No GM products are allowed in organic foods.

Many people purchase organic to avoid excessive use of pesticides and to ensure the produce they choose has not been genetically modified. I choose organic produce when there is a lot of surface area for the pesticide to infiltrate. Broccoli, cauliflower, and raspberries, for instance, have a lot of nooks and crannies for pesticides to seep into that may be hard to wash away. I also choose organic when I purchase produce items I know are big GM crops such as corn, potatoes, papayas, squash, beets, soy, and, coming to your table soon…salmon.

Outside of the produce section, if a product contains corn, soy, canola oil, or cottonseed oil and isn't labeled organic, it has most likely been genetically modified. As the organic food market continues to grow and demand for these products increases, so does the potential for corruption so organic may not always be reliable. Therefore, I encourage you to support your local farmers and ranchers and get involved at a local level to see what you can do to support your community's ability to sustain itself.

Many countries are watching the U.S. to see what will happen to us as a result of consuming GM foods; for now it seems we are a part of one big experiment in which the results won't be uncovered for a long time. Unfortunately, tracking the impact of GM foods is especially difficult in the United States because the foods are not labeled.

Because genetically-modified foods have the potential to cause harm, they are not considered *Good Decisions*.

Hybridization of Wheat

As of May 2013, no genetically-modified wheat is authorized for cultivation anywhere in the world. However, some wheat fields have been found to contain GM wheat regardless of the fact that it has not been approved.

When the biotech industry tried to genetically-modify wheat, some grains became so inbred they could not grow so they went back to hybridization. By 1980, thousands of new hybridized grains had been created. Some were bred to resist pathogens and environmental conditions, others to increase yield.

After thousands of experiments, it was discovered that with hybridization, the gluten proteins had undergone significant changes. These were the proteins that had been altered in order to hybridize. When researchers compared two parent strains of wheat, 95 percent of the proteins expressed in the offspring were the same, but 5 percent were unique, not found in either parent. This situation is like giving birth and finding that the genes in your child were never seen before!

Continued breeding has increased the amount of foreign proteins found in the offspring. These altered, foreign gluten proteins may be one of the primary reasons for the increase in celiac and autoimmune disease we have seen in the last fifty years. It certainly correlates to when the problems with gluten started.

While wheat is not classified as a genetically-modified crop, it can be just as problematic. I was told once that *The New England Journal of Medicine* listed fifty-five diseases that can be caused by eating gluten found in wheat. When I went to its website to verify this, I lost count after twenty. The top five were celiac disease, irritable bowel syndrome, chronic diarrhea, Hashimoto's thyroiditis, and diabetes.

The scary thing is, wheat is the most consumed grain on the planet, and people continue to talk about how healthy it is. Wheat products such as pasta, breads, flour, and other refined products made from conventional wheat are linked to too many diseases for it to be considered a healthy food.

Conventional hybridized wheat is not a Good Decision.

Heirloom Grains

While this information may seem overwhelming, it is important to note that while it may be difficult to tell what your whole grain has been through before it ends up in your grocery cart, a whole grain is still a much better decision than fast foods, processed foods, and refined foods. Everything is relative. So grains don't need to be avoided completely, just selected carefully.

Many organic heirloom grains are entering the marketplace, and while the term "heirloom" is not well-regulated, it is often associated with companies that encourage biodiversity and preservation of our ancient food supply. We are experiencing a movement toward a more health-conscious nation. The fact that you are reading this book indicates you are a part of this movement!

The more conscious we become about the food we eat, how we grow it, preserve it, and transport it, the more solutions we will find when it comes to feeding the world and sustaining local communities. It seems like there is an awakening, as if Americans are waking up from fast food befuddlement, looking around them, and demanding something different.

Agricultural methods are changing, and creative, sustainable, bio diverse methods are feeding millions of people. We are becoming increasingly aware that the health of our planet and food supply is imperative if we wish to ensure our survival as a species.

Small communities are banning together and asking for raw milk, raw cheese, and local fruits and vegetables grown creatively without pesticides. And when there is demand, supply is usually not too far behind. So it is always a good idea to ask yourself, "What am I demanding?" and "How does it contribute to the health of my planet and my people?"

There are many whole grains to choose from, and many levels of refinement that grains go through. Let's look at whole grains and the different levels of refinement so we can make *Good Decisions…Most of the Time.*

Levels of Grain Refinement

There are many different levels of refinement. From cracked whole grains to flour, knowing at which point to say no to a grain can be somewhat confusing. The following information will help.

Whole Grains

Whole grains contain the entire grain kernel: bran, germ, and endosperm. Loaded with fiber, iron, thiamin, riboflavin, niacin, and folic acid, whole grains are very nutritious. Whole grains undergo the least amount of processing because only the outer hull is removed, while the bran, germ, and endosperm remain intact. When they are soaked and cooked properly, they are the most nutritious form of grain because the nutrients are not removed, and the amount of fiber, protein, vitamins, and minerals is at its highest. Whole grains are also referred to as hulled grains.

Organic whole grains are very *Good Decisions*.

Pearled Grains

Pearled grain is grain that has been polished to remove its outer layer, known as the bran. The resulting grain has less fiber, proteins, vitamins, and minerals than whole grain. After pearled grain is produced, it can be ground into grits, flour, flakes, and a variety of other products. It is important to purchase 100 percent whole grain products, not pearled grain. With pearled grain, many vitamins and minerals are lost for convenience sake or for a softer, sweeter product. Pearled barley is an example of a pearled grain.

Pearled grain is not a whole grain and is not considered a *Good Decision*.

Grain Flakes

Grain flakes are made when whole grain is steamed and rolled to produce flattened or flaked kernels, which allows the grain to cook faster. Grain flakes are also known as rolled grains. These are most often made from pearled grains and are used in cereal products, so be wary and study the label to avoid these. It's easy to find organic whole grain flakes online and in many grocery stores. The most common grain that is flaked is oats, but any grain can be flaked. I find these make tasty breakfast porridges, and the nutrients remain intact. For those who don't like the chewy texture of the whole grains and grain grits, flakes are a wonderful alternative.

Organic whole grain flakes are *Good Decisions*.

Grits

Grits are a form of grain in which the grain or kernels are cut into smaller pieces so they'll cook faster. Grits are typically coarsely ground and used as traditional breakfast foods made of ground dried corn kernels, but they can be made from any grain. Coarsely-ground polenta is an example of grits. Southwestern Indians soaked their corn in a light water/lye mixture before drying and stone-grinding into grits. Unfortunately, grits are often made from pearled grains and lack whole grain nutrition. Be wary of these products and search for organic, whole grain grits.

Organic whole grain grits are *Good Decisions*.

Meal

Meal refers to grain that has been ground until it has a course, sandy texture. Meal is often used in breads and cereals, and it is most often ground from corn. Again, as long as the meal is ground from an organic whole grain, it's a nutritious choice. Read your labels well. Meal has a lot of surface area and will break down quicker in the body to increase blood glucose levels than whole grains, so you don't want to go crazy with meal. This is where we get to the tipping point where if the grain is refined any further, it becomes flour, which is an unhealthy decision because of its impact on blood sugar levels.

Organic, whole grain meal is a *Good Decision*.

Farina

Farina is a milled cereal grain. Farina is usually made from wheat germ and the endosperm (the starchy inner parts of wheat kernels), which is milled to a fine granular consistency and then sifted. Because the bran and most of the germ are removed, this cereal is often enriched with Vitamin B and iron. Farina, by itself, is most often served as a breakfast cereal.

In the past, farina was made primarily from wheat grains to produce Cream of Wheat® and Malt-O-Meal®. Today, several delicious whole grain farina products are available for many uses. Corn farina, made from whole organic corn, can be cooked like polenta. Whole brown rice farina is a tasty nutrient-dense alternative to Cream of Wheat, which is processed. Like meal, farina has a lot of surface area that breaks down quicker in the body to increase blood glucose levels, so don't go crazy with Farina either. Use Farina and meal to add interest to your diet, and when possible, cook them with a little bit of fat and protein to slow the entrance of sugar into the bloodstream.

Organic whole grain farina is a *Good Decision*.

Flour

Flour is created by grinding and sifting grains into a powdered form that varies in texture from very soft to coarse. Flour is the main ingredient in bread, cakes, pastries, and other types of baked goods. Flour is the most processed form of the grain.

Good Decisions does not recommend any flour, regardless of the grain that it was ground from, because flour has a much greater surface area. This means it will be quicker to absorb into the body and, therefore, more prone to elevating blood sugar levels. It occurs too often in foods such as pastries, cookies, cakes, bread, and pasta, where in many cases sugar has been added.

When you do have your weekly treat, feel free to indulge in flour products if you desire. I encourage you to make an unhealthy decision better by experimenting with 100 percent whole grain, organic, soaked or sprouted quinoa, teff, buckwheat, or rice flour in your recipes. You may be pleasantly surprised by how delicious they are.

Flour is not a *Good Decision*.

Now let's talk about all of the wonderful variety of *Good Decisions* grains you can choose from and how to use them! We will start with some of the grains that contain gluten.

Grain Varieties

Gluten Grains

These are best avoided if you suspect a sensitivity or allergy to gluten, your digestion is not working well, the grain is genetically-engineered or overly hybridized, or the grain has not been properly prepared.

Barley

After wheat, rice, and corn, barley is one of the largest cereal grain crops in the world and is generally pearled and processed, so it's important to find this grain in its 100 percent whole grain organic form. Timeless Food is a company I trust. I love its heirloom purple prairie barley.

Barley has a nutty, sweet flavor and has a texture similar to pasta. The color of the heirloom grain ranges from tan to various shades of brown or purple. With nearly 13 grams of fiber per cup, barley is a very good source of fiber. (This makes Metamucil® powder look wimpy, considering that one adult serving of Metamucil powder contains only 3 grams of fiber.) Barley is also is a good source of phosphorus, selenium, copper, and manganese.

Barley is great for use as a substitute for hamburger. It makes wonderful vegetarian tacos, taco salads, chili, or side dishes and salads. It is also great in pilafs or cooked like oats for breakfast.

Organic whole grain heirloom barley is a *Good Decision*.

Purple Prairie Barley Risotto

Serves: 6
Total Time: 45 minutes

Ingredients

- 2 tablespoons extra virgin olive oil
- 1 large yellow onion, finely chopped
- 3 garlic cloves, minced
- 3 cups sliced shitake mushrooms
- 1 cup dry red wine
- 4 cups purple prairie barley, cooked al dente
- 4 cups vegetable broth
- Salt and freshly ground pepper
- ¼ cup chopped fresh parsley

Directions

1. Heat the oil over medium heat in a large, heavy nonstick skillet or saucepan, and add the onion, garlic, and mushrooms. Cook, stirring, until tender, about five minutes. Add the barley and red wine. Cook, stirring, until the wine has evaporated. Add the broth, and cook, stirring often, for 10 minutes. Continue to simmer until the broth has been absorbed by the barley. There should still be some creamy liquid surrounding the grains of barley. Add salt and pepper to taste. Stir in the parsley, remove from the heat, and serve.

Spelt

Spelt is a wheat grain species that originated as wheat (such as emmer wheat) and a type of wild goat-grass. Spelt is an excellent source of manganese, which plays an important part in how your brain functions. Spelt is also a good source of niacin, copper, phosphorus, protein, and fiber. Spelt has a mild and nutty taste, with a slight hint of hazelnut.

Spelt goes well with earthy ingredients such as mushrooms and strong sauces, such as those made with garlic and olive oil. Stuffing, risotto, and pilafs are great when spelt is the main ingredient.

Organic whole grain spelt is a *Good Decision*.

Khorasan Wheat

Khorasan wheat, also known as Kamut®, is a whole grain closely related to wheat. Its origins can be traced back to ancient Near Eastern countries. Kamut is high in protein, selenium, zinc, and magnesium, and has an unmistakable buttery flavor.

Kamut is excellent in soups, salads, pilafs, or savory side dishes. Kamut is a relatively large chewy grain that almost resembles pasta more than a grain and, therefore, makes a good substitute for pasta.

Organic whole grain khorasan wheat is a *Good Decision*.

Rye

Rye grass originated as a weed found in grain fields. It is now used for flour, rye bread, sourdough bread, beer, and some vodkas and whiskey because it ferments easily. Rye grain has a very aggressive and hearty flavor with a slightly bitter taste. The color of the grain ranges from beige to dark gray.

Rye is processed into a variety of forms including whole kernels (berries), flakes, meal, and flour. The whole grain requires longer cooking time than other grains, so soaking the berries overnight is essential.

Rye berries are used in stew, rice, and vegetable stir-fry. Rye flakes cook faster than rye berries, and they can be used in a variety of dishes, including soup.

Organic whole grain rye is a *Good Decision*.

Oats

While oats do not contain the gluten found in wheat, they are a close relative to wheat and contain a protein similar to gluten called *avenin*. This protein can trigger a reaction in some people. Oats are frequently processed in the same facilities as wheat, barley, and other grains and, as a result, can become contaminated with other glutens. Because of this, oats are officially listed as a crop containing gluten. Some people react to the proteins in oats, and for these people, oats can be very inflammatory. If you feel mentally foggy, anxious, headachy, itchy, and/or have trouble focusing, you may not do well with oats and they are best avoided.

There are hundreds of varieties of oats. The two main classifications are winter oats and summer oats. About 90 percent of the oats grown in the U.S. are used for animal feed. The remainder is processed with a number of methods, including steaming, rolling, cutting, and grinding, to produce products for human consumption, such as oat bran, oat flakes, oatmeal, steel cut oats, and oat flour.

Nutritional Nugget

Oats have reduced the pain and irritation of poison oak, poison ivy, eczema, shingles, rashes, and other skin conditions for years. The milk within the oat is harvested usually in late August when the seeds are premature. These milky oat extracts can nourish the nervous system when dealing with stress, depression, nervous debility, and exhaustion. The extracts have also been used as a sexual tonic! So bring on the oatmeal! Vavavroom!

Because oats contain polyunsaturated fatty acids, they tend to go rancid easily. To prevent this problem, many companies use heat up to 200°F to treat their oats. This process prevents the polyunsaturated oils from going rancid and spoiling the oats.

Unfortunately, it also kills the enzyme phytase that is needed to break down phytic acid. Because of this issue, oats are considered a low phytase grain, so it is important to:

- Find oats that have not been heat processed.
- Add phytase rich whole buckwheat groats or phytase producing probiotic bacteria in the form of yoghurt or kefir to the soaking liquid.
- Soak oats for a full 24 hours.

I love oatmeal, but finding true raw rolled oats can be difficult. Even some Irish and Scottish oatmeal brands promoted as "unheated" actually are heat-treated to minimize rancidity. A good source of authentic raw rolled oats can be found at http://www.bluemountainorganics.com or http://sproutpeople.org. Keep in mind, these oats do spoil easily so they are best kept in the fridge.

Oats have enjoyed popularity because of their cholesterol-lowering ability. In addition to the fiber benefits, oats are also a very good source of selenium. Selenium works with vitamin E in numerous vital antioxidant systems throughout the body. Selenium is helpful in decreasing asthma symptoms, supporting the thyroid gland, and in the prevention of heart disease. In addition, selenium is associated with a reduced risk for cancer, especially colon cancer. Oats are an excellent source of selenium and manganese, and a very good source of magnesium, phosphorus, and protein.

Oats are very diverse and can be used to make oat bars, thicken soups, and add crunch to toppings in replacement of breadcrumbs. My favorite use for oats is as a breakfast grain. Oatmeal with coconut oil, raisins, and cinnamon, topped with an egg cooked over easy, just doesn't get any better or any more nutritious!

Organic whole grain oats are a very *Good Decision*.

Non-Gluten Grains

No need to worry about gluten sensitivities here; the following whole grains are all *Good Decisions!*

CHAPTER FIVE

Organic Corn

There are many different types of corn.

Dent corn is named for the indentation on the top of the kernels that develops as the corn dries in the field.

Flint corn, known for its multicolored ears, is used as a popular decoration in the fall months. The decorative ears, often referred to as "Indian corn," contain kernels of vibrant colors that range from yellow, orange, and red to blue, purple, and black. The kernels are very hard, but they can be ground into meal and used for human consumption.

Flour corn, as the name indicates, is grown solely for the production of corn flour. The kernels are starchy and much softer than other types of corn, which allows flour milling to be an easier process.

Popcorn, white and yellow, is a special variety of dried corn with high moisture content. About 15 percent of the kernel is water, which creates steam when the kernel is heated. This heating causes the kernels to explode and pop open because the steam cannot escape.

Sweet corn is often considered a vegetable rather than a grain because it is most often eaten fresh like a vegetable. Sweet corn has a higher sugar content than other types of corn, but the sugar begins to convert to starch after it is harvested, so it is best when eaten fresh. Although there are many different varieties, the three types of sweet corn that are readily available are white corn, yellow corn, and a hybrid of both white and yellow corn.

I remember growing sweet corn in our backyard when I was a child. It was so crisp and sweet and delicious! Now, most corn has been genetically modified to be resistant to pests, weather, and drought. While this makes for a hardier corn, it's just not as tender and doesn't taste as good. Organic corn can be very difficult to find and is often limited to local farmers' markets. As a result, I limit my corn consumption to the summer months when I can obtain local organic corn and then freeze it for use throughout the winter.

The Italian dish polenta is most often made from cornmeal ground from flint corn. Cornbread is a cornmeal classic that can be topped with plain yogurt and berries for a creative dessert.

When organic and properly prepared, corn is a very *Good Decision*.

Teff

Teff is a gluten-free grain belonging to the grass family. It is one of my favorite grains to cook with. The grain is the size of a poppy seed and comes in a variety of colors from white and red to dark brown. The word "teff" means "lost" in the Amharic language. This name refers to the fact that because the grains are so tiny, they are lost if dropped.

Teff is high in dietary fiber, iron, calcium, and protein, and your body can absorb the iron in teff relatively well. Teff is similar to millet and quinoa in cooking, and considering its size, teff is a nutritional powerhouse.

Teff is often prepared as a hot cereal or as polenta because the sticky cooked grain can be easily formed and stay shaped. The white grains have a mild flavor, while the red and brown grains have a very pronounced flavor that goes well with full-flavored, spicy foods.

Whole grain organic teff is definitely a *Good Decision* and an All-Star grain to keep well stocked in the pantry.

Rice

Rice is such an important part of the diet that nearly half the world's population receives nearly 50 percent of its daily calories from it. Rice is grown in river deltas, flooded or irrigated coastal plains, and terraced hillsides. It is most often cultivated in subtropical locations and in temperate areas with long, hot, humid growing seasons.

Asia supplies most of the world's rice, and there are thousands of varieties to choose from. Some of the most nutritious rice are the colored varieties. Bhutanese red rice, brown Kalijira rice, Madagascar pink rice, and many other varieties are extremely dense nutritional choices. I love these rice varieties and get excited any time I can cook with them.

In ancient China, nobles commandeered every grain of a variety of black rice for themselves and forbade the common people from eating it, so it became known as "Forbidden Rice." According to Zhimin Xu, an associate professor at Louisiana State University, a spoonful of black rice bran contains more health-promoting antioxidants than are found in a spoonful of blueberries, but with less sugar and more fiber and vitamin E.

Rice can be used to make puddings, stuffing, pilafs, and even in replacement of oatmeal as a breakfast grain.

Organic whole grain rice is definitely a *Good Decision*!

Wild Rice

Wild rice is not actually a type of rice, but the edible seed of an aquatic grass that grows in marshy areas of lakes and rivers. Almost always sold as a dried whole grain, wild rice is high in protein and dietary fiber and, like true rice, it does not contain gluten. It is also a good source of the minerals potassium and phosphorus, and the vitamins thiamine, riboflavin, and niacin. It may vary in color and can be yellow, tan, brown, or almost black.

Wild rice has a pleasant, chewy texture and a distinctive earthy, nutty flavor. It is eaten alone or used as an ingredient for soups, stuffings, and casseroles. A small quantity added to steamed vegetables makes an excellent side dish. It also adds a nice flavor to tossed salads and is one of the best sides for poultry and fish.

Whole grain organic wild rice is a *Good Decision*.

Seed Grains

Seed grains do not contain gluten and are therefore much easier to digest. They do contain phytates and need to be soaked, but do not need to be soaked as long. A 6-12 hour soak is all these seed grains need.

Job's Tears

Also known as Hato mugi, the seed of this plant is similar to barley. It has many names, including Coix or Job's Tears because its shape is similar to a teardrop. It is used in traditional Chinese medicine for certain conditions of the stomach and spleen, and it is said to help reduce inflammation and arthritis and help stabilize blood sugar levels.

Nutritional Nugget

This is a fantastic grain that can be used to support diabetics. In fact, hato mugi works so well at lowering blood sugar levels that if you take medicine for diabetes, be careful to monitor your blood sugar levels closely, as your need for medication may decrease.

Job's tears are also rich in protein, iron, calcium, B vitamins, and fiber and come in several colors including yellow, brown, white, and purple. It can be cooked alone or combined with other grains in soups, stews, salads, and side dishes and is an excellent substitute for pearl barley.

Organic whole grain hato mugi is a very *Good Decision.*

Job's Tears and Whitefish Stew

Serves: 8
Total Time: 1 hour, 25 minutes, plus soaking time

Ingredients

- 1 teaspoon olive oil
- 2 cups chopped onion
- 3 garlic cloves, chopped
- 1 tablespoon finely chopped fresh ginger root
- 8 cups organic vegetable broth
- 1 cup Job's Tears, soaked in water overnight and drained
- 16 ounces cubed white fish (halibut, black cod, pollock)
- 1 cup fresh shiitake mushrooms, sliced
- 6 cups baby bok choy
- ¼ cup fresh lime juice
- Sea salt and pepper to taste
- 1 cup cilantro
- 3 green onions, finely sliced for garnish

Directions

1. In a large stockpot sauté onion, garlic, and ginger in olive oil until onions are tender and translucent. Add broth, Job's tears, and bring to a rolling boil. Reduce heat to low, cover, and simmer for 45 minutes to an hour. Add fish and shiitake mushrooms and simmer for an additional 15 minutes. Add baby bock choy, lime, salt, and pepper. Simmer for 5 minutes, and then remove from heat. Ladle into individual serving bowls and garnish with cilantro and green onion. Serve hot.

Millet

Millet refers to a variety of related plants bearing small seeds used as a grain. In the U.S., millet is often used as a popular type of birdseed.

Varieties of millet include:

Foxtail – most often used for birdseed or for brewing beer

Pearl – primarily used in India as a food source

Proso – available in the U.S. for human consumption, livestock feed, and birdseed

Finger millet – a red-colored variety most often found in Eastern Europe or Asia

Bulrush millet – found mainly in Europe, Africa, and Asia

Millet is a good source of manganese, tryptophan, magnesium, phosphorus, and fiber.

Millet has a mild sweetness and crunchy texture, and it is eaten as a cereal, side dish, or polenta. It can be added to soups, stews, and desserts. Toasted millet seeds are especially good. The grain's consistency depends on the cooking method; it can be creamy like mashed potatoes or fluffy like rice.

Whole grain organic millet is a *Good Decision*.

Quinoa

Quinoa is not a true grain, but its seeds are often used as grain. The plant is actually a part of the same botanical family as beets and spinach. It produces clusters that contain thousands of tiny bead-shaped seeds that range in color from light beige and yellow to rust or almost black. It has superior nutritional qualities and, when cooked in water, the seeds increase in size significantly, swelling three- or four-fold. When cooked, the seeds become springy and tender.

Quinoa has gained popularity in the U.S. because it supplies complete protein, which means it contains all nine essential amino acids. Quinoa's amino acid profile is well-balanced, making it a great choice for vegans. Quinoa is packed with the amino acid *lysine*, which is essential for tissue growth and repair. In addition to protein, quinoa contains other health-building nutrients such as manganese, magnesium, iron, copper, and phosphorus.

Quinoa makes fantastic salads, stuffing, casseroles, cereals, and desserts. It is a very tasty, diverse grain that can also be used to thicken soups and stews.

Whole grain organic quinoa is a very *Good Decision*.

Amaranth

Amaranth is actually the seed of an herb, but it is often mistaken for a grain. Hunter-gatherers ate amaranth at least eight-thousand years ago. Today, amaranth leaves are gathered, boiled, and fried. It is popular in Mexico and Peru, where only popped seeds are eaten. One amaranth plant may produce as many as half a million seeds. The amaranth seed is light tan to red in color and has a mild tangy or peppery flavor. Amaranth is a good source of iron, magnesium, phosphorus, and manganese. One cup of Amaranth contains a powerful 26 grams of protein. By comparison, one egg has 17 grams of protein!

Amaranth is delicious toasted as a snack, or used in pilafs, salads, soups, and stews.

Whole grain organic amaranth is definitely a *Good Decision*.

Buckwheat

Buckwheat, which is a native plant of Russia, is actually not a grain but the seed of a fruit related to rhubarb and sorrel. Most people are pleasantly surprised to find it does not contain gluten. Buckwheat that has been roasted is known by the Russian name kasha and unroasted buckwheat is simply called buckwheat. Buckwheat contains 22 grams of protein, 17 grams of fiber, and almost 86 milligrams of magnesium in a one-cup serving. Those are some serious nutrients!

The magnesium in buckwheat relaxes blood vessels and improves blood flow while lowering blood pressure, making it great for a healthy cardiovascular system. Some of buckwheat's health benefits are due to its rich supply of flavonoids, particularly rutin, a medicinal chemical used for vascular disorders.

In culinary terms, buckwheat can be considered a grain. It is cooked and prepared in the same manner as whole grains. Buckwheat is gluten free and does not require soaking for long periods but is most healthful when soaked overnight for seven to eight hours to neutralize the phytates and begin the sprouting process that makes seeds so nutrient dense. Don't be alarmed if the water seems a little slimy. This is normal when soaking buckwheat; just make sure that you rinse it before use.

Buckwheat is used in many Russian and Indian dishes and is a popular grain for salads, stuffing, and even soups. The groats are delicious cooked as a breakfast grain or used as a substitute for pasta in risotto.

Whole grain organic buckwheat is a *Good Decision.*

Cleaning and Rinsing Grains

Always rinse whole grains before soaking or cooking them in order to clean the grain and to remove any debris that may be present. Rice is often rinsed before cooking, but there are some instances when this is not necessary. Before you rinse rice, consider the type of rice and how you plan to cook it. Some types of rice that are high in starch content, such as Asian rice, can be rinsed to remove some of the stickiness of the rice. This can be done with other grains as well, depending on what consistency you desire in your finished product.

If I want to use grain to thicken a dish, I give it a quick rinse to retain the starch. Asian cooks often rinse rice several times, not because they are overly fearful of contaminants in the rice, but because extra rinsing is an important step in producing light and fluffy perfectly-cooked rice.

Repeated rinsing allows the grain to be cooked in a smaller quantity of water, which improves the taste and results in a lighter, fluffier grain. A quick rinse allows the grain to retain the starch, which results in a thicker, heavier grain. This is good to keep in mind when considering a recipe with grain and the characteristics you want from it.

Grain Storage and Tips for Purchasing Grains

- Buy grain from a source that has rapid turnover. Whole grains lose freshness more quickly than refined flours, so buy the freshest product possible.
- Never buy grains in bulk bins found at your grocery store where they are more exposed to oxygen and more likely to go rancid.
- Purchase your grains in well-sealed packages.
- For storage, use glass containers with tight lids and store whole grains in a cool, dry, dark location.
- Refrigerate whole grain flours and most grains if you cannot use the entire package in two months. In the summer, store whole grain flours in the refrigerator or a dry cool location. Warm temperatures can quickly turn some whole grains rancid.
- Read packaging to determine the shelf life of the grain. Some grains, even when stored perfectly, have a shelf life of only a few months, while others, like popcorn, can keep for several years if stored correctly.

Reading Labels

Thousands of products line our grocery store shelves. Often they are laden with any number of additives, preservatives, food dyes, sugar, etc. Familiarize yourself with labels the next time you take a trip down the bread aisle of your local grocery and read a few ingredient lists. You may see: calcium propionate (a preservative), potassium sorbate (a preservative), DATEM (diacetyl tartaric acid ester of mono- and diglycerides, an emulsifier), sodium stearoyl lactylate, ascorbic acid, potassium iodate, azodicarbonamide (dough conditioners), natamycin (a natural mold inhibitor), silicon dioxide (an anticaking agent), caramel coloring, refinery syrup, and a number of other substances designed to increase the shelf life and artificially flavor the product.

When looking at these labels, the nutrition facts may lead you to believe that a product is healthy based on calorie information. A closer look at the ingredient list will tell what's really in the product. Bring your eyeglasses if you wear them since much of this information is in fine print.

If you do buy grain products such as breads and pasta products on those not-so-most-of-the-time occasions, look for products that use soaked or sprouted whole grains such as buckwheat, teff, rice, or quinoa—and the fewer the ingredients, the better.

The Psychology of Food

Letting Go of Judgment

We have all experienced judgment in one form or another, from the beautiful skinny woman walking by that we label "bitch" to the overweight slovenly person we deem "lazy." Judgment can be a difficult thing to escape. Whether we are the one doing the labeling or the one being labeled, it has become so normal that most of us don't even know we are doing it, let alone why we do it.

An Emotional Maneuver

Judgment is actually a maneuver we do subconsciously to manage our emotions and make ourselves feel better. But herein lies the rub; relief is temporary. Judgment does not address the underlying issues, which are strong feelings and emotions we have not been taught to manage properly.

When you diminish another individual, you subconsciously elevate yourself to increase your own sense of worth and value. Often you may not be conscious that you are doing this. That skinny bitch we see serves as a trigger, which may dredge up feelings of envy, resentment, or jealousy.

Let's follow the feelings of shame and envy. I see the beautiful skinny woman; I immediately compare her to myself and sense a feeling of lack. I may feel shame that I let myself go and gained weight. I may feel fear that I may never be able to control my eating habits or be that beautiful. I envy her because I am comparing her to myself and judging her as beautiful and skinny, which I deem "good," and me as overweight and ugly, which I deem "bad." This makes me feel like I may never measure up. I feel uncomfortable and my nature is to avoid pain, seek pleasure, so I turn the tables and label beautiful and skinny to be "bitch" and overweight and ugly to be nice or "good." I have effectively turned the tables on this woman, and she is now deemed "bad," and I am now "good."

My feelings of shame and envy diminish. I have effectively soothed myself and managed my emotions by diminishing another person.

But we don't have to diminish or devalue the other person to create the illusion that we are enough. We simply already are enough. There is nothing we need to do or become to achieve worthiness. It is not performance based; it is not based on physical attributes, or anything else for that matter. We are all of equal value, and we will always be of equal value.

Think of this concept from a soul perspective. Think of yourself as a spirit within a physical body and others as spirits within physical bodies. While we may all have different physical bodies on the outside, we are all spirits on the inside. Now, this physical body and spirit is born into life with a sense of wonder, joy, and unconditional love. Children will look at a ninety-year-old man, a person of a different ethnicity, and even a dangerous mountain lion with curiosity and openness. This is who we are: the spiritual presence within the physical body. When children learn from the previous generation that has been influenced by historical events, cultural phenomena, and social trends, they begin to identify with things or beliefs. Judgment becomes the means by which we value ourselves and others.

The ironic thing about judging others is that we are really judging ourselves.

For instance, we judged ourselves as not being good enough when we labeled the beautiful woman "bitch." Another example is if your partner does something that makes you feel embarrassed or upset, your discomfort is really fear that others may judge you—guilt by association. You may judge yourself as having chosen your partner poorly.

When you feel irritated with other people for an anxiety that wells up inside of you, whether it is worry about what the group or others think or how they view you, it *always* has something to do with you and how you are judging yourself.

There are two types of emotional maneuvers that we use to increase our perception of our own worth and value: negative maneuvers and positive maneuvers.

Negative Maneuvers

"The world would be better without me" is the mentality that describes this category well.

The emotional aspect of negative maneuvers is used to judge and beat up yourself. This is the type of maneuver that usually precedes overeating. Why do we do this? Because when we have these negative emotions, we sometimes feel better because the inflicting of pain releases pain. It is similar to anger. When you feel angry, yelling at someone gives you a feeling of release, no matter how temporary. Beating yourself up uses the same release mechanism. If you feel horrible about yourself for being overweight, it may cost you ten emotional units, but beating up on yourself or yelling at someone else releases twenty emotional units. Cutters and smokers who burn themselves or inflict pain on themselves use this maneuver to release the pain inside. Overeating can be a form of release that brings short-term relief from negative self-talk.

Punching the wall, kicking the dog, yelling at your spouse, or emotional eating expends energy and releases the inner turmoil that may have arisen from your own feelings of inadequacy. This is simply a maneuver used to release the emotional discomfort inside of us.

Positive Maneuvers

"I am better than you" (the holier-than-thou or righteous stance) is what this category is about. It may manifest as egocentric and focused on the self.

Relative to food, an individual may be obese and his or her actions may say, "Look at how frugal I am because I drive a crappy car." What that person is really saying is "I am better than you." While driving a crappy car has nothing to do with obesity, it can be a way of managing emotions and bringing relief from feelings of unworthiness.

The enhancement of the self for the purpose of social reinforcement is another way we try to elevate our worthiness. For instance, it is one thing to have a little two-door convertible to zip around town in because it's fun to do so. It's another thing to have it so you can be seen in it.

Whether someone is living below his or her means or swimming in wealth, this form of emotional maneuvering is used to bring the same relief as a negative maneuver.

One method elevates others, the other elevates us.

Practicing Good Decisions

Practice Judgment Neutrality and Assessment

So how do we allow others to be who they are without judgment? How do we find within us the inner knowing that we are worthy, no matter what we do or look like, so our temptation to judge our behaviors or ourselves is reduced?

The most effective way to let go of judgment is to observe when you do it. The simple act of observing your inner dialogue dissipates it. Observe yourself when you judge others and the habit will lessen over time. When you catch yourself judging, back up and see whether you can assess the situation instead and identify whether it is a positive maneuver or a negative maneuver. Ask yourself how you may be using judgment to manage your own emotions.

This is called *judgment neutrality*. Nothing is good or bad; it is just cause and effect. Thus, instead of beating ourselves up for eating too much, which doesn't do anything but manage our emotions ineffectively, we practice observing and managing our emotions without harsh judgment. We simply observe and say, "Well, I just overate." There are many situations you might judge.

You may judge yourself:

Judgment: You look in the mirror and feel uncomfortable emotions. So you tell yourself how fat and unworthy you are. You harshly judge your worth based upon your appearance. (*Negative maneuver*)

Assessment: You look in the mirror and notice you are heavier than you have been in the past. There is no good or bad attached to the observation; it just is. (*Judgment neutrality*)

You may judge certain foods:

Judgment: Sugar is bad. Looking at sugar from this perspective elicits an emotional response that you connect to sugar. It may even cause you to identify with the label "bad" and make you feel "bad" and beat yourself up when you eat it. (*Negative maneuver*)

Assessment: Sugar is not nutrient dense, and when over-consumed, it can lead to obesity, addiction, and disease. It is not good or bad; it just is—cause and effect. (*Judgment neutrality*)

You may judge other people:

Judgment: You see a mother yelling at her child in the grocery store and label her a bad mother and a horrible person. It elicits a strong emotion from you and you feel like you would be a much better mother than she is. (*Positive maneuver*)

Assessment: You see a mother yelling at her child in the grocery store and don't attach any label to it. It just is. You could even take this a step further and send compassion to the mother for having a rough day or whatever hardships she may have endured in her life. *(Judgment neutrality with compassion)*

Judgment neutrality saves all the energy we put into judging others and ourselves, and we start removing judgment from things that don't need to be judged. Foods are not good or bad; it is our thoughts about them that make them good or bad.

Processed foods make us feel lethargic, dull, and heavy. Vegetables and fruits make us feel light, sharp, and energetic. This is not good or bad; it is cause and effect. Truth and knowledge tell us it's not the food itself, but the frequency at which we eat certain foods that contributes toward dis-ease or wellness in the body. Judgment neutrality and assessment can be powerful tools we can use to make food decisions easier.

Being judgment neutral takes practice. In the beginning, when you start to notice how often you judge things, it may get worse before it gets better. Often what we think about is what we bring about, and what we focus on gets bigger. Approach this conundrum by focusing on assessing situations instead of trying to force yourself not to judge.

Assessing utilizes intellect, and judgment arises from emotion. Pay attention to your emotions, and when you feel yourself being triggered, i.e. feeling a powerful emotion, judgment is most likely involved. If you can catch yourself at this point, you are doing great! Pause for a moment and observe what you are feeling in the moment. Being aware of what is happening emotionally is most of the battle! Now instead of responding or reacting from emotion, see whether you can assess the situation instead.

You may be relieved to find when you stop judging others, you also stop judging yourself. Fear and resistance become emotions simply to sit with, just as you would any other uncomfortable emotion, until it dissipates.

You have your own personalized measuring system, and the more you increase your awareness of this and stop measuring yourself and your behaviors against other people or their behaviors, the less you will judge yourself. The less you judge yourself, the more confidence and freedom you will have to be your authentic self, and the more joyful the walk down your hallway of life will be!

Chapter Six

Balancing Minerals with Legumes, Nuts, and Seeds

In this chapter, we explore mighty legumes. We will discuss why they are considered "All-Star" protein sources, and you'll learn how to prepare them in a way that won't make your belly bloat or your partner run from the room. We will talk about the benefits of eating legumes and discuss the third nutritional foundation: mineral balance. Because the body is unable to manufacture them, minerals must come from the diet. You will also learn delicious ways to prepare legumes and a few tips to increase legumes' digestibility, taste, and texture. We will end with more on the psychology of food.

Benefits of Eating Legumes

Legumes are a class of vegetables that includes beans, peas, and lentils. They are among the most versatile and nutritious foods available. It always surprises me that they rarely get the attention they deserve. One of the many reasons I shine the spotlight on legumes is because they are so rich in fiber, which aids digestion and can both ease constipation or firm up diarrhea. Legumes are high in protein, which aids blood sugar regulation, and they are chock-full of minerals. Legumes are also a good source of folate, known as one of the "feel good" vitamins used to counter symptoms such as irritability, mental fatigue, confusion, depression, insomnia, and muscular fatigue. It is no wonder nutritional therapists have been encouraging people to consume legumes for years.

Because legumes pack such a huge nutritious punch, they can be consumed as much as you desire—and they are easy to prepare! Let's look at the many ways legumes contribute to our health and wellbeing.

Heart Health

One study examined food intake patterns and risk of death from heart disease. In this study, researchers followed more than 16,000 middle-aged men in the U.S., Finland, The Netherlands, Italy, former Yugoslavia, Greece, and Japan for twenty-five years. Typical food patterns were:

- Northern Europe consumed the most dairy products.
- The U.S. consumed the greatest amount of meat.
- Southern Europe consumed the most vegetables, legumes, fish, and wine.
- Japan consumed the greatest amount of cereal, soy products, and fish.

When researchers analyzed the data, they found that legumes were associated with a whopping 82 percent reduction in the risk of death from heart disease.

Blood Sugar Regulation

In addition to beneficial effects on the heart, the fiber in legumes helps stabilize blood sugar levels. This is because fiber slows the entrance of sugar into the bloodstream. Legumes also contain abundant amounts of trace minerals that play a role in blood sugar regulation. If you have insulin resistance, hypoglycemia, or diabetes, legumes can really support you. In one study, researchers compared two groups of people with type 2 diabetes who were given different amounts of high fiber foods. One group ate the Standard American Diet (SAD), which provides 24 grams of fiber each day, while the other group ate a diet containing 50 grams of fiber each day. Those who ate the diet higher in fiber had lower levels of both blood sugar and insulin. I would also wage their digestion improved dramatically with all that fiber to bulk things up and move things along!

Energy

Legumes can help increase your energy by replenishing the iron in your body. You may already know that iron is an integral component of hemoglobin, which transports oxygen from your lungs to all parts of your body, making it a vital component of good health. I've known many women who complained of being tired all the time, only to find out they had an iron deficiency. However, if you've ever taken iron supplements, you know they can cause you to be miserably constipated. Legumes help alleviate this problem by providing both iron and fiber—without the constipation. Women who are still menstruating are often at greater risk of iron deficiency.

Mental Clarity

Legumes are a good source of folate or vitamin B9. This is one of the "feel good" B vitamins, important for mental health and energy. Folate deficiency symptoms include mental fatigue, forgetfulness, confusion, and more.

Insomnia, Depression, and Anxiety

Tryptophan is one of the ten essential amino acids found in food that your body uses to synthesize the proteins it needs. It is especially well-known for its "after-Thanksgiving-Dinner" effects on the body, obvious when the person washing the dishes comes out of the kitchen to find everyone crashed on the couch in an after-dinner daze. This effect, however, is mostly due to the carbohydrates consumed that triggered the release of tryptophan rather than the turkey's actual content of tryptophan.

Tryptophan plays a role in the production of nervous system messengers that relates to relaxation, restfulness, and sleep. Because of its ability to raise serotonin levels, tryptophan has been used therapeutically in the treatment of a variety of chronic conditions, most notably insomnia, depression, and anxiety. Not consuming enough tryptophan can also cause irritability, impatience, inability to concentrate, and weight gain. Legumes are a great source of this vital nutrient.

Protein

Legumes are a wonderful protein source for vegetarians and non-vegetarians alike. One cup of lentils has almost 17 grams of protein. When you consider that two eggs have roughly 12 grams of protein, the mighty legume becomes very impressive indeed!

Nutritional Nugget

Anise seed, cardamom, coriander, cumin, fennel, and ginger are among the spices that are especially effective in preventing the formation of gas. These can be used not only to increase the flavor and nutrients of the dish, but aid digestion and decrease family flatulence as well!

CHAPTER SIX

Mineral Balance

Building the Third Nutritional Foundation

Legumes, nuts, and seeds are phenomenal sources of minerals. When people think of mineral balance, they think of bone health, which is not surprising considering our body stores minerals in our bones. What many people don't realize is that calcium requires many things in order for the body to absorb and utilize it. Ironically, most people consume enough calcium, but lack the ability to absorb or use it. Let's look at some of the conditions that need to be in place in order for our bodies to utilize calcium.

- *Digestion must be working.* Calcium, zinc, and certain other minerals are only absorbed in an acid environment. If digestion is sluggish and production of hydrochloric acid low, calcium may not be absorbed by the body.
- *Blood sugar levels need to be balanced.* The acidy or alkalinity of our blood is affected directly by what we eat. High blood sugar levels increase acidity of blood. When the blood becomes too acidic, it pulls calcium from tissues and bones to neutralize the acidic pH, leading to osteoporosis and tooth decay. When blood sugar levels are not regulated, hormone levels are often also out of balance.
- *Consumption of fats is necessary*. Fatty acids are necessary to transport certain minerals across cell membranes into cells. This increases delivery of minerals to tissues. In the chapter on grains, we discussed how fat in butter and cream can increase our ability to utilize minerals found in grains. This is also true for legumes.
- *Minerals are needed for the production of digestive juices.* Certain minerals also play key roles in blood sugar regulation. Both of these determine whether hormones decide to pull calcium from bones, put it into bones, or excrete it from the body.
- *We need large amounts of water to digest what we eat.* Water is also the medium in which all nutrients, including calcium, are absorbed.

Are you starting to see how one nutritional foundation can be directly affected by another? All five foundations are interdependent, so if one foundation is weak, it can lead to weakness in the other foundations. Don't be overwhelmed by this; simply know that **Good Decisions...Most of the Time** is designed to address all of the foundations and take you where you need to be. For instance:

- The No Sugar Challenge is designed to regulate your blood sugar levels.
- The section on Improving Digestion gives you the tools you need to ensure adequate digestion.
- The information on fats and oils shows you how to provide your body with quality fats.
- The section on water will show you how to stay well-hydrated and decrease toxicity in the body.
- This chapter emphasizes minerals as the spark plugs of the body. They help to maintain pH balance in the body, bone health, contract and relax muscles, and much more.

Legumes, nuts, and seeds are nutrient dense and great sources of minerals. When a little dairy or quality fat is added to legumes when you consume them, it aids their absorption and provides other nutrients essential for mineral balance. Legumes are truly amazing!

Nutritional Nugget

Cooking beans with kombu (a type of sea vegetable) adds *galactosidase*, an enzyme needed for digesting complex sugars. This enzyme can improve the digestibility of beans even more. Adding kombu to your beans will also increase their nutritional value by adding trace minerals to your dish. Most grocery stores and Asian markets carry kombu.

Legumes and Gas

So, if legumes are so great, why don't we eat them very often? The main reason appears to be the havoc they wreak on our digestive systems. Let's face it; eating beans isn't the first thing you want to do before an important meeting or a first date. If you're an athlete, it doesn't matter how good this superfood is for you because if it produces gas and bloating, you're not going to consume legumes or view them as a way to reach peak performance. This situation is unfortunate because legumes are high in carbohydrates and protein, which is perfect nutrition for an athlete.

Fortunately, it is possible to eat beans without having embarrassing flatulence. Gas occurs because beans contain *oligosaccharides*—complex carbohydrates that aren't easily processed by the human digestive system.

As we discussed in the section on grains, many plants contain natural toxins that can interfere with our ability to digest them. These toxins are a part of the plant's natural defense system to protect them against fungus, bacteria, and other predators, which also makes them less easy for us to digest.

As a high-fiber food, beans are broken down by bacteria and absorbed lower in the digestive tract. The large intestine is responsible for breaking down these high fiber foods through a process called fermentation, which means those noxious gases are a byproduct of digestion. Fortunately, you can lessen this effect by soaking the beans before you eat them. When beans go through fermentation on your countertop, less fermentation happens in your intestines, which means less gas.

As with seeds and grains, legumes also contain phytic acid and have enzyme inhibitors to prevent them from sprouting in unfavorable conditions. Simply soaking beans neutralizes phytic acid and enzyme inhibitors, which aids in digestion and breaks down the complex sugars responsible for gas.

Pigeon Peas and Pork Rib Stew

Serves: 6
Total Time: 45 minutes, plus soaking time

Ingredients

- 2 pounds pork spareribs
- 2 tablespoons coconut oil
- 2 large onions
- 8 garlic cloves, crushed
- 1 teaspoon fresh minced ginger
- 1 cup dry red wine
- 4 cups presoaked, cooked green pigeon peas or three 15-ounce cans rinsed and drained
- 3 cups chicken broth
- ¼ cup chopped cilantro
- Salt & Pepper

Directions

1. Remove the bone and outer rind from the pork ribs. Cut into 1½-inch cubes. Pat dry and season with salt and pepper. Sear pork in coconut oil over medium heat in a large skillet until it is browned. Add onions, garlic, and ginger to the pan and cook until the onions become transparent. Add the wine, pigeon peas, and broth. Bring to a boil, reduce heat, and simmer for 30 minutes. Add cilantro, season with salt and pepper, and serve.

Nutritional Nugget

The antimicrobial properties of *coconut oil* can also help fight gas-producing bacteria and decrease gas and bloating. Therefore, cooking beans in coconut oil may also help reduce gas in certain individuals.

Like seeds, beans have a long shelf life and are an important part of any survivalist's food list. They are a wise choice—as long as there's water available for soaking the beans. Otherwise, that might be one emergency shelter to avoid! Okay, all joking aside, legumes are an extremely valuable source of nutrition and should be frequently incorporated into your meal plans.

Preparing Legumes

Most people seem to have a preconceived notion that soaking beans is hard work and takes lots of time. Quite the opposite is true. All that's required is a little planning the day before. Dried beans aren't difficult to prepare. For the most part, all you really need to do is rinse the beans a few times to remove any foreign matter that might have accumulated on them. Then soak them in warm water in a warm location for 12 to 24 hours.

Why Soak?

Minimizing gas is a good reason to soak legumes and, while it's true that soaking does help break down the indigestible complex sugars, it's certainly not the primary reason to soak. Another important benefit of soaking is that it reduces the phytic acid content and allows for shorter cooking times, which increases nutrient availability and results in a tender, tastier bean.

Dried beans are harvested from mature pods when the beans inside have dried and hardened. The pods are then opened so the dried beans can be removed. Before they arrive at the store for purchase, the beans go through a series of threshing and sifting processes. After sorting, the beans are stored in plastic bags or containers. Notice that none of these steps includes washing the beans because any moisture would cause the beans to start sprouting.

Thus, soaking beans is an easy way to clean beans, and you get the double benefit of allowing the beans to absorb the liquid slowly, which begins to pre-digest starches and complex sugars that cause intestinal discomfort. This process also helps the beans cook evenly and completely so they don't split open, lose their skins, or cook only the outer surface while the middle remains hard.

How to Soak Beans, Peas, and Lentils

You can use these instructions for any legume (beans, peas, lentils).

1. Rinse 1 cup of legumes and add 2 cups warm water.

2. Add 2 tablespoons of one of the following: lemon, vinegar, cultured buttermilk, yogurt, or kefir.

3. Cover and soak the legumes for a minimum of 12 hours, preferably 24 hours.

4. Drain, rinse, and cook the legumes, utilizing butter and broth for maximum nutrition and mineral absorption. These ingredients are particularly flavorful with legumes.

Cooking Tips

- After soaking, rinse beans thoroughly and put them into a large pot. Cook the beans with two times their volume of bone broth.
- Add carminative herbs and spices to reduce gas and increase flavor.
- Add acidic ingredients such as vinegar, tomatoes, or juice near the end of the cooking time, when the beans are just tender. While acid ingredients help to decrease phytic acid and increase digestibility while soaking, this water should be discarded. Acid ingredients when added too early while cooking, may slow the cooking process.
- Beans are ready when they can be easily smashed between two fingers or with a fork.
- One pound of dried beans generally yields about five or six cups cooked beans so keep in mind when soaking legumes, the volume of the legumes increases very substantially!

Nutritional Nugget

Easier to digest than most other beans, the *mung bean,* when cooked, takes on the consistency of porridge. This is eaten for its nutritional value and ease of digestion in both India and China. The Chinese eat mung beans as a food for detoxification. In India, it is traditionally used as a restorative food after illness. Add the digestive herbs and spices mentioned earlier to this dish and you have an All-Star meal!

Storing Beans

To store dried beans, simply seal them in a plastic bag or an airtight glass container and store them in a cool, dry location until you're ready to soak and cook them. I find Mason jars work well. Food experts say that dried beans, if stored properly, can be kept for about thirty years without losing their nutritional value!

To freeze cooked beans for later use, immerse them in cold water until cool, then drain well, dry, and freeze.

What About Canned Beans?

There is much discussion among nutritionists over how much the canning process reduces phytate levels in beans. Studies on the subject are scarce. Some people say that canning reduces phytate levels even more than that produced by soaking and rinsing raw beans. I have not seen studies to back up this claim, but it does make sense that they might have low levels of phytates.

Prior to canning, dry beans are generally soaked (using various soaking procedures) to moisten the seed, then blanched in hot water, put into cans or jars, and immediately covered with hot brine (salt water). Then the containers are hermetically sealed and thermally processed under extreme heat and steam pressure. The processing times and temperatures for canned beans generally exceeds the minimum requirements necessary for commercial sterility. Thus, the process includes an extended cooking time to achieve the desired bean tenderness, which breaks down those complex carbohydrates. It is difficult to say how much phytic acid may or may not remain in the bean when you open the can, but it does make sense that canning would reduce phytic acid content to a significant degree.

Problems with Canning

Today, tin-coated steel is most commonly used for commercial canning. Tin is chemically similar to germanium and lead. One problem in commercial canning arises when the chemicals in the can migrate into the food. This migration, or movement of substances from the can into the food, can cause health problems. Common unhealthy substances found in canned food are lead (which can cause lead poisoning) and the industrial chemical Bisphenol A. or BPA (a potential endocrine disruptor), found in the epoxy commonly used to coat the inner surface of cans. As an endocrine disruptor, BPA can mimic the body's own hormones and may cause negative health effects.[1]

BPA is used primarily in making plastics and can be found in the lining of food or drink products, water bottles, and other products that contain plastic. In 2009, The Endocrine Society released a statement citing the adverse effects of endocrine-disrupting chemicals, including BPA. This statement contributed to the elimination of BPA in baby bottles as well as in sports bottles.

In May 2010, a report from the National Workgroup for Safe Markets (NWSM) stated that canned foods, many of which are labeled as "healthy" or "organic," contain an average of 77 parts per billion (ppb) of BPA.

A study by researchers at the Harvard School of Public Health indicates that canned food absorbs BPA, which is then ingested by consumers. The experiment involved seventy-five participants, half of whom ate a lunch of canned vegetable soup for five days, followed by five days of fresh soup; the other half did the same experiment in reverse order. "The analysis revealed that when participants ate the canned soup, they experienced more than a 1,000 percent increase in their urinary concentrations of BPA, compared to when they dined on fresh soup."[2]

Consumer Reports magazine published an analysis of the BPA content in some canned foods and beverages. The study found that in specific cases, the content of a single can of food could exceed the current FDA Cumulative Exposure Daily Intake.[3]

Many manufacturers no longer use BPA, and the exposure we face today is much lower than in 2010. Some products, however, do still contain it in dangerous amounts so it is good to choose BPA free products.

Identifying BPA in Containers

How do you know whether a can or bottle contains BPA? Polycarbonate, which is made from BPA, is a hard, clear plastic that may be tinted in many colors and used as a lining in canned goods. This lining may indicate the presence of BPA in canned goods. When it comes to plastic bottles, look at the recycle number on the bottle. If it is a number "*7*" and has the letters "PC," then the bottle contains BPA. While all polycarbonate bottles are number "7," some companies do not add the "PC" label. Also, not all plastic with a number "7" label contains BPA. But if the container is clear, hard, and has the number "7," it could contain BPA, and you may wish to choose another type of container that states that it does not contain BPA.

It can be difficult to tell whether a canned good product has BPA in the lining of the can. I find it easier to call the company and ask whether it uses BPA than to play the guessing game. Eden Organics and Native Forest are two companies that do not use BPA to line their canned products. Trader Joe's is also conscientious about its products, but there is no guarantee regarding all products in the store.

Scientists continue to refine their studies of BPA to evaluate toxicity and exposure. Many companies, in response to consumer pressure, are removing the BPA from their products and Congress is considering legislation that would ban BPA from food packaging altogether. Until then, BPA will continue to be found in food packaging and plastic containers. This doesn't mean you should avoid canned beans, just choose them wisely and look for products that do not contain BPA.

Six-Bean Salad

Serves: 12

Total Time: 10 minutes plus time to chill

Ingredients

- One 14.5-ounce can French-style cut green beans
- One 14.5-ounce can kidney beans
- One 14.5-ounce can garbanzo beans
- One 14.5-ounce can lima beans
- One 14.5-ounce can wax beans
- 1 cup bean sprouts
- 1 medium white onion thinly sliced
- 1 chopped green pepper
- ¼ cup olive oil
- ¼ cup red wine vinegar
- ¼ cup white wine vinegar
- ¼ cup grade B maple syrup
- Salt and pepper to taste
- Butter lettuce leaves, 1-2 leaves per serving

Directions

1. Drain and rinse beans and sprouts. In a large bowl, combine beans, sprouts, onion, green pepper, oil, vinegars, syrup, and season with salt and pepper. Marinate in refrigerator overnight or for at least 2 hours. Place butter lettuce leaves on individual salad plates and spoon bean mixture onto lettuce. Serve.

I have many recipes that call for canned beans and use them from time to time when I forget to soak them the day before. When using canned beans, be sure to rinse them well to remove the "tin" taste canned beans can pick up.

While dried legumes are your best decision, it is better to eat canned beans than no beans at all. Dried beans are superior for various reasons.

- Dried beans taste better.
- Canned beans contain more sodium.
- Minerals such as lead migrate into the food from canned beans.
- Dried beans produce less waste.
- Dried beans are cheaper.

Roasted Garbanzo Bean Snacks

Yields: 3.75 cups
Total Time: 50 minutes

Ingredients

- Two 14.5-ounce cans garbanzo beans, rinsed and drained
- 1 tablespoon melted ghee or butter
- 1 tablespoon fresh squeezed lemon juice
- 1¼ teaspoon smoked paprika
- ½ teaspoon cumin
- 1/8 teaspoon cayenne pepper (more if you like spicy beans)
- 1 teaspoon unrefined sea salt

Directions

1. Preheat oven to 350°F. Place all the ingredients in a large bowl and toss until the garbanzos are evenly coated. Place the garbanzos on a rimmed baking sheet in a single layer and bake for 45 minutes; turn them occasionally so they do not burn. Cool slightly and serve. If you like a crunchier bean, cook them longer.

Adapting to Legumes

When you first begin to eat beans, you may experience some intestinal discomfort, even after you've soaked and fermented them. Have no fear; this is simply a result of the high fiber content in beans. If you experience discomfort, incorporate beans slowly to allow your body to adjust to them. This usually happens within two to four weeks.

Some people use Beano®, the well-known flatulence fighter, to help them reduce the symptoms of beans. This product is simply digestive enzymes that helps break down complex sugars found in legumes and cruciferous vegetables, such as broccoli, cauliflower, and cabbage. While I love the company's intention and approach, Beano tablets have a wheat filler, which contains gluten, and it isn't an All-Star digestive enzyme supplement.

For those who do not tolerate gluten and want a purer product, there are many digestive enzyme formulas free from fillers. Some brands can help digest complex sugars, as well as fats, vegetables, proteins, and dairy. These are available online and in some nutritional supplement stores. Digestive problems such as flatulence, bloating, and reflux often go away when the suggestions to improve digestion in Chapter 3 are followed.

Recommended Amounts of Legumes

Good Decisions recommends consuming as many legumes as you desire. Daily consumption of legumes contributes to improved digestion, mineral sufficiency, heart health, mental health, and increased energy levels. There is no limit as long as the legumes have been properly prepared.

Mineral balance is a vitally important nutritional foundation. While carbonated beverages and high sugar sports drinks can decrease bone density, legumes, nuts, and seeds can increase bone density and contribute to overall bone health and muscle performance. The absorption of nutrients in legumes can be enhanced by cooking legumes in a little quality fat. Adding other mineral rich foods to your diet such as sardines, anchovies, salmon, spinach, Swiss chard, yogurt, and cheese also contribute toward mineral balance. Combining these foods can create delicious nutrient dense meals that not only feed your taste buds, but your body's performance as well!

Nuts and Seeds

Grains and legumes are well-known when it comes to phytic acid. Nuts, although less known, are no different, and in some cases contain higher levels of phytic acid than do grains. The amounts of phytic acid and enzyme inhibitors are different with each grain, legume, nut, and seed. When it comes to health benefits from soaking nuts, there isn't enough information about soaking times to know whether phytic acid and enzyme inhibitors are reduced or eliminated completely as a result of soaking. Therefore, these recommendations are more of a guideline than exact science. Traditional methods for soaking nuts typically involve using salt water as a soaking medium to neutralize the enzyme inhibitors that protect the seed from sprouting in unfavorable conditions.

How to Soak Raw Nuts

1. Place 4 cups of raw nuts or seeds in a bowl.
2. Add 1 tablespoon unrefined sea salt.
3. Pour enough warm non-chlorinated water over them to cover them.
4. Cover with a towel and let them soak in a warm place for at least 7 to preferably 24 hours. (Please see the note on cashews below.)
5. Drain off the water and spread nuts out on a stainless steel cookie sheet and dry them in a warm oven on the lowest heat possible for 12 to 24 hours, or place in a dehydrator. The temperature should not go above 150°F; otherwise, the nuts will burn.
6. Ensure the nuts and seeds are totally dried before storing them or they will have a tendency to become moldy.
7. Store nuts and seeds in glass containers with tight-fitting lids, and keep them in the refrigerator.

Cashews

Cashews are the exception to long soaking because they've already been through one soaking during their initial processing. Do not soak them longer than seven hours. If they soak too long, they will be bitter. They may be crisped in the oven at a higher temperature because they have already had their enzymes destroyed by the high temperature used during commercial processing.

Spiced Mixed Nuts

Yields: 4 cups
Total Time: 25 minutes

Ingredients

- 1 pound mixed *raw* unsalted nuts soaked and dried (or pre-packaged sprouted nuts)
- ½ teaspoon ground coriander
- ½ teaspoon ground cumin
- 2 tablespoons melted butter
- ¼ teaspoon cayenne pepper
- 1 teaspoon salt

Directions

1. Position a rack in the center of the oven and heat the oven to 350°F. Combine all ingredients in a large bowl and stir well to coat nuts. Scatter the nuts on a rimmed baking sheet and bake, shaking the sheet a couple of times during baking, until the nuts are nicely toasted, 15-20 minutes.

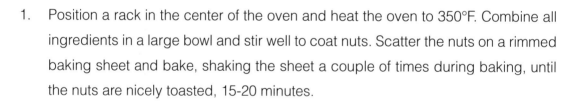

Purchasing Raw and Sprouted Nuts

Purchasing raw or sprouted nuts is the best possible choice for your nutrition. Almonds and some other nuts now go through a process called *pasteurization*. This involves steaming the nuts or spraying them with propylene oxide (PPO) to get rid of any stray bacteria. This chemical was used as racing fuel until it was banned for safety reasons. Sometimes it is disconcerting to know what your food goes through before it reaches your table! Doing a little research is always a good idea regardless of what you find. It is better to be informed than sick. One way to ensure that your nut or seed product hasn't been overly treated with chemicals is to buy raw and organic nuts. Purchasing raw and organic will also ensure that your food has not been genetically modified and that pesticide use has been kept to a relative minimum.

Recommendations for Nuts and Seeds

Good Decisions recommends consuming nuts and seeds daily. How many you consume depends on your size, activity level, protein and fat needs, and other factors. If weight loss is your desired goal and you are consuming a lot of vegetables, legumes, and fruits, then you can eat nuts in small amounts throughout the day to curb your appetite and prevent binging. The protein and fat in nuts can be very satiating, so an ounce here and there will be very satisfying and keep you away from the donut that may be taunting you from the breakroom.

Nuts often get a bad rap because they tend to be high in fat, which means more calories. This is not necessarily a bad thing as you will learn in the chapter on fats. So don't let this stop you from enjoying all of the health benefits of nuts.

The primary concept of the *Good Decisions…Most of the Time* way of life is that a person learns to be in tune with his or her body and practices eating only until he or she is full. It is not about limiting fat, but excluding "poor fats" and incorporating healthy essential fats.

Eating a little protein, such as nuts and seeds every two hours in the beginning, will help regulate blood sugar levels, and can be very helpful for those trying to get off the blood sugar roller coaster ride.

Nutrients Found in Popular Nuts and Seeds

Almonds

Aside from fantastic fat and precious protein, one ounce of almonds provides roughly 36 percent of your Daily Value (DV) of Vitamin E. Vitamin E is an antioxidant that protects cell membranes from the destructive effects of free radicals. This explains why it is used to achieve younger looking skin. One ounce of almonds also provides 20 percent of your DV of magnesium. Magnesium is a mineral that many naturopaths look at when their clients' muscles are "tight" or constipation may be an issue. This is because magnesium relaxes muscles and nerves, making it essential for muscle function and heart health.

Almonds are also a good source of manganese, an antioxidant enzyme nutrient that plays an integral role in eliminating environmental toxins and free radicals. It also helps the body form connective tissue, bones, and sex hormones. Manganese is necessary for normal brain and nerve function, and also plays a role in fat and carbohydrate metabolism, calcium absorption, and blood sugar regulation. Whew! That's a lot of nutrients in one nut!

Brazil Nuts

This is my favorite nut. When I can find an All-Star food that provides a huge amount of nutrients in a very small portion, I get very excited! Therefore, the Brazil nut really does it for me, with one nut providing 137 percent of your daily value of selenium. Selenium helps regulate thyroid function[4] and incorporating selenium-rich foods with iodine-rich foods may be very beneficial to thyroid health. Selenium is also important for vitamin C metabolism, enhancing immune function, and slowing the aging process. That's right, one Brazil nut a day could help to slow the aging process. Sounds much better than a facial peel or Botox®. In fact, scientists have shown that a daily Brazil nut is a better source of selenium than taking a supplement.[5] One Brazil nut a day in exchange for slowing the aging process and improved thyroid health? That doesn't seem like a bad deal!

Cashews

A one-ounce serving of cashews also delivers a hearty dose of magnesium and manganese, along with iron, phosphorus, and potassium. These minerals are vital for bone, blood, and muscle health. Nuts are amazing when it comes to minerals and quality protein. Vegetarians wisely include nuts and seeds in their diet daily for just this reason.

Hazelnuts or Filberts

Also rich in Vitamin E, one ounce of these tasty treats provides a whopping 86 percent of your DV of manganese, 11 percent magnesium, 8 percent phosphorus, and 7 percent of your daily iron needs, as well as small amounts of B vitamins. Because the majority of the calories from nuts comes from fat, nuts are perfect carriers for fat soluble vitamins A, E, and K.

Macadamia Nuts

Again, manganese is the highlight of the macadamia nut, with thiamine coming in second. Thiamine is important for energy production and plays an essential role in the body's ability to convert food into energy. When not consumed in sufficient amounts, thiamin and other B vitamins can leave you feeling very tired. Symptoms of thiamine deficiency include muscles that become very easily fatigued, loss of muscle tone, and heaviness in arms or legs.

Pecans

Pecans are also a good source of thiamine, but their real claim to fame is manganese. Clearly, nuts are a phenomenal source of manganese, that antioxidant enzyme that plays a role in eliminating environmental toxins and free radicals. Copper, zinc, iron, magnesium, and potassium are also often found in nuts.

Therefore, when you're looking for a food source rich in minerals, go nuts! Rich in iron, nuts can also be a valuable source of iron for those needing this nutrient, but who want to avoid constipating supplementation.

Pistachios

These nifty nuggets are a phenomenal source of B6. One ounce will provide you with roughly 24 percent of your DV of this vitamin. Without B6, your body cannot make amino acids, thus all 20 amino acids would be considered essential. B6 also helps break down *homocysteine* (the amino acid associated with cardiovascular disease and hardening of the arteries) in the body. High homocysteine levels are associated with low B6 and B12 levels. So increasing foods rich in B6 lowers your risk of heart disease, stroke, Alzheimer's disease, and osteoporosis. Pistachios are also good sources of thiamine, copper, manganese, and phosphorus with small amounts of magnesium, potassium, iron, zinc, and selenium.

Walnuts

This is another favorite nut because one ounce contains 2542 mg Omega-3 fatty acids. To put this in perspective, two capsules of fish oil in supplement form typically contain anywhere from 500 to 1000 milligrams, making walnuts an All-Star food for vegetarians and carnivores alike. Walnuts are also a good source of magnesium, phosphorus, and iron, with small amounts of selenium and B vitamins. Don't you just love knowing you can get a huge amount of nutrients in such a small portion? Not to mention the protein and fat within nuts are satiating and can help with blood sugar regulation.

Sunflower Seeds

Now I'm really getting excited! While all of the nuts above are known for being a great source of one or more nutrients, sunflower seeds are a great source of many nutrients. This happy kernel provides a very high quality protein that is ideal for vegetarians. Almost a complete source of essential amino acids, one ounce of sunflower seeds will provide you with roughly:

- 47% of your daily value of Vitamin E
- 28% thiamine
- 27% manganese
- 25% copper
- 23% magnesium
- 21% selenium
- 19% vitamin B6
- 18% phosphorus
- 16% folate

Wow! You can now see why I chose this chapter to introduce the third nutritional foundation: *Mineral Balance*. Remember, you can't absorb minerals if you don't eat them! I sprinkle sunflower seeds on my salads, and you can add them to anything if you want a boost of energy and nutrients.

Pumpkin Seeds

Between pumpkin seeds and sunflower seeds, vegetarians can have their protein/ essential amino acid bases pretty well covered. When combined, these seeds lack only one essential amino acid–lysine. Lysine can be found in brewer's yeast, seaweed, and spirulina. Pumpkin seeds' main claim to fame is the amount of iron they contain (1 ounce provides 23 percent of your DV of iron). They are also rich in manganese, phosphorus, magnesium, and zinc. (Zinc is a trace mineral that helps with digestion.)

Peanuts

While peanuts are a great source of protein, B vitamins and minerals, the health benefits may not outweigh the concerns. Peanuts, unfortunately, have a tendency to mold, which can contribute to toxicity caused by a nasty mold called aflotoxin, which is more toxic than DDT. They also contain oxalates, substances that can crystalize and cause kidney or gallbladder problems. While peanuts are now being handled more carefully to prevent aflotoxin growth, and oxalate concerns don't seem to be high, the inflammatory nature of peanuts is something to keep in mind.

I just love nuts and seeds. They are so nutrient-dense in such little packages that you really don't have to eat that many to get huge benefits.

Today, more and more companies cater to health-conscious individuals, and sprouted nuts and seeds are available at some grocery stores. The law of supply and demand may have been a casual concept in school, but in real life it dictates what you will find on the shelves at your local grocery store. And, not unlike Kevin Costner's inner voice in the movie *Field of Dreams,* "If you build it, they will come" when it comes to healthy soaked and sprouted nut, grain, and legume products, if you demand them, they will be supplied.

If you cannot find these products near you, you may consider having a conversation with your local grocers, requesting they provide more organic sprouted nuts, seeds, and legumes. Sprouted nuts can also be found online and are only an Internet search away.

Legumes, nuts, and seeds are heart-friendly; they regulate blood sugar levels, increase mental clarity, and provide nutrients that can help fight insomnia, depression, and anxiety. They are a phenomenal source of fiber, contribute to healthy digestion, and are extremely rich in minerals, which means more energy for you!

Legumes, nuts, and seeds are very *Good Decisions*.

CHAPTER SIX

The Psychology of Food

The Voice in Your Head

Our minds have been conditioned into ways of thinking, thought patterns we have developed based upon what we learned or experienced as children and young adults. Often we don't even know what the mind is saying; it just drives us, and our emotions, straight to the fridge, where the compulsion to serve up four scoops of ice cream instead of one happens almost unconsciously. The key word to pick up on here is **unconsciously**.

We have talked about how weight loss isn't about managing food, but emotions. Now let's talk about where those emotions come from; let's talk about that voice in our heads that is constantly talking, most often about nothing, incessantly. This is the voice that labels things as "bad" for us, yet drives us to eat those things anyway!

Sometimes this voice boosts us to make us feel better, and sometimes it may put us down and tell us how unworthy we are. The voice in your head is what drives your sense of self-esteem or self-importance. So what does this voice have to do with food? This voice is constantly in a state of not enough; it always seeks something else or something more to fill itself, such as things, experiences, emotional maneuvers, etc. It is never satisfied. Food is one of those things and experiences this voice uses to fulfill itself.

Practicing Good Decisions

Eating Consciously

To experience how this inner voice relates to food and weight loss, try this experiment: Sit in front of a large serving of French fries (or whatever your favorite indulgence might be). You are going to make an exercise or meditation out of eating them, so give yourself permission to eat them.

To prepare yourself, sit in front of the French fries and look at them with an alert presence, as if you have never seen them before. Pretend you are a curious child experiencing them for the very first time. Take several long deep breaths and relax as you breathe out. Can you smell the French fries? As you place one in your mouth, feel your taste buds perk up. What is the texture like? Can you feel your mouth water? When you swallow it, can you feel it move from your throat to your stomach? Look at the next French fry; what does it look like? When you place the next one in your mouth, savor it and pay attention to the flavor of it. Continue to eat the French fries slowly; enjoy them fully, and maintain an awareness of your body and how it feels while you eat them.

You may find that at a certain point, the French fries no longer taste as good as when you first started. Pay attention to your stomach and your body. Is it sending you a signal that it is full or done with the experience? This is the satiation signal! Continue to stay in a state of alert presence. See whether you can become aware of the moment when your body tells you it has enjoyed the French fries fully, but has now had enough.

When you receive this message from your body, you may find that while your body may not want more, the voice in your head wants to eat them all! You may become aware of the little angel and devil on each shoulder arguing over whether or not to continue eating. Now, set aside the French fries and sit back and maintain your awareness of what is going on in your head. Listen to the voice in your head that always seeks something more to fill itself. Is it making you uncomfortable? Is the drive to continue eating strong? Stay present and allow the feelings to wash over you; observe them. If the waitress wants to remove the French fries, tell her to leave them. Sit with the discomfort as long as you can, and really pay attention to what is going on inside you.

You may find that a great struggle will occur within you. If this happens, allow it to happen and wait for the discomfort to pass. We do not need to struggle. In fact, the more we resist, the worse the discomfort can be. When we stop resisting or labeling things as bad, we can experience them more fully. The French fries are not bad; it is the thought in your head that deems them bad.

Using truth and knowledge, we know that if we over-consume French fries, weight gain and other health issues may arise. This is the intellectual piece of the puzzle. The emotional piece of the puzzle is driven by the voice in your head that tells you to continue eating, long after your body tells you it is content.

When you practice being alert to your body's satiation signal and what it is experiencing, you become in tune with your body and understand how to respond to its desires. Practice tuning in to how your taste buds come alive when you first begin to eat. Then, as your body gets enough, feel how the food doesn't taste good anymore. When you pay attention to how food tastes, the desire to continue eating will diminish.

Pretending you are experiencing the food for the first time can also be helpful. If your mind tries to convince you to continue eating, the voice has returned and you are no longer present. Gently return your attention to your body and be as present with this experience as much as possible. Do not struggle. Release any resistance within you, and allow the experience and any uncomfortable emotions to wash over you. Managing emotions involves just waiting for them to pass. And they *always* pass.

Know that when you bring your alert attention to the discomfort, it will diminish significantly. When you have mastered paying attention and begin to eat consciously versus unconsciously, food becomes something you enjoy, not something you have no control over, and the voice in your head begins to fade.

Chapter Seven

Healthy Proteins for All Lifestyles

When you think of protein, you might think of the chicken you enjoyed for dinner last night, the hamburger you had for lunch, or the eggs you ate for breakfast. And you're right; these items contain protein, but protein can also be found in legumes, nuts, and seeds, and even fruits and vegetables.

In this chapter, we will talk about the protein basics and the many roles protein plays in the body, from brain function and mental clarity, to younger-looking skin, and strong muscles. You will learn how protein is connected to sexual function and how to avoid the afternoon slump or fatigue. Best of all, you will learn how to cook the perfect protein. We will discuss organics and provide information about seafood that may help you determine which seafood products are right for you and your family. We will end with an exercise that will help you to become more in tune with your body's satiation signal in the psychology of food.

What Is Protein?

Proteins, found in both animal and plant foods, are composed of building blocks called *amino acids*. When you eat food that contains protein, the digestive juices and enzymes in your digestive system break down the protein into these basic building blocks. Your body then uses these amino acids ("building blocks") to build muscles, produce blood, create hormones, and generate other substances your body needs to function.

Why Is Protein Important?

Next to water (which accounts for more than 60 percent of our body weight), protein accounts for roughly 17 percent of our body weight. Organs, hair, skin, nails, and ligaments are also composed of protein. Without protein, we'd be little more than water balloons, with no ability to move! Proteins play a crucial role in many bodily functions; let's look at just a few.

Muscles and Organs

Every muscle in your body contains protein. These proteins contract and relax as you move, blink, or chew. Postural muscles are constantly at work, even as you sit at your desk. Other proteins build heart muscles that contract with each beat of your heart, or lung muscles that expand with each breath you take. As you are reading now, can you feel your heart beat or your lungs expand with each breath you take? Protein is responsible for these actions.

Bones

Your bones are composed of a *latticed protein*, which makes up about 35 percent of the bone and gives it its flexibility. This lattice (similar to a fishnet) traps the mineral known as calcium phosphate, which is about 65 percent of the bone mass, and gives the bone strength. In addition to calcium phosphates, your bones store other minerals needed by the body, including magnesium, sodium, potassium, and more. The latticed protein in your bones—not calcium—prevents fractures and gives your bones flexibility.

Blood

Your body uses protein to create different protein molecules that have specific jobs. Hemoglobin, the protein in blood that transports oxygen, is one of them. Without hemoglobin, oxygen would not be delivered to important tissues.

Hormones and Sexual Function

Hormonal proteins help coordinate certain bodily activities. For instance, insulin is a protein that regulates how blood sugar is used. Sex hormones such as estrogen, progesterone, and testosterone are composed of proteins. Without protein, your sex drive would significantly diminish. Now, this doesn't mean you should start pushing large amounts of protein onto your partner in hopes of increasing sex drive! However, ensuring adequate amounts of quality protein in your diet is important for sexual function.

Growth and Development

Growth hormone (GH) is a protein hormone responsible for stimulating growth, cell reproduction, and regeneration, which makes protein especially important for children.

Unfortunately, most school lunch programs offer a dismal assortment of quality proteins. While pizza and hamburgers are quite tasty, they offer little support for the growing bodies and brains of our children.

Immune System

You also need proteins to keep your immune system healthy. *Antibodies* are special proteins that help your body fight off illness and infection. We would lose the battle against the common cold without our protein friends, the antibodies. When I think of consuming highly processed proteins, such as chicken nuggets or fast food hamburgers, I visualize the body trying to make antibodies from what's left of the protein after processing. The final antibody looks more like a crippled Frankenstein monster than a warrior ready to go to battle.

Enzymes

Enzymes are proteins that speed up chemical reactions. For instance, *lactase* is an enzyme that helps breaks down the sugar lactose found in milk. The enzyme *pepsin* works in the stomach to break down the protein in your food. And as we learned earlier, phytase helps break down phytic acid. Without enzymes, we would not be able to digest and utilize all we eat.

Bodily Fluids

Proteins help control the amount of fluid in the body, which is why a lack of protein can cause swelling of the legs, feet, and ankles.

Memory

In order to communicate, your brain and its spiderweb-like brain cells need protein. Nerve cells communicate with each other using electrical impulses and chemical messengers called *neurotransmitters*, which are made of amino acids. Special neural connections are necessary for your brain to function at its best. To strengthen these connections, your brain cells require proteins. That's why there's a connection between memory and protein. You can improve your memory and increase mental clarity very easily by simply removing sugar from your diet and incorporating high-quality proteins.

The Afternoon Slump

Neurotransmitters, created by the protein you consume in food, can excite or calm your brain. They play a role in whether you are focused and motivated or calm and sedate. To experience their role firsthand, pay attention to what you had for lunch and how you feel afterwards. Have you noticed that a high-carbohydrate lunch can make you feel sleepy and sluggish? Or that eating quality protein in the middle of the day can keep you more alert through the afternoon?

Carbohydrates can make you feel tired because they increase your brain's level of the amino acid *tryptophan*, which causes your brain to make the calming neurotransmitter *serotonin*. Serotonin is important for normal sleep patterns, which may not be what you need to make it through a busy day at work.

Eating protein, however, raises the levels of the amino acid *tyrosine*, which prompts your brain to manufacture the neurotransmitters *norepinephrine* and *dopamine*, which keep you energized by promoting alertness and activity. Protein is the perfect food to avoid the afternoon slump! What you eat affects not only your energy, but your mood and energy levels throughout the day. So if you want to take a nap after lunch, carbohydrates would be a good choice. But if you want to remain alert and need to make important decisions, adding a small amount of quality protein to your lunch will serve you better.

How to Cook the Perfect Protein

Now that you know a few healthy ways proteins nourish the body, the next thing to know is how to prepare them. If you don't like to cook, this section is for you. Many clients who don't like to cook ask me for some simple ways to prepare healthy animal proteins. Teaching them this method for cooking animal proteins gives them the confidence they need to overcome their fears and master the art of cooking proteins. This method is great for individual portion sizes and works with any animal protein, from a fish fillet and boneless chicken breast to steak and a pork chop. It is important to use a quality fat such as ghee that maintains its stability at high temperatures. Beef and lamb tallow or red palm oil may also be used.

How to Cook Animal Proteins Perfectly:

1. Preheat oven to 425°F.
2. Clean and pat dry the animal protein of your choice with paper towels.
3. Season protein with salt and pepper.
4. Heat one teaspoon ghee in an oven safe skillet over medium high heat.
5. Use a paper towel to soak up any excess ghee so you are using just enough to coat the pan.

6. Place protein presentation side down (skin side up if it is fish) into the pan; it will sizzle.

7. Cook for four minutes or until nicely browned.

8. Flip the protein over and place pan in preheated oven for 10 minutes per inch of thickness. (If the protein is ½-inch thick, cook it for 5 minutes; if it is 1½-inches, cook it for 15 minutes.)

9. Remove from oven, cover loosely with foil, and allow protein to rest for 5 minutes. Do not cover protein too tightly; otherwise, it will sweat and you will lose precious juices.

The high heat will seal in all the juices and make it moist and tender. It may not look done when you remove it from the oven, but it will continue to cook while you let it rest for a perfect medium rare. Cast iron, stainless steel, Scanpan at www.chefscatalog.com, or Caphalon pans are pans you can sauté with one moment and place in a hot oven the next.

How long to rest?

This all depends on size. A steak or individual portion should rest between 5 and 10 minutes, while a roast, cooked for much longer, should rest for anywhere from 20 to 30 minutes depending on size.

Nutritional Nugget

When meat is cooked, the proteins heat up and begin to denature, or change shape, which results in a tightening up or shrinking of the meat. This drives all the juices toward the center of the meat. Removing the meat from heat and allowing it to "rest" allows the protein fibers to relax and the juices can be redistributed and be reabsorbed. When meat is not rested, the juices cannot be reabsorbed and juice will be lost when you slice into it—all over your plate instead of in your mouth!

Peppercorn Beef with Balsamic Reduction Sauce

Serves: 4
Total Time: 35 minutes

Ingredients

- Four 4-ounce trimmed beef tenderloin or rib eye steaks about 1½ inch thick
- 1 teaspoon unrefined sea salt
- 3 tablespoons crushed peppercorns
- 1 teaspoon ghee
- ¾ cup balsamic vinegar
- 1 tablespoon honey
- 2 tablespoons butter
- 2 tablespoons fresh sliced green onions to garnish

Directions

1. Preheat oven to 425°F. Wash and pat dry steaks with paper towels. Season steaks with salt and press the peppercorns all over them. In a large ovenproof skillet, heat ghee to medium high heat. Add the steaks and sear until browned. Flip steaks and place in preheated oven for 15 minutes. Remove from oven and let rest for 5-10 minutes.

2. Meanwhile, in small saucepan, bring vinegar and honey to a boil. Reduce heat and simmer until reduced to 1/3 cup. Remove sauce from heat and incorporate butter 1 tablespoon at a time. Transfer steaks to plates and drizzle with balsamic reduction sauce. Garnish with green onions, and serve.

The Quality of Your Protein Matters

I have used the term "quality protein" a couple of times. I do this to distinguish between healthy protein decisions and unhealthy protein decisions. The *quality* of your protein is just as important as *how much* protein you consume. For instance, has the animal protein been pumped full of genetically-modified corn, animal byproducts, growth hormones, and antibiotics? Or was it in a field, leisurely eating bugs and grass? Is it a fresh, crisp, soaked bean salad, or an overly-processed tofu hot dog laden with additives and preservatives?

Eating a little bit of protein every two to three hours is a great way to balance blood sugar levels and get you off the sugar roller coaster ride. However, if it is the wrong kind of protein, you may be setting yourself up for a fall and doing your body more harm than good.

The types of proteins we consume today are different from the proteins people consumed 200 years ago. Animals we once had to hunt or herd now live in small, enclosed spaces and receive food that bears little resemblance to their natural diets. Growth hormones, antibiotics, and a host of other substances are fed to these animals, and when we eat them, these substances do get into our bodies.

More than 60 percent of the typical American diet consists of processed foods. This

Nutritional Nugget

Get to know your local butcher. He/she will be able to tell you where your proteins come from and how they have been handled. Often, if you develop a relationship with your butcher, you may be able to ask that special cuts be saved for you or specialty items ordered if you ask. It is always best to visit your local butcher and get your beef ground at the time you need it. It will reward you in health and will taste much, much better.

includes meat products made by grinding meat scraps and connective tissues together with ammonia, then "gluing" the substance together with transglutaminase, aka "meat glue." Furthermore, many meat and meat products are irradiated to control bacteria and parasites. This causes lipid (fat) oxidation and can grossly affect the flavor of the resulting product, let alone its nutritional value. Nitrates are used as preservatives, and artificial colorings are used to create a "fresher" looking product. Most people don't know what happens to their proteins during the production process, and as for those who do know—well, they wish they didn't.

Fast foods are the biggest culprits in the obesity epidemic and are good examples of what not to eat. The lunch menu in most schools is a long list of foods supplied by fast food chains: from pizza and burgers to hot dogs and chicken nuggets, all of which contain these processed animal proteins. Teaching children to avoid these foods and sending them to school with a healthy lunch made at home will keep your children healthy and often improve their concentration and grades.

Pink slime is another product made by the food industry. Pink slime, officially called "lean finely textured beef," is made of the "bits and pieces" left over after the cow is butchered. In the old days, these were used to make mineral-rich bone broths, which are very healthy. Today, they are simmered, centrifuged, and treated with ammonia to form this cheap meat filler found in 70 percent of the ground beef sold at most supermarkets and found in up to 25 percent of each American hamburger patty. Ammonia is a toxin that is very dangerous for the environment and an inflammatory irritant to humans. Other preservatives may also be used.

Yes, protein is an essential part of a balanced diet, but the quality of protein is just as important. So let's learn what to look for on food labels.

Choosing Safe Animal Proteins

Local Food from Local Farms

An animal protein may bear the label "local." This label says nothing about how the animal was treated, simply that it was produced locally. But that doesn't mean it is bad. In fact, finding a local farm that cares well for the animals you eat is an excellent decision. When you see this label, ask some questions: Where is the farm? How do the farmers treat their animals? What do they feed their animals, and how much room do the animals have to move about? Taking the time to do this will support local farmers, the animal's welfare, and your community's self-sustainability. It also gives you the ability to visit the farm and see for yourself how your food comes to your table. Kids love to do this. For parents, it is a fun way to expose your children to the idea of knowing where food comes from and how it is handled. So if you consume animal protein, finding a local farm to provide your family with beef, chicken, milk, eggs, pork, and even your Thanksgiving turkey is the best decision of all.

Often, if a local farm is not certified as "organic," it may still utilize organic methods but choose not to go through the rigorous organic certification process. If you are uncertain, ask how the animals are raised. Those who cannot afford organic foods find that a quarter-side of well cared for local beef is affordable and will feed the family for a year. Whole chickens can often be purchased for less than grocery store prices when you cut out the middleman and go straight to the farm. Farmers' markets are also wonderful places to find local free-range eggs, whole chickens, pork, and even seafood, depending on where you live.

Organic

The "organic" label is regulated and somewhat reliable, but as the organic industry grows, it needs to be watched since it has the potential to be—and has been—exploited.

According to the U.S Department of Agriculture Organic Certification, USDA Organic Livestock plans[1] and practices include:

- Mandatory outdoor access when seasonally appropriate. Producers are required to allow the stock to graze throughout the entire grazing season for the geographical region.
- No use of antibiotics, growth hormones, slaughter byproducts, or feed products utilizing plastic pellets for roughage or formulas utilizing urea or manure. Food containing genetically-modified organisms (GMO) is prohibited. If antibiotics are used, the animal must be removed from the organic program.
- Only 100 percent organic feed and approved organic feed supplements are allowed.

- Sound animal husbandry and preventative health care must be practiced. Organic management is required from the last third of the gestation period or the second day after hatching.
- Rotating animals between organic and non-organic management is not allowed.
- The producer must establish and maintain preventive livestock health care practices, including conditions that allow for freedom of movement and stress reduction. When preventive practices, veterinary vaccines, and other biological substances are inadequate to prevent sickness, a producer may administer synthetic medications. All appropriate medications must be used to restore an animal to health when methods acceptable to organic production fail. Livestock treated with a prohibited substance must be clearly identified and shall not be sold, labeled, or represented as organically produced. Farmers may not withhold medical treatment from a sick animal in an effort to preserve its organic status.

Organic farmers must meet strict standards to get this label, and many organic farmers take the organic label seriously. Many consumers are equally passionate about supporting organic methods, but organic livestock practices still have issues. For instance, if an animal is sick, it may need antibiotics, which would remove the animal from the organic program. Therefore, the animal may not receive the medication it needs. Animal living quarters, while typically less crowded, may still be tight.

When it comes to produce, herbicides and pesticides used on fruits and vegetables are still used but to a lesser degree, and many companies may label food organic that is not organic. For instance, Whole Foods grocery stores sells its own brand, 365 Organic® frozen vegetables. A closer look at the label shows the product came from China, where organic regulation is not only questionable, but also highly unlikely. This doesn't mean you should avoid the organic label; just carefully monitor what you purchase and read labels carefully. Organic still means that animals receive better treatment than conventional animals and less potent herbicides and pesticides are used on vegetables and fruits. You can also rest assured that the product has not been genetically modified, or fed genetically-modified food, antibiotics, or growth hormones.

Seared Halibut on Navy Beans with Lemon and Tarragon

Serves: 4

Total Time: 35 minutes

Ingredients

- 1 tablespoon extra-virgin olive oil
- ½ cup finely chopped red onion
- 1 cup organic chicken broth
- 1 tablespoon apple cider vinegar
- 2 tablespoons lemon juice
- Two 14.5-ounce cans navy beans, drained and rinsed
- 1 teaspoon finely grated lemon zest
- 2 tablespoons chopped flat-leaf parsley
- 1 tablespoon chopped tarragon
- Salt and freshly ground pepper to taste
- Four 4-ounce halibut fillets, each 1½ inch thick
- 1 teaspoon ghee

Directions

1. Preheat oven to 425°F. Rinse the beans and drain. Heat olive oil over medium heat in a large saucepan and add onion. Cook until onion starts to brown. Stir in the broth, vinegar, and lemon juice and simmer for 5 minutes. Add beans, lemon zest, parsley, tarragon, salt, and pepper. Stir to coat beans and simmer 5 minutes.

2. Pat the fish dry and season lightly with salt and pepper. In a large oven-safe sauté pan, heat the ghee over medium-high heat, place the halibut presentation side down (skin side up) into the pan, and sear until nicely browned. Flip the halibut and place into preheated oven for 10-15 minutes. If it is a thick fillet, cook for 15 minutes; if it is closer to 1-inch thick, only cook it for 10 minutes. Remove fish from the oven and let rest loosely covered for 5 minutes. Place ½ cup of the bean mixture in the center of a plate and place the halibut fillet on top. Garnish with tarragon and serve.

Grass-Fed

"Grass-Fed" was once a voluntary label to describe what the animal ate, not its living conditions. In 2007, the U.S. Department of Agriculture changed the requirements for this designation, stating that animals must graze in a live pasture during the growing season in order to use the "Grass-Fed" label.[2] This was a victory for farmers and ranchers who don't utilize feedlots to fatten up animals for the last three or more months of their lives. Grass is the native diet of cows; corn is used only because it fattens animals quickly.

Nutritional Nugget

Zinc is a nutrient linked to digestive health, reproductive health, and sexual competence. One 3-ounce serving of beef tenderloin provides 28 percent of your daily need of zinc!

According to the grass-fed standard, "grass and/or forage shall be the feed source consumed for the lifetime of the animal, with the exception of milk consumed prior to weaning."[3] However, the standard doesn't restrict the use of genetically-modified (GM) forage such as alfalfa, Bahia grass, or other grasses. The animals may be given antibiotics or synthetic hormones to promote growth and to prevent or treat disease. Many farmers take pride in their grass-fed status, and they only utilize items such as antibiotics if necessary for the animal's health. Other labels may accompany the grass-fed label to reassure the consumer that the animal was grass-fed and that hormones or GMOs were not utilized. The grass-fed claim is only reliable if the product has a "USDA Process Verified" label; otherwise, the verification is only voluntary. Grass-fed animal products are a better choice than conventional products. Only a small percentage (estimated at 5 percent) of our beef comes from grass-fed cows. Grass-fed is great for those who insist on a healthier, more humane process and product.

Grass-Fed Organic

Animal products may be labeled as "Grass-Fed Organic." This term means that the animals are solely fed a diet of organic grass or forage, and that no antibiotics, growth hormones, slaughter byproducts, or GMOs are utilized. Further, the animals have mandatory outdoor access during the grazing season. "Grass-fed organic" is a very *Good Decision*.

Certified Humane Raised and Handled®

This label indicates the producer meets the rigorous standards of care established by the Humane Farm Animal Care Program, a national "nonprofit organization created to improve the lives of farm animals by setting rigorous standards, conducting annual inspections, and certifying their humane treatment."[4] A committee of animal scientists and veterinarians with expertise in farm animal issues developed these standards, which require that animals have ample space, shelter, and gentle handling to limit stress. The standards additionally state:

- The use of growth hormones and antibiotics is prohibited.
- Animals must be free to move and not confined. Cages, crates, and tie stalls are prohibited. This means that chickens are able to flap their wings and dust bathe, and pigs have the space to move around and root.
- Livestock must have access to sufficient, clean, and nutritious feed and water.
- Animals must have sufficient protection from weather elements and an environment that promotes their wellbeing.
- Managers and caretakers must be thoroughly trained, skilled, and competent in animal welfare.
- Farmers and ranchers must comply with food safety and environmental regulations.[5]

The program provides independent verification that animals were raised and handled humanely. Qualifying products bear the organization's official logo. The goal of this program is to improve the lives of farm animals by driving consumer demand for kinder and more responsible farm animal practices.[6] Humane standards might include no cages, natural feed, less painful methods of slaughter, or prohibition of practices such as tail docking or debeaking. Animal care standards require that animals be allowed to engage in their natural behaviors, have sufficient space, shelter, gentle handling to limit stress, and have ample fresh water and a healthy diet. Vegetarians who have chosen not to eat animal proteins because of the way they are treated may find these farm products worthy of support. Animal products that bear this label are very *Good Decisions*.

American Humane Certified

The American Humane Society has been a leader in animal welfare programs, and it has a program called the American Humane Certified® program. (Formerly known as the Free Farmed program.) "American Humane Certified works closely with its independent Scientific Advisory Committee, industry professionals, and producers to ensure that industry advancements and best practices are part of American Humane certification standards. Based on the American Humane Society's 132-year legacy of being the gold standard for humane behavior, consumers trust the American Humane Certified label."[7]

I like these standards-setting organizations, as they advocate for and represent a healthier animal, which in turn means healthier products for me as a consumer. American Humane Certified products are considered very *Good Decisions*.

Animal Welfare Approved

The Animal Welfare Institute (AWI) is a non-profit charitable organization founded in 2006 in response to growing consumer interest in how farm animals are raised and a desire to know where food is coming from and how it is produced. Animal Welfare Approved (AWA) is a separate AWI division dedicated solely to certifying and promoting family farms that raise their animals with the highest welfare standards.

AWA standards are said to be the most rigorous and progressive animal care requirements in the nation, and they require animals be raised outdoors on pasture or range. The organization is consistently ranked as the most stringent of all third-party certifiers by the World Society for the Protection of Animals.[8] Scientists, veterinarians, researchers, and farmers work collaboratively to develop AWA standards, incorporating best practices and recent research. Annual audits by experts in the field cover birth to slaughter. I am impressed by the rigorous standards farmers adhere to in order to use this label. AWA encourages the use of homeopathic and herbal remedies and is considered a very *Good Decision*.

Biodynamic® Farming

In the United States, Demeter Association, Inc. represents Demeter International, a not-for-profit organization that sets the high standards for farmers wishing to practice biodynamic practices and principles, with "the mission to enable people to farm successfully, in accordance with Biodynamic® practices and principles. Demeter's vision is to heal the planet through agriculture."[9]

> "Disease and insect control are addressed through botanical species diversity, predator habitat, balanced crop nutrition, and attention to light penetration and airflow. Weed control emphasizes prevention, including timing of planting, mulching, and identifying and avoiding the spread of invasive weed species."[10]

> "De-horning, de-beaking, and wing clipping of poultry are prohibited, as is tail cutting of piglets and docking of lambs. Homeopathic remedies in place of vaccines are strongly recommended, and the use of antibiotics is prohibited. If an animal is being raised for the sale of meat, eggs or milk, a minimum of one-half of its feed must come from the farm, and the remainder must be Demeter certified (minimum of 80% of the total ration) or cNOP certified organic (no more than 20% of the ration)."[11]

Many farms utilize biodynamic methods and strive to create a farm "ecosystem" in which the farm is able to sustain itself. These farms may also utilize similar holistic methods but may not bear any label. These farms are sprouting up across the nation in response to consumers who are willing to pay a higher price for a superior product. Biodynamic farming is a very Good Decision.

I get a feeling of satisfaction when I purchase animal protein sources from producers that care about the animal and work collaboratively to provide sustainable, healthy products; it means a better product and planet for you and me.

Proteins to Be Aware of

Conventional Animal Proteins

More than 70 percent of the animal proteins in the U.S. are raised using conventional methods. There is no label to look for when it comes to conventional products. You may see the words "Natural," "Fresh," or "Family Farmed," along with a host of other words that are not regulated.

Conventional industrial farming methods for animal proteins allow the following:

- Dairy cows may be fed antibiotics, pig and chicken byproducts, hormones, pesticides, sewage sludge, and genetically-modified organisms (GMO), including a now-discredited genetically-modified (GM) bovine growth hormone (rBGH).
- Beef cows may be fed antibiotics, pig and chicken byproducts, steroids, hormones, pesticides, sewage sludge, and GMO products.
- Pigs may be fed antibiotics, animal byproducts, pesticides, sewage sludge, arsenic-based drugs, and GMO products; growth hormones fed directly to the animal are prohibited. Tail docking, a practice in which farmers remove piglet tails using pliers or a hot docking iron, is often done to prevent pigs from chewing on each other's tails in close quarters.
- Broiler chickens may be fed antibiotics, animal byproducts, pesticides, sewage sludge, arsenic-based drugs, and GM food products; growth hormones are prohibited. Chickens are often de-beaked to prevent them from hurting other birds in close quarters.
- Egg-laying hens may be fed antibiotics, animal byproducts, pesticides, sewage sludge, arsenic-based drugs, and GMO products. These animals are often de-beaked and crowded into very small pens where they must live their entire lives.
- Dairy cows may be given a genetically-engineered hormone called recombinant bovine growth hormone rBGH to increase milk production.

While increased milk production equates to higher profits for the beef and dairy industries, what do these practices mean for you and me?

According to The European Union's Scientific Committee on Veterinary Measures Relating to Public Health, the use of six natural and artificial growth hormones in beef production poses a potential risk to human health.[12] The committee questioned whether hormone residues in the meat of "growth-enhanced" animals can cause developmental problems in *humans*, disrupt *human* hormone balance, interfere with the reproductive system, and lead to the development of breast, prostate, or colon cancer.[13] The European Union has banned hormone-treated meat and meat products from the U.S. since 1988. The ban remains in place today.

Here at home, the American Academy of Pediatrics found American girls reach puberty much earlier now than in the past.[14] Some health experts suggest that this is due to the consumption of dairy, which is packed with growth hormones and other chemical contaminants.

The FDA approved rBGH in 1993, despite much opposition from scientists and government officials. The FDA based its approval on an unpublished study by the Monsanto Corporation, and many still wonder how this was possible when rBGH is prohibited in most of the world. Cows are also fed a diet high in genetically-engineered corn products, which some scientists believe has contributed to outbreaks of mad cow disease.[15] Others believe mad cow disease is a result of feeding cows the remains of other cows. As a result, this is no longer allowed; however, feeding conventional cows the remains of pigs and chickens is still allowed. Cows are herbivores; they are only given these remains because it makes them grow bigger, faster.

What an animal eats *does* end up in the meat and milk of that animal. When cows are fed plastic filler pellets, genetically-modified corn, byproducts of other slaughtered animals, and are injected with antibiotics, growth hormones, and other substances—and when they are crowded into small spaces where they often stand in their own feces for hours while the acid rots away their hooves—a high quality, healthy, nutritional product cannot result.

The research I have done on how animals are treated with conventional farming methods makes me truly understand the vegetarian stance. There is no question about it; the way many conventional animal proteins are processed is horrific, for the animals and for humans.

Good Decisions recommends avoiding conventional animal products.

What about Seafood?

Today, there's a lot of confusion about the healthfulness and safety of seafood. Fish and shellfish are an important part of a healthy diet, as they contain high-quality protein, are mineral rich, and contain Omega-3 fatty acids. On the other hand, seafood can also contain unhealthy substances such as mercury, polychlorinated biphenyl (PCB), chlordane, dioxins, and dichlorodiphenyltrichloroethane (DDT). Each year, dangerous quantities of pollutants are emitted into the air. When it rains, this pollution gets into our rivers, lakes, and oceans, where it contaminates the fish and shellfish that live there.

National Geographic, in an article titled "Fukushima Fallout Not Affecting US Caught Fish," reported that in August of 2013, "the Japanese government reported that the Fukushima plant was leaking approximately 300 tons, or 71,895 gallons, of contaminated water each day. That's a lot of water—except when you compare it to the Pacific Ocean, which is estimated to contain 187,189,915,062,857,142,857 gallons."[16] Is the ocean so vast and the pollutants so minimal in comparison that our seafood really is safe? To eat or not to eat seafood can be a tough decision.

One thing to consider when making this decision is your digestive health. Certain species of probiotic bacteria, such as Lactobacillus naturally occurring in the gut, mouth, and vagina are known for their ability to bind to and detoxify some of these toxins.[17] If you have a condition where repeated use of antibiotics may have depleted your stores of good bacteria, the substances in seafood may not sit well with you. Another person with strong digestion and abundant gut flora may be able to handle the substances in seafood just fine.

It is a good idea if you eat a lot of seafood to ensure that you also eat plenty of fiber to cultivate these heathy organisms as well as fermented foods such as yogurt, kefir, sauerkraut, kombucha, miso, and tempeh.

Much effort is going into cleaning up our environment, especially in developing countries. Research is underway to determine how these friendly bacteria may be used to bind to and detoxify pollutants in our environment, and alleviate the effect of contamination in our food. For now, seafood is best consumed with an awareness of the potential problems.

Mercury

Mercury has been used to manufacture products from thermometers to automotive light switches. Mercury makes its way up the food chain and to your table when large fish eat contaminated smaller fish, and you eat the large fish.

Nearly all fish and shellfish contain traces of mercury. For most of us, the risk from mercury by eating fish and shellfish is not an issue. But for children, it's a different story. Certain shellfish and fish contain higher levels of mercury, which may harm an unborn baby or child's developing nervous system. The risks posed by mercury in fish and shellfish depend on the amount of fish and shellfish eaten and the levels of mercury in the fish and shellfish.[18,19]

Nutritional Nugget

Dandelion, that little weed in your back yard, is known within the herbalist community as a detoxifying herb. It works because it improves liver and gallbladder function as well as helps clear excessive waste products and estrogens from the blood for elimination. Some stores now carry dandelion greens in the produce section. While they are a little bitter, they are still quite delicious! Dandelion salad or tea to go with your seafood, anyone?

When we eat fish that contain mercury, the mercury enters our body and acts as a neurotoxin, which is basically a poison that can interfere with brain and thyroid function. Mercury poisoning can adversely affect memory, fertility, blood pressure regulation, and can cause tremors, vision loss, and numbness of the fingers and toes.[20] Mercury is a well-known neurotoxin.

You can't see mercury, so it is not easy to know how much of it may be in your food. The best way to avoid high levels of mercury is to avoid seafood listed in the tables below that are known to contain high amounts of mercury.

Nutritional Nugget

If you are not a fish eater, you may choose to supplement with fish oil supplements instead. If you do this, be sure you choose a fish oil or cod liver oil supplement that has been tested and is free of mercury. Reputable fish oil supplements are Carlson and Nordic naturals. They are expensive but worth it.

Farmed Fish

As an alternative, many people have turned to farmed fish, especially salmon, in hopes of avoiding mercury. But this product may not be the solution we'd hoped for. In the most comprehensive analysis of farmed and wild salmon to date, a study, sponsored by the Pew Charitable Trusts,[21] analyzed toxic contaminants in approximately 700 farmed and wild salmon (totaling 2 metric tons) collected from around the world to be representative of the salmon typically available to consumers. The study examined salmon produced in eight major farmed salmon-producing regions and obtained from retail outlets in sixteen major North American and European cities. The study found that concentrations of several contaminants associated with serious health risks, from neurological effects to cancer, were significantly higher in farmed salmon than in wild salmon.

The authors concluded that concentrations of several cancer-causing substances were high enough to suggest that consumers should consider restricting their consumption of farmed salmon. Another concern regarding farmed salmon is that they are fed an unnatural diet of corn. Not just any corn, but genetically-modified corn, along with artificial coloring used to create the bright-orange color of wild salmon. Farmed salmon are also fed GM soy, antibiotics, and other unnatural substances found in food pellets.

In most cases, consumption of more than one meal of farmed salmon per month could pose unacceptable cancer risks, according to U.S. Environmental Protection Agency (EPA) methods for calculating fish consumption advisories.[22] So even though wild salmon may still contain mercury, it is less of a risk than farmed salmon. Most restaurants use farmed salmon, so don't forget to ask before you place your order.

The newest concern with farmed fish is the pending approval of genetically-engineered (GE) salmon, which would be the first approval of a genetically-engineered animal for consumption. There are unanswered questions about what would happen if GE salmon, which is injected with a growth hormone gene so it will grow large and get to market faster, got into the wild. I can't help but wonder what this GE fish, designed to get big fast, would do to me if I ate it. Would I, like the GE salmon, quickly grow big?

Whole Foods, Trader Joe's, and Target have all pledged not to carry GE salmon if approved, and the movement away from this is strong because many feel not enough testing has been done and the potential of GE salmon to impact the environment adversely if accidentally released into the wild is too big a risk. Too many questions left unanswered, too many studies yet to be done, and too many risks yet to be mitigated will keep this product off my table until I feel substantial studies have been done to ensure its safety.

Farmed fish is not a *Good Decision.*

Making Safe Seafood Decisions

The best thing to do is to be aware of, and try to avoid, fish that contain high amounts of contaminants. Instead, choose fish that contain low amounts of contaminants. The Natural Resources Defense Council (NRDC) offers a downloadable wallet card that lists the mercury levels in fish, and it offers recommendations on how often to eat those types of fish and how to choose sustainably. The site also provides information about which species are endangered and should be avoided. This information is updated frequently, so it's a good website to follow. Knowing which seafood products will support your overall wellbeing, as well as the sustainability of the planet, is of paramount importance. The following guidelines were taken from the NRDC website and were current as of April 2014.

Seafood That Contains the Least Amounts of Mercury			
Anchovies	Butterfish	Catfish	Clams
Crab	Herring	Mackerel	Oysters
Sardines	Squid (Calamari)	Tilapia	Trout
Scallops	Whitefish	Salmon	Shrimp

Seafood That Contains Moderate Levels of Mercury (Limit to six or less servings per month)				
Bass	Cod	Croaker	Halibut	Lobster
Snapper	Mahi Mahi	Perch	Sablefish	Tuna

Seafood That Contains High Levels of Mercury (Choose these seafood items three times or less per month)		
Bluefish	Chilean Sea Bass	Grouper
Spanish Mackerel-Gulf	Tuna - Canned Albacore	Tuna - Yellow Fin

Seafood That Contains the Highest Levels of Mercury			
King Mackerel	Marlin	Orange Roughy	Shark
Swordfish	Tilefish	Tuna -Bigeye (Ahi)	

While all this talk about environmental pollutants and mercury may be a bit disconcerting, seafood is still a much better decision than processed foods, fast foods, and even most cereals on the market. Everything is relative.

Good Decisions feels that seafood offers many benefits to health and is a very *Good Decision* when eaten within the Natural Resources Defense Council's recommendations.

Seared Salmon with Lemon Caper Butter Sauce

Serves: 4
Total Time: 25 minutes

Ingredients

- Four 4-ounce wild salmon fillets
- 1 teaspoon ghee
- 3 tablespoons butter, divided
- 2 cloves garlic chopped
- 1 cup dry white wine
- 2 tablespoons drained capers
- 2 tablespoons fresh lemon juice
- 1 tablespoon freshly minced parsley
- Salt and pepper to taste
- 4 thin lemon slices

Directions

1. Preheat oven to 425°F. In a large ovenproof skillet, heat 1 teaspoon ghee over medium high heat, soaking up any extra with a paper towel. When a drop of water dances on the surface of the pan, you are ready to place the salmon in the pan, presentation side down, skin side up. Sear salmon until nicely browned, then flip so the skin side is down. Place in preheated oven for 5 minutes. Remove from heat, cover loosely with foil, and let rest for 5 minutes.

2. In medium skillet, melt 1 tablespoon butter over medium heat. Add garlic and sauté until fragrant. Add white wine and raise heat to medium high. When wine has reduced to ¼ its original volume, add capers. Remove from heat. Enrich sauce by adding the remaining butter one tablespoon at a time, allowing each piece to melt completely before adding the next. When butter has been incorporated, add lemon juice, parsley, and salt and pepper to taste. Serve sauce over fish and garnish with lemon slices.

Choosing Safe Plant Proteins

As we discussed previously, legumes, certain grains, nuts, and seeds are All-Star protein sources. These tasty proteins contain many health-giving substances. They can be quick and easy to prepare, have a long shelf life, and do not spoil as easily as animal proteins. Choose organic to ensure the products were not genetically modified and that pesticides, herbicides, and other pest management substances were kept to a minimum.

Plant proteins are very *Good Decisions.*

What about Soy?

Soybeans are high in phytic acid and other natural toxins known as "anti-nutrients." In an effort to remove the anti-nutrients from soy products, soybeans are taken through a series of chemical processes that include acid washing in aluminum tanks,[23] which puts an undesirable heavy metal into the final soy products.

For human consumption, soybeans must be fermented to reduce the mineral-blocking effects of phytates. Raw soybeans, including the immature green form, are actually toxic to humans. Soybeans also contain hemagglutinin, which causes red blood cells to clump together. And, while these substances are reduced in processing, they are not completely eliminated. Soy also contains goitrogens, which frequently lead to depressed thyroid function, a common occurrence among women today.

In addition, autoimmune disease has been associated with compounds (environmental estrogens) found in soy that, when eaten, display estrogen-like activity. While some may deem environmental estrogens beneficial for the reduction of hot flashes or female hormonal balance, it may be of concern.[24] More than 90 percent of soybeans in the U.S. are genetically modified, and genetically-modified soybeans contain one of the highest levels of pesticide contamination of all foods. Processed soy products, such as soy milk and tofu, may be a good source of protein, but they are not quality protein and are *not* considered *Good Decisions.*

Safe Soy Products

Many women have found relief from menopausal symptoms, such as hot flashes, by utilizing soy products. While organic, properly-prepared soy products are difficult to find, in time, as consumer demand increases, they will become readily available. For now, if you choose to utilize soy, choose from products that are fermented, which include Natto, Amakaze, Miso, and Tempeh.

Cost Considerations

Many people tell me that they cannot afford organic. That's okay. If organic is not an option for you, then choosing conventional animal and plant proteins is still better than choosing processed foods—it's a big step in the right direction. Choosing conventional protein is better than choosing no protein at all.

Vegetarian Lifestyles

There are many types of vegetarians.

Total vegetarians eat only plant food. They do not eat any animal foods, including fish, eggs, dairy products, and honey.

Vegans avoid all animal products. They do not eat eggs, dairy products, and, in some cases, honey. Many vegans also avoid anything made from animal products, such as gelatin, leather, fur, and wool. Many vegans also refrain from eating food that may not contain animal products in the finished process, but is made using animal products. There is some debate as to whether honey fits into a vegan diet.

Raw vegans eat a diet of unprocessed vegan foods that have not been heated above 115°F. "Raw foodists" believe that foods cooked above this temperature have lost a significant amount of their nutritional value and are harmful to the body.

Fruitarians eat only fruits, seeds, nuts, and other plant components that can be gathered without harming the plant.

Lacto vegetarians include dairy products in their diet of plant foods, but not eggs. ("Lacto" comes from the Latin for milk.)

Ovo vegetarians include eggs, but not dairy products, in their diet of plant foods. ("Ovo" comes from the Latin for egg.)

Lacto-Ovo-Vegetarians eat both eggs and dairy products in addition to plant-based foods. When most people think of vegetarians, they think of lacto-ovo-vegetarians.

Buddhist vegetarians (also known as *su vegetarians*) exclude all animal products as well as vegetables in the allium family: onions, garlic, scallions, leeks, and shallots.

Pescetarianism, or Pesce-vegetarianism, includes fish and some other forms of seafood. The Italian word "pesce" means fish. Pescetarians typically do not eat meat or animal proteins, but do eat fish.

Vegetarians may eat fowl, such as chicken and turkey, but avoid red meat and pork.

Pollo Pescetarians include poultry and fish or "white meat" only in their diets.

Semi-Vegetarian Diets

Individuals may describe themselves as "vegetarians" while practicing a semi-vegetarian diet, since some dictionary definitions of vegetarianism vary. Some definitions include the consumption of fish, while other definitions exclude fish and all animal flesh. In other cases, individuals may describe themselves as "flexitarians." This type of diet may be followed by those who reduce animal flesh consumption as a way of transitioning to a complete vegetarian diet or for health, environmental, or other reasons.

What About a Vegetarian Lifestyle?

While there are many types of vegetarians, I will use the term to mean an individual who does not eat animal proteins.

Are humans supposed to be vegetarians? Or are we designed to be meat eaters? The debate has gone on, and will continue to go on, for many more years as people hold steadfast to their beliefs. Wanting to understand the issue, I did a little research into the mystery of what our bodies are and are not designed to eat. Following is what I found.

Some vegetarians believe a human's intestinal length is more like a herbivore's (six times our body length), and is therefore designed for digesting vegetables, grains, and fruits.

When looking into this, I discovered the intestinal length of a meat-eating animal is three times its body length to allow for quick removal of waste that can putrefy in the intestines.

I then found a human's intestinal length to be just under eight times our body length (assuming a "mouth to anus body length" of three feet). This puts us between animal-eaters such as cats (three times their body length), dogs (3.5 times their body length), and plant eaters such as cattle (20 times their body length) and horses (12 times their body length). Perhaps this makes humans more adaptable; perhaps our bodies evolved to accommodate both meat and plants.

According to a 1999 article in the journal *The Ecologist,*[25] several of our physiological features "clearly indicate a design" for eating meat.

> First and foremost is our stomach's production of hydrochloric acid, something not found in herbivores. Furthermore, the human pancreas manufactures a full

range of digestive enzymes to handle a wide variety of foods, both animal and vegetable. While humans may have longer intestines than animal carnivores, they are not as long as herbivores; nor do we possess multiple stomachs like many herbivores, nor do we chew cud. Our physiology definitely indicates a mixed feeder, or an omnivore, much the same as our relatives, the mountain gorilla and chimpanzee (who have been observed eating small animals and, in some cases, other primates).[26]

So it appears we are quite capable of consuming and digesting both meat and plant life. We don't have to choose between the two. Both omnivores and vegetarians have all the tools they need to digest and absorb their food. So the diet and lifestyle you choose is completely up to you!

It really boils down to personal choice, and as we have seen throughout this book, we are all biochemically different. One problem I've encountered in my practice, however, is that many meat eaters eat too much poor quality meat and processed fast foods, and many vegetarians are what I call "junk food vegetarians." They've chosen not to eat meat, but they aren't too fond of vegetables, nuts, and legumes, either. They're usually addicted to bread, chips, processed foods like rice cakes, and even soy, which may give them protein, but at a high cost to their overall health. These vegetarians can be vulnerable to protein deficiency, which can result in weakness and fatigue, headache, apathy, depression, anxiety, decreased mental alertness, hair loss, brittle hair, ridges of deep lines in fingers or toenails, dry flaky skin, difficulty sleeping, and other symptoms.

If you choose a vegetarian lifestyle, it's imperative to learn about essential amino acids and where to find them. With this knowledge, you can make informed, conscious food choices to ensure you get enough protein-rich plant sources each day. Some plant sources, such as nuts, beans, quinoa, and seeds, contain quite a bit of protein. By combining them, you can get complete coverage of all the essential amino acids.

The only potential hole in the vegetarian diet is vitamin B12. This vitamin can be found in laver (seaweed), miso, tempeh, tamari, and shoyu. Think of anything that is fermented by bacteria, and you most likely have a plant source of vitamin B12. However, the amounts of B12 in plant sources are very small and can lead to deficiency if one is not diligent. Nutritional yeast is grown on cane or beet molasses and, as with brewer's yeast, some brands are fortified with synthetic vitamin B12. This vitamin does not occur in nature, but is used as a food additive and as a supplement because of its lower cost and stability. Still, nutritional yeast is a good way to ensure B12 sufficiency as long as the product has been fortified.

If you are a vegetarian and aren't good about soaking grains and legumes or consuming a diverse source of plant proteins, I recommend incorporating nutritional yeast, brewer's yeast, spirulina, sunflower seeds, pumpkin seeds, quinoa, and parsley into your diet.

You may also visit my website at www.gooddecisions.com to find information on foods that will provide both animal and plant sources of the essential amino acids, vitamins, and minerals.

Additionally, organic eggs are one of the most complete and perfect protein sources and contain every essential amino acid. When I come across junk food vegetarians, if I can't talk them into plant-rich protein sources like quinoa, beans, nuts, seeds, and vegetables, I introduce the idea of adding organic eggs or whole fat dairy products to their diets, in small amounts. I don't do this to change their belief system, but rather to ensure their bodies get what they need to enjoy optimal health.

It's easy to understand why many people choose a vegetarian lifestyle. Until we all demand humane treatment of our animal protein sources, inhumane and unhealthy methods will not change. To locate a reliable source of quality animal proteins, visit any of the humane certified programs' websites for a list of certified farms near you where you can find quality local proteins. You can often visit the farm to see how the animals are treated. Personally, I want to know that the chicken I am about to eat was running around, happily eating bugs, and the cow that becomes my source of complete proteins and B vitamins was grazing on grass and had room to roam. I want to know that the milk I drink is filled with the same healthy nutrients the cow ate. I agree with vegetarians: animals should be treated well. I appreciate the resources that are saved by their efforts. Many Americans would do well to eat a little less animal protein and a few more vegetables.

Scrambled Eggs with Tarragon

Serves: 4
Total Time: 10 minutes

Ingredients

- 8 large eggs
- 1 tablespoon unsalted butter
- 1 tablespoon chopped fresh tarragon leaves
- Salt and pepper to taste

Directions

1. Heat a medium nonstick frying pan over medium-low heat until hot, about 2 minutes. Add butter to the pan and, using a rubber spatula, swirl until it's melted and foamy and the pan is evenly coated. Crack the eggs into the pan, lightly scramble with spatula, and sprinkle with tarragon. Let sit undisturbed until the eggs just start to set around the edges, about 1 to 2 minutes. Using the spatula, break up the eggs and flip eggs to cook evenly. Season to taste with salt and pepper. Serve immediately.

Recommended Protein Amounts

The various recommendations made by health practitioners regarding the daily allowance for protein may be anywhere from 10 to 35 percent of your daily calories. Using the standard 2000 calorie diet as a reference, this can be anywhere from 50 to 175 grams per day. It's a broad range because everyone is different. When nutritional therapists make recommendations, we must consider size, activity level, as well as several other factors. Because many people consume too much protein, I tend to recommend serving sizes that start around 3-4 ounces of meat or fish, 1-2 eggs, ½ cup presoaked and cooked beans, peas, or lentils, and 1 ounce nuts or seeds. I find these recommendations to be a good place to start, but they may need to be tweaked for the petite grandma or seven-foot male athlete.

Nutritional Nugget

How do you know whether you're consuming too much protein? If you have bad breath and consume a lot of protein, odds are you are eating too much. Increase your vegetable intake until the offensive odor goes away!

Everyone is different, which is why I try to guide you to listen to your own body. When you eat real foods and listen to your body's satiation signal, calories do not need to be counted and portions do not need to be rationed. You will just stop eating when your body tells you to.

Many of my clients gleefully report to me that they eat more than ever before, but are losing weight. This is because they are eating real food: vegetables, fruits, legumes, nuts, seeds, and animal proteins and yes—even fat! They are also avoiding processed foods such as pasta, bread, fast food, and sugar. Most people don't have a problem getting adequate protein in their diets. A handful of nuts here, a hardboiled egg there, sunflower seeds on a salad, bean soup, smoked salmon, hummus, and even organic, local beef are all *Good Decisions* and, when spaced throughout your day, will do much to regulate your energy, blood sugar levels, hormones, and more. Here are a few All-Star proteins to keep in mind.

Good Decisions Quality Proteins

- Seafood: Wild salmon, sardines, anchovies, and herring, mackerel, trout, crab, shrimp, oysters, clams
- Eggs, organic chicken, turkey, duck, pork, venison, elk, bison, beef, liver
- Nuts and Seeds
- Legumes: Soaked or sprouted beans, peas, and lentils
- Grains: quinoa, amaranth, wild rice, and teff

Portuguese Sardine Salad

Serves: 4

Total Time: 40 minutes

Ingredients

- 1½ pounds fingerling potatoes, halved lengthwise
- 2 tablespoons melted ghee
- 1 teaspoon unrefined sea salt
- 2 tablespoons olive oil
- 4 tablespoons fresh lemon juice
- 2 tablespoons minced shallots
- ¼ teaspoon smoked paprika
- 2 garlic cloves, minced
- 8 fresh whole sardines
- 4 cups mixed baby greens
- 2 large eggs, hard-boiled and halved
- 8 cherry tomatoes
- 8 lemon wedges
- Freshly ground black pepper

Directions

1. Preheat oven to 425°F. Combine potatoes, ghee, and salt; toss well to coat. Place on a rimmed baking sheet and bake for 15 minutes. Stir potatoes; bake an additional 10 minutes or until golden brown and tender.

2. Combine olive oil, lemon juice, shallots, paprika, and garlic in a large bowl; stir to combine well. Add warm potatoes to bowl; toss to coat.

3. Heat a large nonstick skillet over medium-high heat. Pat sardines dry with paper towels; sprinkle with salt. Coat pan with ghee and add sardines to pan; cook 3 minutes on each side or until crisp and done. (Sardines could also be broiled if desired.)

4. Arrange 1 cup mixed greens on each of 4 plates. Place ¾ cup potatoes on each salad serving. Top each salad with 2 sardines, 1 egg half, and 2 cherry tomatoes. Serve with lemon wedges; sprinkle with pepper. (Adapted from www.myrecipes.com.)

The Psychology of Food

The Life That You Are

By now you are probably more aware than ever of the voices in your head. Most people will admit to hearing voices; others, wanting to avoid being judged and who are run by the ego, will not. When I first became aware of the voice in my head, it became bigger. It got louder, more annoying, and more like a spoiled child screaming at me when the voice could not have its way or I would not soothe it with a larger portion or a hit of sugar.

This voice tends to live in the past and future. It is either seeking something more in the future where it imagines itself being fulfilled, or it is dwelling in the past where it chews on events or experiences and creates mental movies about how it could have responded or what could have happened in past situations.

The secret to finding peace from this voice is to pay attention to it. While this seems counterintuitive, it actually works really well. When you bring awareness to what the voice is saying, it immediately begins to recede. Only when you are aware of the voice do you become free of it.

Eckhart Tolle, in his book *A New Earth*, tells us, "When you can no longer feel the life that you are, you are more likely to fill your life with things" I can't think of anything that describes compulsive eating better. Food is simply a thing that we try to fill ourselves with in an effort to fill the void.

Because we have moved so far away from our inner being, we no longer feel the life that we are. We feel empty, and have a strong desire to avoid this discomfort and fill the emptiness, often times with food. Instead of filling the void with food, let's see whether we can get rid of it altogether.

Practicing Good Decisions

Feel the Life That You Are

Today I am going to ask you to sit in silence and "feel the life that you are." This requires setting aside 15-20 minutes of time before a meal, without any disturbance. Prepare your meal first so all you have to do is sit down to enjoy it after this exercise. This will help you become more in tune with your body.

Be sure that you will be free from any distractions for 20 minutes. Do not lie down, as the temptation to sleep may be too strong. This is not about relaxation, but increasing your alertness; you want to sit in silence, alertly waiting for the "life that you are" to reveal itself. Turn the heat up or wrap yourself in a warm blanket so the cold will not distract you.

Now, sit in a comfortable position. Listen to the silence that surrounds you. Try not to rush through this; really take your time. Take a few deep breaths and feel your body and heartbeat begin to slow. Now, close your eyes and bring your attention to your toes; can you feel the blood circulating through them? Wiggle your toes and see whether you can feel the blood flow circulating through your lower legs and thighs. Spend a few moments here just feeling your legs and listening to the stillness.

When you feel inclined, move your attention to your stomach; is it gurgling? Can you feel any digestive movement? Again, spend several moments paying alert attention to your stomach and its sounds and movements. When you are ready, move your attention to your heart. Can you feel your heartbeat? Stay here for as long as you wish and focus alertly on your heart beating within your chest. Can you feel the energy of blood moving throughout your body? If the voice interrupts your focus, bring your attention to what it is saying, and notice how when you bring your attention to it, it dissipates and fades away.

Next, bring your attention to your arms and your fingers. If you felt your heart beating in your chest, can you feel the blood as it is pumped into your arms? Keep your focus on each of these body parts as long as you wish. Feel the energy as it courses through your body. Now, bring your attention to your lungs. Do you feel your lungs expand and deflate with each inhalation and exhalation? Pay particular attention to the pause between your exhale and your inhale. Don't force your breathing; relax and stay alert. Observe your breathing for as long as you wish. The life that you are *is* the life force pulsating through your body; it *is* the aware presence within your physical body.

Now, slowly open your eyes, and maintaining your state of quiet alertness, slowly get up and sit down to your meal. Appreciate the look, smell, and taste of it. Slowly eat it, one bite at a time. Feel the food moving into your belly. Pay attention; can you tune in to your body's satiation signal that tells you it has had enough? It is usually shortly after the food starts losing its taste. When you receive your satiation signal, stop eating and put the rest of your meal away for a different time when your body tells you it is hungry and would like something to eat.

Practice this awareness as often as possible, and you will no longer need to count calories or restrict your portions. *Good Decisions...Most of the Time* is a way of life in which you eat wholesome natural foods and tune in to your body so that you stop when you are full. By paying more attention to the now, and bringing an awareness to now, you begin to sense your own nature, you become in tune with your body and its needs, and action can be much easier because it is taken from truth and knowledge rather than emotion and ego.

Be aware that wanting to be somewhere else, with someone else, doing something else, is the mind's way of disliking where you are now. This is interesting when you realize that the now is really all we have. The past is simply an accumulation of now moments that have gone by. The future is nothing more than now moments that haven't happened yet, so you see, all we really have is now.

The desire to overeat or eat unhealthy foods is the mind's way of trying to soothe itself when it feels threatened, or to fill the void. If you have been doing your homework, you have probably encountered many uncomfortable moments. This practice will help with the discomfort immensely. When you find yourself in an uncomfortable food situation, take your attention to the energy within you and feel your heart beat or your lungs expand. Pause and cultivate that alert presence, the keen awareness of what is happening at the time of your discomfort. You will find this relieves the discomfort! Simply bringing your attention to and increasing your awareness of the discomfort releases its hold on you.

When you take your attention away from doing and place it on *being* in the present moment, you will find that your body is very clear about what it wants and needs, and it is easier to fill those needs. When you are aware of the magnificent life that you are, you are already full and the need to fill any void disappears. The chocolate cake or French fries then become friends that can be enjoyed and savored every once in awhile, instead of enemies that you can't control.

Chapter Eight

Fats and Oils

Fat. The mere mention of the word elicits images and emotions—not all of them good—and with good reason. For more than fifty years, physicians and reputable institutions such as the American Heart Association have warned us to stay away from foods that contain saturated fat or cholesterol because they consider them unhealthy. In this chapter, we will look at this old belief and see whether it is still true today. You will learn about the chemistry of fats, the many healthful properties of fats and oils, and how they can be used to lose weight, make skin younger looking, and boost your immune system. We will also look at how fats and oils are refined and processed.

Why Is There Such a Fat Phobia in the U.S. Today?

In the 1950s, doctors, armed with information from the now-famous *Framingham Heart Study*, insisted that their patients avoid saturated fats and cholesterol. Our trusted healthcare providers recommended margarine, Crisco®, and other so-called "healthy" alternatives. As a culture, we believed we were doing the right thing when we consumed these "new" low- and non-fat foods because we thought they were good for us. "Non-fat" became the new "Holy Grail" in the food world. This information caused us to believe that foods high in saturated fats and cholesterol would clog our arteries, result in heart disease, make us fat, and lead us to an early death. And so, fearfully and obediently, we limited or removed saturated fats and cholesterol from our diets. We increased our consumption of so-called "healthy" foods such as pasta, breads, and dairy; yet our cholesterol levels still went up. Obesity has not decreased; obesity has *increased*—and the same goes for heart disease. Millions of people—wanting to lose weight and prevent or control heart disease and other chronic conditions—decreased their fat intake, replaced whole-fat products with low-fat counterparts, and avoided the big "no no" foods like steak, butter, and eggs—only to find that their weight and health did not improve. Why?

It isn't much of a leap to accept that what we've been told is not accurate. When these studies first came out, the edible oil industry and food manufacturers saw a tremendous market opportunity to capitalize on the "no-fat" craze, so they engineered thousands of foods to be lower in fat or fat-free. Additionally, the industry created a new breed of fatty acids: *trans fats*, also known as hydrogenated vegetable oils, which were then marketed as the new "healthy" fats. What many people fail to notice is that these non-fat and low-fat food items are often higher in sugar and artificial flavorings to improve the taste that is lost when fat is removed.

Today, new findings and review of the *Framingham Heart Study* indicate the results of the study are open for a different interpretation. Further, the study's scoring methods vastly overestimated the coronary risk assigned to saturated fats.[1] Many studies have since proven that saturated fat and cholesterol are **not** the primary factors involved in heart disease.

CHAPTER EIGHT

The low-fat approach to eating may help some individuals, but for most, it has not helped control weight or improve health. Today, Americans consume less fat, yet an alarming percentage of us are obese, take heart or cholesterol-lowering medications, and millions have diabetes. At least one in two people is now overweight or obese in over half of Organisation for Economic Co-Operation and Development (OECD) countries. Rates are projected to increase further, and in some countries, two out of three people will be obese within ten years.[2]

Why? Why didn't cutting fat and cholesterol pay off as expected? Could it be because saturated fats and cholesterol are not that harmful? After all, hunters and gatherers of most native cultures consume a significant amount of both, yet heart disease and diabetes are rarely an issue for them. Or could it be because the processed fats that came into the marketplace fifty years ago aren't as healthy as we have been led to believe? The answer is most likely both.

As it turns out, cholesterol is not nearly the villain it is portrayed to be. It is now glaringly obvious that manmade fats peddled as "healthy alternatives" are far from healthy and that cholesterol plays very important roles in the body, hormone production being only one. Trans fats are much worse than the saturated fats they replaced.

The recommendation to decrease saturated fats and increase trans fat consumption has been one of the most dramatic changes in the Western diet over the last fifty years. It has contributed significantly to the fat phobia we experience today. In addition, a new understanding of the serious risk posed by partially hydrogenated oils is coming to light. Derived from vegetable oils and touted as healthy, these fats are chemically-stabilized oils created because they are inexpensive and resist spoilage. These fats may be cheap and they may last longer, but many recognized institutions have found these oils to be anything but healthy. What started as a food manufacturer's dream come true has turned into a health nightmare for generations brought up on hydrogenated fats that do not function well in cell membranes or brain tissue. Today people are uncertain about whom and what they should believe when it comes to fat; it is no wonder we are so afraid of fats today!

In this age of increasing food technology, where man can manipulate fats to be more stable, genetically modify corn to tolerate high levels of pesticides, and add preservatives to increase shelf life, the focus has been on quantity, not quality.

Our political, economic, and social leaders have long maintained that world hunger is a primary concern for all of us who inhabit the planet. A look around our grocery stores tells a different tale. *Quantity* of food clearly exists more so now than any other time in history. Throughout history, only royalty and the wealthiest of society had access to fruit out of season; now many of us take it for granted. Time spent hunting and gathering food is now often spent watching TV.

Still, amid all the modern commercial developments and large-scale food manufacturing, small bakeries, meat and fish markets, and farmers markets are sprouting up locally where people who care about *quality* are selling their products. Food co-ops are in demand, and the assortment of minimally-processed fats and oils is greater than ever. We are becoming more creative regarding how we feed the world, and instead of sending food to certain Third World countries, we are teaching people how to sustain themselves.

Gourmet duck fat and old world cheese made as it was 500 years ago can easily be found today. Quality fats that have been extracted without chemicals are making their way back to the marketplace. Tropical oils that used to be costly are now affordable and easily available. Our grocery shelves offer so many choices that the challenge has become reading labels to determine how the oil was refined and what is actually in it. While we no longer have to hunt animals, milk a cow, or churn cream into butter to get the food we need to survive, we do need to be more diligent about reading labels and avoiding the wrong kinds of fat. Let's find out exactly what fat is so we can stop being afraid of fats and begin to make informed and confident decisions regarding them.

What Are Fats?

Fats may be either solid or liquid at room temperature, depending on their structure and composition. Fats and oils are made up of collections of molecules called *triglycerides*.

If the collection is liquid at room temperature, then we call it an *oil*; if it is solid at room temperature, it is called a *fat*.

The shape of the triglyceride molecule depends on the fatty acids found in the triglyceride. A fatty acid is an organic molecule made from carbon, hydrogen, and oxygen. Hydrogen and oxygen bind to carbon atoms to form chains. Fatty acids are given different names depending on the length of the chain and the degree of saturation. Some of the carbons along these chains have single bonds and are classified as saturated fatty acids. Other carbon chains with at least one double bond are classified as unsaturated fatty acids. If only one bond is unsaturated, it is called a monounsaturated fatty acid. A fatty acid having several double bonds in the carbon chain is classified as a *polyunsaturated fatty acid*.

No fat is 100 percent saturated; when fats are totally saturated, they become hard and wax-like. Most fats are a combination of fatty acids. Their classification is determined by the highest percentage of saturated, monounsaturated, or polyunsaturated fatty acids.

If you had trouble following that, don't worry about it; it gets easier.

Types of Fat

There are four types of fat:

- Saturated fatty acids
- Monounsaturated fats
- Polyunsaturated fats
- Trans fatty acids

Saturated fats

Saturated fats are found primarily in animal food sources such as beef, butter, lard, and tropical oils such as coconut oil and palm oil. They are also found in dairy fats and nutmeg butter. These fats are highly stable and are terrific for cooking since they are not easily damaged by heat, light, or oxygen, and they are endowed with many beneficial nutrients.

When these fats are not refined and processed, they are very *Good Decisions*.

Saturated fats are composed mostly of saturated fatty acids, which are carbon chains with single bonds. This single bond results in a compact, straight shape, which allows them to fit closely together, making them solid or semi-solid at room temperature. Though these fats have been labeled as "bad," they are not the enemy they are made out to be. Quite the opposite, they have come to be known as quite healthy. Because animal fats contain a higher percentage of saturated fatty acids, they are classified as saturated fats.

Saturated fats from animals are typically processed utilizing a process called rendering. While this term may sound technical, it simply means "to give." When you cook bacon, for example, the heat melts the fat away from the meat, or the meat "gives up" its fat. The browned crispy bacon is removed from the pan, and what you have left is bacon fat or lard. This fat can then be "clarified" by pouring it through a fine sieve filter or cheesecloth to remove any brown bits of protein and stored for later use. It will keep in the fridge for about a month. This is the fat your grandpa stored in the coffee can on the countertop to use when frying potatoes, eggs, or anything else that he felt needed it. (Did I just date myself?) Clarifying, of course, is optional.

Typically, pork fat is wet-rendered into lard. Beef and lamb fat are rendered into tallow. Poultry fat from chicken, turkey, and duck is called schmaltz. Duck fat is a very tasty fat that can be rendered as you would the fat from bacon to add flavor and nutrients to other dishes.

Saturated fats from plants, such as coconut and palm oil, are extracted via grinding and pressing, and may or may not involve the use of chemical solvents. We will go over plant oil extraction methods more in a bit.

Duck Cassoulet

Serves: 8
Total Time: 2 hours, plus overnight resting

Ingredients

- 1 teaspoon extra-virgin olive oil
- Four ½-inch thick slices of pancetta, cut into ½-inch cubes
- 2 cups yellow onion, chopped into ½-inch cubes
- 1 pound dried flageolets or Great Northern beans, rinsed and picked over, then soaked overnight and drained
- 1 tablespoon chopped thyme
- 2 bay leaves
- 1/8 teaspoon ground cloves
- 8 cups chicken stock
- 4 cups water
- 4 small garlic cloves, peeled
- Unrefined sea salt
- Pepper
- 4 pieces of duck leg confit, trimmed of excess fat
- ¾ pound French garlic sausage, sliced crosswise into 1-inch thick pieces
- 2 tablespoons chopped parsley

Directions

1. In a large saucepan, heat the olive oil. Add the pancetta and cook over medium heat until the fat has been rendered, about 5 minutes. Add the onion and cook, stirring occasionally, until softened, about 7 minutes. Add the beans, thyme, bay leaves, cloves, stock, and water and bring to a boil. Simmer over low heat, stirring and skimming occasionally, until the beans are al dente, about 45 minutes. Add the garlic cloves to the beans and simmer 5 more minutes. Discard the bay leaves. Season the beans with salt and pepper and let cool to room temperature. Cover and refrigerate 12-24 hours. (If made ahead, this can be refrigerated for up to 2 days.)

2. Preheat the oven to 350°F. Rewarm the beans over moderate heat. Transfer the beans to a large, deep baking dish. Nestle the duck legs and sausage into the beans. Bake for about 40 minutes, until the cassoulet is bubbling and all the meats are hot. Remove from the oven and let rest for 15 minutes. Garnish with fresh chopped parsley. Serve. This dish can also be prepared utilizing individual ramekins instead of a large baking dish.

Short-Chain Saturated Fatty Acids

There are many different lengths of saturated fatty acids. Those with shorter carbon chains, typically from three to twelve carbons, are the type found in butter, coconut oil, and palm kernel oil. These are called *short-chain saturated fatty acids*.

Medium-Chain Saturated Fatty Acids

Slightly longer in length, medium-chain saturated fatty acid lengths vary from eight to fourteen carbons. These are known for their antimicrobial, antibacterial, antiviral, and antiprotozoal properties. They are found in coconut and palm kernel oils, as well as the milk of humans.

These short- and medium-chain saturated fatty acids are not deposited in adipose tissue, and they are not found on chylomicrons unless they are consumed in large amounts. Chylomicrons are distinct carriers in the blood that transport fat through the lymph system to the liver, fat tissue, and other tissues of the body. Instead, medium-chain saturated fatty acids are transported in the portal blood to the liver for conversion into energy. This quick conversion process may prevent weight gain.

Long-Chain Saturated Fatty Acids

Long-chain saturated fatty acids range from 14 to 24 carbons in length. The longer ones make up a significant portion of the membrane fatty acids found in the brain. Because these long-chain fatty acids are found in foods that are more satiating, they have shown to inhibit excess food/caloric intake.[3] Imagine that—eat fat to lose fat. What a concept! These fatty acids are found in tropical oils, meats, dairy, poultry, and fish.

Monounsaturated Fats

Olive oil, sesame oil, and fats found in almonds, pecans, cashews, peanuts, and avocados are examples of monounsaturated fats. These are *Good Decisions* when they have not been processed or refined. Your body can make monounsaturated fatty acids from saturated fatty acids. Monounsaturated fats are composed mostly of monounsaturated fatty acids and are structured with one double bond. This causes the molecule to bend slightly, so these fats do not pack together as well as saturated fats. They tend to be liquid at room temperature but become solid when refrigerated. Monounsaturated oils are relatively stable. They also do well when exposed to heat, light, and oxygen, and can be used in cooking. They are, however, less stable than saturated fats, so they are best utilized at low and medium temperatures.

Nutritional Nugget

How does your body register satiation? When you eat small amounts of healthful fats (such as those found in eggs, meats, nuts, cream, and butter) in response to the fat, your body produces a satiation hormone that sends you a signal indicating you've eaten enough!

Like saturated fatty acids, monounsaturated fatty acids also have different lengths. Foods containing monounsaturated fats are known to reduce low-density lipoprotein (LDL or bad) cholesterol, while possibly increasing high-density lipoprotein (HDL or good) cholesterol.[4] The most popular of the monounsaturated fatty acids is oleic acid, which may be responsible for the blood pressure-reducing effects of olive oil.[5]

An interesting use of oleic acid is as an ingredient in Lorenzo's oil, a combination of two fats extracted from olive oil and rapeseed oil, developed to prevent the onset of adrenoleukodystrophy (ALD), a condition effecting only young boys. ALD attacks the myelin sheaths of the body, causing symptoms similar to those in multiple sclerosis. Though Lorenzo's oil does not cure the condition, it can delay the onset or progression of the disease in those who are not yet symptomatic. This is a powerful example of how oils can be used to prevent disease.

Oleic acid can be found in olive oil, peanut oil, avocado oil, beef tallow, chicken, eggs, butter, lard, and human milk. You may be wondering why beef tallow or lard, which are classified as saturated fats, would contain monounsaturated fats. This is because all fats and oils are combinations of different fatty acids. For instance, olive oil is more than 70 percent monounsaturated fatty acids and 16 percent saturated fatty acids. Remember, fats and oils are classified according to the dominant degree of saturation.

Polyunsaturated Fats

The most famous of the polyunsaturates are linolenic fatty acid (Omega-3) and linoleic fatty acid (Omega-6). Because your body cannot make these, they are called "essential," and they must be obtained from foods. These essential fatty acids are precursors for hormone-like substances known as *eicosanoids*, and *prostaglandins*, which are potent regulators of metabolism and play key roles in inflammation and immunity.

Molecularly, polyunsaturated fats are composed mostly of polyunsaturated fatty acids, ranging from 18 to 22 carbon lengths and have bends at the position of double bonds, which means that they do not pack together well; hence, they remain liquid even when refrigerated. Unpaired electrons at these double bonds are highly reactive and extremely unstable. When they are subjected to heat, light, oxygen, or water in extraction, processing, and cooking, free radicals form quickly. As a result, these fatty acids are unstable even at room temperature and should not be used in cooking.

Polyunsaturated oils that have been cold-pressed and packaged in dark containers are the safest choices because there will be less chance of exposure to heat, oxygen, and light, which damage the oil. These oils should be refrigerated and utilized soon after purchasing. Use them in salad dressings, smoothies, and other recipes that do not use heat.

Nutritional Nugget

The gummy residue in frying pans, cookie sheets, and salad bowls is the result of unhealthy polymers that form when polyunsaturates are not protected. Polymers are more like plastic than food and can be quite unhealthy. If you see such residue, you know your fat or oil is not holding up to heat and is most likely causing more harm than good.

There are *two* polyunsaturated fatty acids:

1. **Alpha Linolenic Acid (Omega-3):** Found in fish, such as salmon, anchovies, sardines, tuna, and halibut, other seafood including algae and krill, and in walnuts and flax seed oils. Eggs, beef, lamb, chicken, and meat also contain small amounts of Omega-3 fatty acids, especially if the animal is grass fed. This fatty acid is a precursor for polyunsaturated fatty acids EPA and DHA.

2. **Linoleic Acid (Omega-6):** This polyunsaturated fat is one you don't need to go out of your way to get. Nuts and seeds, and oils extracted from them, are excellent sources of linoleic acid, and the typical American diet tends to contain 14 to 25 times more Omega-6 fatty acids than Omega-3 fatty acids, typically (and unfortunately) from refined oils and processed foods.

It's important to emphasize that while Omega-3 fatty acids help reduce inflammation, most Omega-6 fatty acids tend to promote inflammation. Reducing the amount of Omega-6 fatty acids from refined oils and processed foods can dramatically decrease inflammation and impact health in positive ways.

The Mediterranean diet has a healthy balance between Omega-3 and Omega-6 fatty acids, and emphasizes foods rich in Omega-3 fatty acids, as well as fresh fruits, vegetables, olive oil, garlic, and whole grains. Many studies have shown that people who follow this diet are less likely to develop heart disease than those who do not follow the same diet.[6] This difference is because the Omega-3 and Omega-6 fatty acids are in balance. Symptoms of essential fatty acid deficiency include fatigue, poor memory, dry skin, heart problems, mood swings or depression, and poor circulation.

With all the fears of a high-fat diet, you may find it surprising that Inuit Eskimos, who get high amounts of Omega-3 fatty acids from eating large quantities of fatty fish, tend to have increased HDL cholesterol (the good cholesterol) and decreased triglycerides[7] (fats in the blood). Large population studies suggest that Omega-3 fatty acids in the diet, primarily from fish, help protect against stroke caused by plaque buildup and blood clots in the arteries that lead to the brain.[8] Eating at least two servings of fish per week may reduce the risk of stroke by as much as 50 percent!

Baked Whole Fish in Thai Garlic-Chili Sauce

Serves: 4
Total Time: 45 minutes

Ingredients

- 2 whole fresh and cleaned red snapper, gray mullet, or trout
- ¾ cup tamari soy sauce
- 2 tablespoons Worcestershire sauce
- 12 cloves garlic, chopped
- 1 tablespoon fresh minced ginger
- 2 tablespoons fish sauce
- ½ teaspoon black pepper
- 3 tablespoons fresh lime juice
- 2 red chilies, sliced (more or less can be used, depending on how spicy you'd like your fish)
- Tin foil and banana leaves
- 1 cup loosely packed cilantro
- 1 cup loosely packed fresh basil
- 8 lime wedges for serving

Directions

1. Preheat oven to 375°F. Place fish on a cutting board and score it by making vertical cuts 1-2 inches or more apart along the length of fish, from head to tail. Turn fish over and do the same on the other side.

2. Combine the next 8 ingredients through red chilies together in a bowl.

3. Place banana leaf on a large piece of tin foil on a baking sheet. Make sure the leaf is big enough to wrap the fish. Place fish in the center of the banana leaf. Drizzle half of the marinade over each fish, covering both sides. Be sure to spoon some into the cuts you've made, as well as into the cavity. Reserve the rest for later. Fold the sides and ends of the leaf over fish to cover it. You want the leaf to come into contact with the

fish, as this adds to the flavor. Place fish in the oven and bake at 375°F for 25 minutes or longer, depending on the size of your fish. Remove fish from oven and check some of the deeper cuts to see whether inner flesh is cooked. It should be opaque, not pink or translucent-looking. Remove fish from oven and open up the banana leaves.

4. Pour remaining sauce over fish and return to the oven. Turn oven to "Broil" setting and broil for 5-8 minutes, or until the fish is nicely browned and crisp-looking. Banana leaves will become quite brown and fragrant. To serve, arrange fresh cilantro and basil on a platter. Place fish on the bed of herbs and garnish with lime wedges.

Fortunately, this essential fat is easy to incorporate into the diet, and the great thing about fish is that a little goes a long way. Two servings per week, or one teaspoon of oil a day, is all you need. Any higher amounts may increase the risk of bleeding; it packs that powerful a punch. While I always recommend trying to get your nutrients from food, there are situations where supplementation is appropriate. If your doctor has recommended fish oil supplementation for you, look for a brand that guarantees the product is mercury-free. As with any supplement, it should only be taken under the supervision of a qualified health care provider.

Omega-3 polyunsaturated fatty acids from whole food sources are very *Good Decisions.*

Trans Fats

Very small amounts of naturally occurring trans fatty acids can be found in ruminant animals, but the majority of trans fats come from partially-hydrogenated vegetable oils. These rearranged fatty acids are produced by bombarding polyunsaturated oils with hydrogen in a process called partial hydrogenation. This process makes the normal bending polyunsaturated fatty acids straighten out and behave like saturated fats in foods (turns an oil into a solid fat). This transformed fat is used to replace the so-called "bad" saturated fats, such as butter, often used in baking.

Mixing butter with sugar and flour creates delightful cookies, pastries, and cakes, but when you try to replace the solid butterfat with a "healthy" vegetable oil, the results are less than impressive. In response, manufacturers found a way around it by creating their version of "healthy" fats. These manmade fats are cheaper to produce, have a longer shelf life, and last indefinitely. Think about a Twinkie for a moment and you will get a feel for the nutritional value of trans fats. These fats are also treated with chemicals and have many additives to increase flavor and texture. Trans fats are processed to the point that, in some cases, bugs won't even touch them! Because trans fats can be made cheaply, the product ended the need for nutrient-dense, stable tropical oils and animal fats. No one ever hunted a Ding Dong or gathered a Twinkie, and if a bug won't touch margarine or Crisco, why should I? The studies now show these fats to be anything but healthy.

Nutritional Nugget

People are often surprised to find that foods provide more nutrients than a supplement. For instance, supplemental Omega-3 fatty acids from fish usually provide 1,000 mg of Omega-3. One three-ounce piece of Atlantic wild salmon contains 1,716 mg of Omega-3 fatty acids. One ounce of walnut halves contains roughly 2,565mg of Omega-3 fatty acids, and one tablespoon of ground flax seeds provides 1,600 mg!

In the *Nurse's Health Study*,[9] women who consumed the greatest amount of trans fats had a 50 percent higher risk of heart attack, compared to women who consumed the smallest amount of trans fats. Some researchers suspect that trans fats increase blood levels of two other artery-clogging compounds as well: a fat-protein particle called lipoprotein (a) and blood fats called triglycerides.[10] Other studies indicate that trans fats may also raise the risk of diabetes. Researchers at the Harvard School of Public Health suggest that replacing trans fats with polyunsaturated fats (such as the fat in salmon) can reduce diabetes risk by as much as 40 percent.[11]

Good Decisions recommends avoiding trans fats like the plague.

You will find these fats in foods such as baked goods, some frozen foods, margarine, chips, mayonnaise, fries, and a host of other processed foods. Numerous studies have shown that trans fatty acids adversely affect blood sugar regulation,[12] coronary heart disease,[13] obesity,[14] infertility,[15] and depression.[16] In response to the public outcry and adverse publicity about trans fats, some manufacturers are eliminating them from their products and replacing them with stable palm oil, which is certainly a step in the right direction, but considering the large body of evidence that trans fats cause disease, it is surprising that so many products still contain it.

In 2005, the Institute of Medicine of the National Academy of Sciences concluded that there is no safe level of trans fat in the diet, and that trans fats are not essential and provide no known benefits to human health.[17] In 2004, an FDA advisory panel concluded that trans fat is more harmful than saturated fats.[18]

Walter Willett is one of the most prolific medical and health researchers of modern times, having published more than 700 scientific papers, as well as a popular book titled *Eat, Drink and Be Healthy*.[19] In 2003, he was awarded the Linus Pauling Institute Prize for Health Research, which recognizes excellence in the field of orthomolecular medicine.[20] Willett once advised consumers to switch from butter to margarine. In a PBS interview in January 2004, he said:

> Unfortunately, as a physician back in the 1980s, I was telling people that they should replace butter with margarine because it was cholesterol free, and professional organizations like the American Heart Association were telling us as physicians that we should be promoting this. In reality, there was never any evidence that these margarines, that were high in trans fat, were any better than butter, and as it turned out, they were actually far worse than butter.

In 2003 Stephen Joseph, a public interest lawyer, created controversy when he filed a lawsuit to make food giant Kraft remove trans fats from its Oreo cookies, which are made by Kraft's subsidiary Nabisco. Just one day after the media coverage about the lawsuit began, Kraft announced that it would reduce or eliminate trans fat in Oreos and hundreds of other products.[21]

Joseph formed BanTransFats as a not-for-profit organization, with himself as President and Chief Executive Officer, and trans fat expert Mary Enig, Ph.D. as consultant. Enig's book, *Know Your Fats,*[22] is a must-have for anyone who wants to know more about fats. An expert in fat research—she is co-founder, vice president, and board-member of the Weston A. Price Foundation (WAPF)—Enig has been a champion for coconut oil and other saturated fats that have been given a bad rap. I highly recommend *Know Your Fats*.

The most common oils that go through hydrogenation are vegetable oils, canola oil, and soybean oil. So, when you are standing in the grocery store aisle in front of the huge selections of oils, be sure to avoid these. Trans fats are listed as "partially hydrogenated oil" among the ingredients on labels and are not *Good Decisions.*

Other Noteworthy Fats

Conjugated Linoleic Fatty Acid (CLA)

CLA is formed in the rumen (stomach) of ruminant animals and should ideally be obtained through animal sources. CLA is known for its weight management properties, which include reducing body fat and increasing lean muscle mass.[23] Yes, another fatty acid that is both satiating AND helps with weight loss.

Anticancer properties have also been attributed to CLA, and studies on mice and rats show encouraging results in hindering the growth of tumors in mammary, skin, and colon tissues.[24] Meat, eggs, and dairy products are a significant source of CLA, especially if the animals have been grass-fed. In fact, meat and dairy products from grass-fed animals can produce 300-500 percent more CLA than those of cattle fed the usual diet of 50 percent hay and silage and 50 percent grain.[25]

Small amounts of CLA are found in safflower oil and some vegetable oils. In supplemental form, this is isolated and extracted and not as stable or reliable as CLA consumed directly from dairy or meat products.

CLA obtained from food delivers fat-soluble vitamins as well as protein and other cofactors that may enhance absorption of CLA, so food-based CLA has a greater impact. Many people afraid of fat may hesitate to incorporate cream in their diets, but consider this: studies done with CLA show promise for use in weight loss because the satiation experienced when one consumes only a small amount of fat may decrease appetite.

This means that it may decrease the desire and potential to overeat. When your body gets what it needs, it sends a satiation signal to your brain that says, "Okay, I'm done!"

Nutritional Nugget

Instead of a 1,500-milligram supplement of CLA that typically contains undesirable ingredients such as artificial coloring, consider two tablespoons of organic or raw cream, which is equal to almost 2,000 milligrams of CLA. This is another good example of how food can pack a much bigger nutritional punch than supplementation!

Cream, butter, eggs, and meat products—consumed in small amounts—can have a significant impact on weight loss, cancer prevention, and immune enhancement—and they taste delicious!

All this may seem challenging because it's counter to what we have been taught all these years. The edible oil industry and food manufacturers bombard us every day, touting the health benefits of certain low fat or processed foods that are anything but healthy, and hydrogenated fats and low fat products have been part of that hype.

Fat Replacements

New fat replacements are coming into the marketplace. Food engineers can be very creative and are using carbohydrate and protein- and lipid-based products to create something that tastes like fat, functions like fat, but is *nothing* like fat. These products are called *lipid analogues*. With all the new information about the adverse health effects of trans fat, we will likely see an increase of these new engineered foods in the future.

Cholesterol

With all this talk about fat, you may be thinking, "But what about cholesterol? If I incorporate more fat in my diet, won't my cholesterol levels go up?" The answer is no, as long as you don't eat more than your body needs. Remember the exercise in Chapter 6 with the French fries? Increasing your awareness of, and waiting for the satiation signal to tell you when your body has had enough will stop you from over-consuming.

Fat is also used mostly in salad dressings and in cooking where it accents the meal more so than dominates it. So don't use the health benefits of fats and oils as a license to go crazy! The key concept here is *quality* fats in *small* amounts.

Let's learn more about cholesterol and its many functions in the body so we won't be so afraid of it.

No-Crust Mushroom Quiche with Baby Greens and Cucumber Vinaigrette

Serves: 8
Total Time: 1 hour, 20 minutes

Ingredients

For the Cucumber Vinaigrette:

Serves: 8
Total Time: 1 hour, 20 minutes

Ingredients

For the Cucumber Vinaigrette:

- ¼ cup orange flavored vinegar
- 1 tablespoon Dijon mustard
- ½ cup peeled, seeded, and minced cucumber
- Unrefined sea salt to taste
- 4 tablespoons expeller pressed walnut oil

For the Quiche:

- 2 tablespoons organic butter
- 1 pound oyster mushrooms, sliced
- 1 pound white mushrooms thinly sliced
- 2 shallots
- 1 tablespoon fresh chopped thyme
- 12 large eggs
- Salt and pepper to taste
- Pinch of nutmeg
- 6 cups tightly packed baby greens

Directions

1. Whisk together vinegar, mustard, cucumber, and salt until well-combined and salt is dissolved. Whisk in oil adding a little bit at a time. Refrigerate.

2. Preheat oven to 350°F. Coat a round cake pan lightly with butter. In a large skillet, heat the butter. Add the oyster and white mushrooms, season with salt and pepper, and cook over medium heat, stirring, until starting to soften, about 7 minutes. Add the shallots and thyme and cook, stirring often, until the mushrooms are tender, about 12 minutes longer. Season with salt and pepper and let cool.

3. In a blender, mix eggs, salt, pepper, and a pinch of nutmeg at high speed until frothy, about 1 minute. Scatter half of the mushroom mixture over the bottom of the cake pan. Pour the egg mixture on top of the mushrooms and top with remaining mushrooms. Bake quiche for 1 hour, or until richly browned on top and the custard is barely set in the center. Let cool.

4. Toss baby greens with cucumber vinaigrette to coat. Cut quiche into 8 wedges and place one wedge on each plate. Serve with ½ cup baby greens.

Functions of Cholesterol in the Body

Cholesterol Helps Maintain Healthy Cell Membranes

Cell membranes are primarily composed of fats. Cholesterol gives these membranes structure and helps maintain cellular integrity. This membrane acts as a barrier that prevents damaging substances from getting into cells and moves waste products out of the cell. Many diseases occur when there is a problem or malfunction with the membrane's ability to regulate this process. A neurodegenerative condition such as Alzheimer's is only one of these diseases. Think of it this way: poor-quality fats and not enough cholesterol make poor-quality membranes. When you consider every tissue and every organ in your body is composed of trillions of cells, this is a big deal.

Growth and Metabolism

Cholesterol is so important for growth and metabolism that 70 percent of mother's milk is cholesterol. For years, baby formula has been made with coconut oil for just this reason.

Hormones (the Body's Chemical Messengers)

The body uses cholesterol to make hormones, which serve as the body's chemical messengers. For instance, the body uses cholesterol to make the sex hormones estrogen and testosterone. A deficiency in cholesterol would also mean a deficiency in these important hormones, which could impact one's ability to enjoy healthy sexual function.

Vitamin D

The body uses cholesterol for making vitamin D and other vital compounds. Since foods rich in vitamin D are also rich in cholesterol, low cholesterol diets are inherently deficient in vitamin D. Sunlight is also required to turn cholesterol into vitamin D, so avoiding the sun will also undermine your ability to synthesize vitamin D.

It's absolutely incredible how fast adequate levels of vitamin D can be restored by sunlight. The human skin produces approximately 10,000 IU of vitamin D in response to 10-30 minutes of summer sun exposure. That's more than 16 times your daily requirement for vitamin D. Even better, six days of 10-30 minutes of sunlight exposure, without sunscreen, can make up for forty-nine days of no sunlight exposure. As your skin gets darker, it produces less vitamin D and you can stay out longer without burning. Sunning yourself for 10-30 minutes is generally recognized as a safe way to obtain more than adequate amounts of vitamin D, but remember, cholesterol is needed for the conversion of sunlight to vitamin D.

Nutritional Nugget

When having trouble sleeping, try this Ayurvedic night cap. In a small saucepan over medium heat, combine ¼ teaspoon ground poppy seeds, ¼ teaspoon ground nutmeg, and 6-8 ounces half and half. Bring to a simmer. Drink 4 hours before bed. The poppy seeds will help you fall asleep; the nutmeg works to keep you asleep, and the half and half will give your body the cholesterol it needs to make important sleep hormones!

Bile Acids

One of the major uses of cholesterol is the production of bile acids, which are synthesized in the liver from cholesterol and are secreted in bile to emulsify fat and aid the absorption of fat in the intestine. A clue to the importance of cholesterol is that most of the bile acids are not excreted with the feces, but are reabsorbed from the lower intestine and recycled back to the liver.

As your intake of cholesterol-rich foods decreases, your body will increase its own production of cholesterol. Likewise, when you consume more cholesterol-rich foods, your body produces less of its own cholesterol. This checks and balances system shows that cholesterol is so important that your body will do what is necessary to ensure adequate amounts.

Blood cholesterol levels are used as a marker for coronary heart disease. When someone has high blood cholesterol levels, it serves as a sign to look at the diet and make some changes. Cholesterol levels in food, however, are not always connected to the levels of cholesterol in the blood.

I find the amount of sugar and sweets in a diet to be strongly linked to high cholesterol levels. When I have a client with a high cholesterol level, we can usually get it under control within a few weeks simply by reducing and eliminating the amount of sweets in his or her diet.

So that bacon-wrapped scallop or asparagus really isn't the enemy we thought it was!

Bacon-Wrapped Cod with Bitter Greens

Serves: 4
Total Time: 35 minutes

Ingredients

For Dressing:

- 1 tablespoon Dijon mustard
- 1 tablespoon raw honey
- 2 tablespoons apple cider vinegar
- 1 cup fresh squeezed pink grapefruit juice
- ½ cup extra-virgin olive oil

For Cod:

- 1 skinless, boneless cod fillet (1¼ pounds and 1½ inches thick)
- Unrefined sea salt and fresh ground pepper
- 3 tablespoons fresh chopped sage
- 12 strips nitrate free organic bacon
- 3 cups mixed bitter greens (radicchio, frisée, arugula)
- 1 cup grapefruit segments

Directions

1. Whisk together mustard, honey, vinegar, and grapefruit juice. Season dressing with salt and pepper. Gradually whisk in oil and refrigerate.

2. Wash and pat dry fish, cut into 4 pieces and season with salt and pepper and fresh sage. On a work surface, arrange 3 slices bacon so they overlap slightly. Place a piece of fish at one short end and tightly wrap with bacon, cutting off any excess bacon. Repeat with remaining fish and bacon. Heat a large nonstick pan over medium-high. Place fish, bacon seam side down, in pan and cook until bacon is deep golden brown on all sides, about 9 minutes, turning occasionally.

3. Toss greens with dressing and grapefruit segments and serve with fish.

Cholesterol and Lipoproteins

Fat and cholesterol do not dissolve in water or blood. The body gets around this basic chemistry problem by packaging fat and cholesterol into tiny, protein-covered particles called *lipoproteins*. Lipoproteins can carry quite a bit of fat, and they mix easily with blood and flow with it. Some of these particles are big and fluffy, while others are small and dense. The most prominent lipoproteins are low-density lipoproteins and high-density lipoproteins.

Low-Density Lipoproteins (LDL)

LDL carry cholesterol from the liver to the rest of the body. Cells latch onto these particles and extract fat and cholesterol from them when they need it. When there is too much LDL cholesterol in the blood, these particles can form deposits called *plaque* in the walls of arteries throughout the body, resulting in narrowing the arteries and limiting blood flow. When plaque breaks apart, it can cause a heart attack or stroke. Because of this, LDL cholesterol is often referred to as *bad*, or harmful, cholesterol.

High-Density Lipoproteins (HDL)

Think of HDL as the garbage trucks of the bloodstream. HDL scavenges cholesterol from the bloodstream, from LDL, and from artery walls, then ferries it back to the liver for disposal. HDL cholesterol is often referred to as *good*, or protective, cholesterol.

In general, the lower your LDL and the higher your HDL, the better your chances of preventing heart disease and other chronic conditions.

Triglycerides

Triglycerides are a type of fat that circulates in your blood. Triglycerides store unused calories in fat cells and provide your body with energy. Because triglycerides (and cholesterol) can't dissolve in blood, they circulate throughout your body with the help of lipoproteins.

Triglycerides are essential for robust health, but an excess of triglycerides can be unhealthy. Foods high in sugar or overconsumption of fat or consumption of trans fats will cause the body to produce more triglycerides. Even a small amount of alcohol can cause a significant increase in triglyceride levels.

High levels of triglycerides are linked to atherosclerosis, heart disease, and strokes. Diets high in simple and refined carbohydrates, with carbohydrates accounting for more than 60 percent of the total energy intake, can increase triglyceride levels.[26]

In my practice, I've found that when clients remove refined carbohydrates and sugar, and incorporate vegetables and quality proteins, triglyceride and cholesterol levels often return to normal within a week or two.

How Are Fats Extracted?

Like carbohydrates and proteins, it is not enough to say that certain fats are *Good Decisions* without looking at how the fat is processed and refined. Making *Good Decisions* regarding fats requires looking at several factors. One of the factors to consider is how the fat or oil is extracted from its source.

Wet or Dry Rendering of Animal Fats

Animal fats are separated from fatty tissues by wet or dry rendering. In wet rendering, the fatty tissue is heated under steam pressure, thus rupturing the cells and liberating the fat.

In dry rendering, the fatty tissue is heated and agitated in jacketed drums until the fats are released. Centrifuges are used to separate the fat from water and protein. Animal fats can then be processed many ways, including filtering, bleaching, hydrogenation, and emulsification. This processing is done to improve shelf life and stability as well as to make the oil look "pretty."

Animal fats are easy to render at home. Simply cooking the animal protein will render a good deal of fat that can be collected for later use. Professional chefs prize bacon fat and duck fat as a way to add richness and flavor to many dishes. When these fats are unrefined, they are rich in fat soluble nutrients and arachidonic acid (one of the most abundant fatty acids in the brain), as well as choline (essential for the construction of healthy cell membranes) and cholesterol.

I'll bet you never thought a nutritional therapist would be telling you to eat bacon fat! Remember, the key word here: *small* amounts. As with fish oils, a small amount is sufficient. Animal fats are exceptional *Good Decisions*—when unrefined—and a smart way to add flavor and nutrients to a dish. A pat of butter here, a teaspoon of duck or bacon fat there, and a little coconut oil on your oatmeal will not do anyone any harm. In fact, as studies continue to show, they are turning out to be quite healthy.

Butter is an animal fat made by churning cream until the fats separate from the liquid (buttermilk), and the butter is in a semisolid state. Making butter is fun to do with kids. In fact, it is still done today in some schools to show kids where butter comes from.

Plant Extraction Methods

Plant fat extraction procedures are more complex and involve a variety of extraction methods. Some of these methods have been used for generations. Others methods have come a long way through new technologies and, while they may make a useful product, may not always be suitable for us.

The following terminology will help you in the grocery store when it comes to making *Good Decisions* about fats and oils and interpreting their labels.

Expeller-Pressed

Expeller pressing is a chemical-free process in which the nut or seed is pressed to force the oil out mechanically, which is why many expeller-pressed oils are expensive. Expeller pressing extracts about 75 percent of the oil and the quality of these oils is exceptional. This method creates a certain amount of heat, and stable fats and oils such as saturated fats (coconut oil) and monounsaturated fats (olive oil), can be extracted using this method. However, this method may not be appropriate for polyunsaturated fats, which are less heat stable.

After the first pressing, there are two processes used to extract the remaining oil from the source or when extracting oil from harder nuts, seeds, or kernels. First, the expeller-pressed method may be used again, or an extraction method may be used in combination with a chemical such as hexane. This substance can cause neurological damage. To avoid it, simply choose oils that have been expeller-pressed instead of solvent-extracted.

Cold-Pressed

Cold pressing is the process of expeller pressing in a heat-controlled environment. To be considered a cold-pressed process, the temperature must remain below 120°F, which prevents the more delicate oils from deteriorating. When purchasing unstable, delicate polyunsaturated oils, such as flax seed oil, it is best to choose oil that has been extracted using cold-press methods.

If you don't see "expeller" or "cold-pressed" on the label, you can assume the oil is solvent-extracted, which involves using a chemical solvent such as hexane, and heat up to 500°F. The result is a less healthy, bland-tasting oil. Also, when you see "cold-pressed" or "expeller-pressed" oils, even in health food stores, it refers to *how* the oil was extracted. It says nothing about *how much* the oil has been refined. Just because you see the word expeller-pressed, it doesn't necessarily mean it has the same benefits as *unrefined* expeller-pressed oils.

Solvent-Extraction

Remember the expeller-press method that removes around 70 percent of the oil? Well, the "cake" that is left over still contains oil, which can be further extracted with the use of solvents. The byproducts of these methods are used to feed animals in feedlots. As you may guess, the flavor and nutritional value of these oils is inferior. The solvent-extraction method produces clear oil, free from rancidity and foreign matter, which is great for shelf life, but not as good for your health.

Solvent-extracted oils are *not Good Decisions.*

Virgin Oil

Virgin is an extraction term used mostly in the coconut and olive oil industry. It refers to an oil product pressed and extracted by purely mechanical means. In comparison, non-virgin oils may come from dried coconut meat, seed, and olive cakes, which are solvent-extracted utilizing chemicals.

Extra Virgin Oil

This term is most often used in the olive oil industry; *extra virgin* doesn't actually refer to the extraction process, but the level of acidity in oil. According to the International Olive Oil Council (IOOC), extra virgin olive oil should come only from virgin oil production and contain no more than 0.8 percent acidity. During the extraction process, no chemicals should be used. Extra-virgin olive oil should be cold-pressed, which means that no heat above a certain temperature is used during processing.

When you purchase olive oil, the "extra virgin" label should denote a better quality product and, typically, a higher price. The reason you are seeing so many *shoulds* under this term is because there are no federal rules that define what is—or is not—"virgin" or "extra virgin" oil, making these two terms less than reliable.

So if you see the terms "virgin" or "extra virgin" on a bottle of any oil, it may or may not indicate a higher quality product.

How Are Fats and Oils Refined?

After fats and oils are extracted, they may go through many levels of refinement.

Unrefined Oils

Unrefined oil is only lightly filtered after it is extracted to remove large particles. These oils can often be identified by a cloudy appearance with visible sediment on the bottom of the bottle when it has been sitting. Olive oil and some sesame oils often have this sediment. This doesn't compromise quality at all; in fact, quite the opposite is true. Unrefined oils are considered "whole" oils, and their color, flavor, and smell are more pronounced than in refined oils. Unrefined oils are more nutritious, but they have a shorter storage life than refined oils and need to be handled with some care.

Unrefined oils are best in salad dressings or when cooking at low to medium temperatures because their natural resins and other beneficial particles burn easily and can create unpleasant flavors and unhealthful properties if overheated. Remember that gummy residue I mentioned earlier?

Unrefined oils are fabulous and have a rich flavor that is distinct, which is why these oils are prized by many chefs. Unrefined oils carry the true bouquet of olives, sesame seeds, peanuts, or whatever plant was the oil's original form, and the strong flavors of these oils can dominate whatever dish is made with them. In some cases, unrefined oils are added to dishes after they are done to protect their flavor and integrity. Unrefined oil contains a full range of bioactive constituents that are responsible for many healthy benefits. As a rule of thumb, when an oil has a strong, natural flavor and aroma, it also has a higher nutritional value.

If you notice oils are a bit cloudy, have a rich aroma, dark color, and deep flavor, you can treat them like the treasures they are—very *Good Decisions!*

Refined Oils

There are different levels of refining that the oil or fat may go through after extraction. Naturally-refined oils are more thoroughly filtered and strained than are unrefined oils. Sometimes additional heat is utilized, but without harsh or damaging chemicals. Refining clarifies the oil, which makes it look more clear and appetizing, but filters out nutrient-rich particles and reduces the oil's flavor. However, by removing particles and resins, naturally-refined oils become more stable so they can be stored longer and are more resistant to spoiling.

Regardless of how the fat or oil has been extracted, most refined oils go through many steps in the refinement process, which may include one or all of the following methods:

Degumming

Degumming is the first step in the refining process of many oils. It is done to prevent gum deposits in the oil from fermenting, which decreases shelf life. Many methods are used to de-gum; some use water, acid, or other substances to prepare the oil for further processing. Phosphoric or citric acid or silica gel are often added to enhance this process, which produces the commercial emulsifier lecithin.

Alkali Refining

The degummed oil may be further treated with an alkali to remove free fatty acids, glycerol, carbohydrates, resins, metals, phosphatides, and protein meal. The oil and alkali are mixed, allowing free fatty acids and alkali to form soap. The soap is then removed through centrifuging. Any residual soap is removed with hot water washings. This is done to remove Free Fatty Acids (FFA) responsible for the acidity of the oil.

Nutritional Nugget

Does your stomach get upset when you eat fatty foods? The gallbladder (a small organ just below your liver) must release sufficient amounts of bile in order for fats to be properly emulsified and utilized. If this bile becomes thick and sluggish, fat absorption and utilization is impaired, and you may experience an upset tummy or even nausea when you eat fatty foods. What to do? Beets, beet juice, lemon, and dandelion greens are wonderful foods that thin the bile and support the liver and gallbladder.

Bleaching

Trace metals, color bodies such as chlorophyll, soaps, and oxidation products from previous steps are removed using bleaching clays, which absorb the impurities. Bleached oils are nearly colorless. Bleaching is done to remove substances, which can affect the look and taste of the oil. Canola (rapeseed) oil goes through this process to remove the green color due to the presence of chlorophylls, and to moderate the distinctive taste of the oil that was unacceptable in the 1950s.

Depending on the finished product, oils may be then subjected to one or more of the following four processes:

Fractionation

Also known as *winterization*, some oils, such as salad oils or oils that are to be stored in cool places, may undergo this process so they will not become cloudy when chilled. The refined, deodorized oils are chilled with gentle agitation, which causes higher melting fractions to precipitate. The fraction that settles out is called *stearin*.

Nutritional Nugget

How do you know whether oil has gone bad? Smell the oil. If it's rancid, the yummy richness will have turned to a crayon-like, bitter yuck that is easily discernible.

Hydrogenation

The treatment of fats and oils with hydrogen gas in the presence of a catalyst results in the addition of hydrogen to form a carbon-carbon double bond. This bond produces trans fats, those not-so-good fats we discussed earlier. Hydrogenation of unsaturated fats and oils increases their melting points and hardness. This process is often used to produce shortenings, which are generally defined as plastic materials made wholly from fats and oils. Hardness can be controlled by varying the ratio of solid to liquid glycerides.

Deodorization

Deodorization is a steam distillation process carried out in a vacuum. It removes volatile compounds from the oil, resulting in bland oil with a low level of free fatty acids, which is more stable. This step also removes any residual pesticides or metabolites that might be present. Deodorization produces some of the purest food products available, and, unfortunately, the least nutritional or tasty. Few products are as thoroughly clean as refined, bleached, and deodorized oil.

Lard Interesterification

Interesterification is often done within the oil industry to produce standardized oils that may be blended with other oils for use in margarine and cooking fat. This process is most often accomplished by catalytic methods at low temperatures: the oil is heated at 90°C, agitated, and mixed with the catalyst (to speed up the process). It does not change the degree of saturation of the fatty acids, but it is said to improve the functional properties of the oil, which means that the resulting oil will be more stable when heated and have a longer shelf life.

Refined fats and oils are not *Good Decisions.*

The Bottom Line on Fats

Refined oils and hydrogenated fats are not healthy.

Saturated fats found in animal products such as beef, pork, and duck are not the villains they have been portrayed to be.

In *small* amounts, quality fats and oils provide the body with many valuable nutrients needed to support optimal health. Good old-fashioned butter, unrefined coconut oil, olive oil, walnut oil, and other unrefined oils are not bad for you. They bring flavor and nutrients to a dish and will be more satiating than a meal without fat.

Quality fats are defined as *unrefined, non-hydrogenated, cold pressed,* or *expeller pressed* oils and fats.

Again, this doesn't mean you should go crazy with fats; while I have used bacon and other fats in recipes to make the point that cholesterol and saturated fats are not the villains they have been portrayed to be, common sense should still be used and fats consumed in small amounts as accents to your diet to provide nutrients, satiation, and flavor.

Nutritional Nugget

Do you have light or gray-colored stools? Bile gives stools the brown pigment. If bile production is inadequate, thick, or sluggish, your stools will be light or gray in color. This means your ability to use fats may be impaired. If left unchecked, this impairment can result in essential fatty acid deficiency. What to do? Remove or decrease consumption of hydrogenated or deep fried foods, refined foods, and processed foods, and start reaching for high-fiber foods, beets, lemons, dandelion greens, and Omega-3 fatty acids in small amounts.

The Psychology of Food

Your Dopamine Center

Dopamine is a neurotransmitter that plays a powerful role in controlling the brain's reward and pleasure centers. When you eat something sweet or highly pleasurable, the sensation travels up to your brain to your dopamine center and tickles it! Your brain giggles (simplified terms here) and likes it very much, so it releases dopamine, which imprints the experience as "important" and creates a lasting memory of it. This sensation is pleasurable, so dopamine will command the brain to "Do it again!" Like a child who wants to be swung around by a parent, dopamine heightens the possibility of taking one more bite, even after the satiation signal has told you to stop!

"Interestingly, dopamine is not just a messenger that dictates what feels good; it also tells the brain what is important and what to pay attention to in order to survive. And the more powerful the experience is, the stronger the message is to the brain to repeat the activity for survival."[27] This means certain individuals who don't have anything exciting in their lives may be more vulnerable to things that give them a dopamine rush. Food can be one of those things.

This rush explains how someone can become so addicted to food that it can be detrimental to his or her health. It also explains why exercise, yoga, massage, and acupuncture can be helpful tools in the fight against addiction; they can help to create a new healthy dopamine-tickling activity that causes the memory of old activities to fade over time. These activities also create a new set of experiences for the brain to register as important and pleasurable.

Practicing Good Decisions

Finding New Ways to Tickle Your Dopamine Center

Your next homework assignment involves a little personal contemplation. Sit down and think about what unhealthy foods tickle your dopamine center. Then find a healthier replacement and see whether it can elicit the same response. For instance, if you love sugary desserts, substitute a roasted pear for cake. Wait until you are very hungry to eat the pear, and when you do eat it, eat it slowly and enjoy it thoroughly. Were you able to get the same dopamine reaction as a slice of cake?

Finding substitutions, healthy ways to tickle your dopamine center, dulls your memory of unhealthy foods and lessens the compulsion to overeat or eat unhealthy items. You can also replace food with activities you enjoy, but haven't participated in lately. Art, music, exercise, or even a class at the community college can help you feel excitement toward life and therefore reduce dopamine's ability to drive you.

Other things to keep in mind about dopamine:

- Exercise increases dopamine levels; incorporating a brisk 20-minute walk at the same time every day can have dramatic effects.
- Stress can make you more prone to relapse. Avoid stress whenever possible.
- Reward yourself once a week with a food you really desire.
- Practice, practice, practice finding new healthy ways to tickle your dopamine center.
- Increase your awareness of your dopamine center and what it feels like when it is tickled.
- Be patient; it will take time for the old memories to fade.
- Create a new routine. The same activity at the same time of day creates a habit the brain recognizes; this in itself can be a tickle that the mind will enjoy.

Making *Good Decisions…Most of the Time* will naturally promote the fading of old memories and patterns. As your cravings for certain foods go away, it will become easier and more enjoyable to walk down your hallway of life toward improved health. As you choose fruit over sugar, home-cooked meals over fast food, and nuts over potato chips, your body will begin to heal and your mind will adapt to a more vibrant and alive lifestyle.

Chapter Nine

Cooking with Fats and Oils

Now that you know how fats and oils can be extracted and refined, we can focus on why it is important to incorporate healthy fats into your diet and how they can be used to relieve pain, boost your immune system, and sharpen your mind. You will learn how fats can be used to prevent strokes and heart attacks, slow the progression of certain cancers, treat sexual phobias, and how they can be used as sexual tonics! Most importantly, the information in this chapter will give you greater clarity on how to cook with fats and oils so they don't go from being good, healthy decisions to rancid, not-so-good decisions. You will learn which fats and oils are best utilized at low, medium, and high temperatures and which oils should not be used for cooking at all. We will talk about beliefs and discover how you want to live your life relative to food and habits when we end with the psychology of food.

Almost all foods, even vegetables, contain some fat. Quality fats play many prominent roles in the body, so it's hard to believe we have limited our consumption of healthful fats for so long. Let's look at a few reasons why quality fats and oils are foundational to health and vitality.

Quality Fats and Oils
Building the Fourth Nutritional Foundation

When people talk about fats, the essential fatty acid Omega-3 steals the spotlight, and for good reason. But other unrefined fats are also extremely valuable and have much to contribute to the health and wellbeing of the body. In the past, we resisted fats because we were told for years that they will harm us. Today we have a much greater knowledge of fats and oils and how they play many essential roles in the body. Let's look at a few of these roles so we can become more comfortable with the idea of fats as foundational to our health and wellbeing.

Cell Membrane Structure and Function

Fat plays an essential role in how your cell membranes function. Think for a moment about how many cells you have in your body. It is estimated that there are over 50 trillion cells in the human body. Each of these cells has a membrane or cell wall made up of fat. When you don't consume enough fat, these membranes can become weak. If you over-consume hydrogenated fats, your body will have no choice but to make membranes out of this manmade compound. As a result, your body will create substandard cell membranes. Your cell membranes have an impact on what gets into and out of your cells, which is of paramount importance when it comes to nutrient absorption and metabolism. Incorporating quality fats into your diet contributes directly to the quality and health of your entire body and is absolutely foundational.

Inflammation

Some fats, such as hydrogenated fats, refined fats, and Omega-6 fatty acids, create inflammation; other fats, such as fish oil, walnut oil, and flax seed oil decrease inflammation. Controlling inflammation in the body is particularly valuable when it comes to treating heart disease, muscle and joint injuries, and inflammatory diseases such as arthritis, bronchitis, colitis, and tendinitis. Many people who have knee and joint issues think their problems are a result of getting older when inflammation is often the cause. Incorporating Omega-3 fats from salmon, sardines, and walnuts and decreasing processed foods can help keep inflammation to a minimum. These are the oils that can help prevent strokes and heart attacks.

The Brain

Your brain is 60 percent fat. Myelin, the fatty coating of the neurons (brain cells), is 75 percent fat. The composition of the fat in your brain is a direct reflection of the fat you consume in your diet. For example, if you consume a diet rich in saturated and unsaturated fats from tropical oils, meats, eggs, fish, nuts, seeds, and dairy, then your brain has the best possible nutrients. On the other hand, if you consume hydrogenated fats, refined fats, or fats that have gone rancid, then your brain will have no choice but to use these fats to make brain tissue, and the health of your brain may suffer. Doing nothing else but removing sugar and adding a small amount of quality fats to your diet will do wonders for increasing mental clarity and build the foundation for mental health.

The Heart

Fat is the preferred fuel for your heart. It's interesting to realize that for years we have been told to avoid fat for the heart's sake, but now we know the heart prefers to use fat as energy. Richard L. Veech of the National Institutes of Health has shown that the heart works 28 percent more efficiently using ketones (also known as ketone bodies) as fuel than it does using glucose.[1] *Ketones,* a product of fatty acid metabolism, are the result of the body burning fat for energy or fuel. You may remember from the last chapter that coconut oil is a marvelous source of ketones and, contrary to Western belief, improves HDL, the good cholesterol in your body.[2]

The role of Omega-3 fatty acids in cardiovascular disease is well-established. One of the best ways to help prevent heart disease is to eat foods that are rich in the monounsaturated and polyunsaturated fats mentioned in this book. Clinical evidence suggests that Omega-3 fatty acids, DHA, and EPA help reduce risk factors for heart disease, including high cholesterol and high blood pressure.[3] Fish oil has been shown to lower levels of triglycerides (fats in the blood) and to lower the risk of death, heart attack, stroke, and abnormal heart rhythms in people who have already had a heart attack. Fish oil also appears to help prevent and treat atherosclerosis (hardening of the arteries) by slowing the development of plaque and blood clots, which can clog arteries.[4]

Weight Loss

Unlike carbohydrates, which you could eat all day without ever feeling full, fats have the potential to stop the carnage, so to speak, and prevent binging. Have you ever gone on a vegetable diet or cleanse? By the second day, you are ready to rip someone's head off for a bowl of ice cream or a juicy steak. When you eat cream, butter, meat, or eggs, it doesn't take much to send you to the couch purring like the cat that ate the cream! Feeling satisfied is a marvelous sensation—so is enjoying your meals! Life is too short not to enjoy animal fats, tropical oils, and organic whole fat dairy products. You don't have to feel guilty when you consume these items. The great thing about fats is that a little goes a long way, and it doesn't take much foundational fat to make a dish taste great, deliver a powerful punch of nutrients, and make you feel satiated, which can prevent overeating and aid the weight loss process.

Skin and Hair

Fat helps maintain healthy skin and hair. When people practice *Good Decisions*, they report that their skin has improved, and their hair feels healthier than it has in years. Fat helps the body absorb and move vitamins A, D, E, and K through the bloodstream, all very beneficial for healthy skin and wrinkle prevention. But remember, it has to be the right fat—not any old fat will do.

Ghee, a type of clarified butter, has been used for centuries for healthy skin. In addition to using it in cooking, you can apply ghee topically after a shower. Same goes for coconut oil. These are much better options than chemically-laden lotions. Incorporating a little healthy fat into your diet daily can give skin and hair a healthy glow and prevent wrinkles!

Immunity

The medium-chain saturated fatty acids found in coconut oil and palm kernel oil have antimicrobial, antiviral, and antiprotozoal properties similar to the medium-chain fatty acids found in breast milk and can be invaluable when trying to boost immunity. These fatty acids keep the "bugs" at bay so your immune system can focus on other things. Butter is rich in conjugated linoleic fatty acid, which supports the immune system and also provides nutrients.

Energy

Fat is one of the three macronutrients (along with protein and carbohydrates) that supply energy in the form of calories to the body. Fat provides nine calories per gram, which is more than twice the number provided by carbohydrates or protein. Most people believe this is a bad thing. "Why should I consume fat when it will just give me more calories?" they wonder. But if you think of the nutrients the body gets from those calories that feed hormones, liven up the skin, and clarify the brain, then you understand why they are important. One hundred calories from coconut oil is a much better decision than 100 calories from sugar. One will feed the body nutrients it can use, while the other will head straight into storage—as fat.

Many people don't feel satiated when they eat certain carbohydrates. As a result, they keep eating, often ingesting so many calories that they feel full, but get only half the nutrients. Adding a little healthy fat to your oatmeal, salad dressing, and vegetables may add more calories, but this is not a bad thing when those calories are nutrient dense, taste delicious, and will give you more energy.

Diabetes

People with diabetes often have high triglyceride and low HDL levels. Omega-3 fatty acids from fish oil can help lower triglycerides and apoproteins (markers of diabetes) and raise HDL, so eating fish or taking fish oil supplements may help people with diabetes.[5]

Pain Relief

Most clinical studies examining Omega-3 fatty acid supplements for arthritis have focused on rheumatoid arthritis (RA), an autoimmune disease that causes inflammation in the joints. A number of studies have found that fish oil helps reduce symptoms of RA, including joint pain and morning stiffness.[6] One study suggests that people with RA who take fish oil may be able to lower their doses of non-steroidal anti-inflammatory drugs (NSAIDs).[7] An analysis of seventeen randomized, controlled clinical trials looked at the pain-relieving effects of Omega-3 fatty acid supplements in people with RA or joint pain caused by inflammatory bowel disease (IBS) and painful menstruation (dysmenorrhea). The results suggest that Omega-3 fatty acids, along with conventional therapies, such as NSAIDs, may help relieve joint pain associated with these conditions.[8] This means incorporating fish oil on a regular basis may be a valuable tool in pain management.

Attention Deficit/Hyperactivity Disorder (ADHD)

Too many refined carbohydrates and not enough essential fatty acids have been implicated in ADHD in adolescents. Getting kids off sugar and getting them to consume more quality natural fats, vegetables, and proteins can have an enormous impact on their behavior and ability to focus. Children with ADHD may have low levels of certain essential fatty acids (including EPA and DHA).[9] In a clinical study of nearly 100 boys, those with lower levels of Omega-3 fatty acids had more learning and behavioral problems (such as temper tantrums and sleep disturbances) than boys with normal Omega-3 fatty acid levels.[10,11] Fats are foundational to the growth and development of our children.

While the easiest way to get fish oils into your kids' diets may be supplementation, it is always best to get these nutrients from food sources such as salmon, halibut, sardines, walnuts, and freshly-ground flax seeds.

Incorporate a Variety of Fats into Your Diet

As you have seen, fats play many important roles in the body and are foundational to maintaining health and vitality. Different fats provide different health benefits so it is important to incorporate a variety of fats into your diet.

So, how much of this good stuff should you incorporate into your diet daily?

Nutritional Nugget

If you tend to get achy legs at night, try taking a fish oil capsule before bed. It thins the blood, increases circulation, and can ease leg pain or achiness associated with poor circulation. It's also easier on the tummy than aspirin!

Recommended Amounts of Foundational Fat

Good Decisions recommends consuming quality unrefined healthy fats and oils every day. Essential fatty acid deficiency is epidemic, so consuming adequate amounts of fish oils, walnut oils, and flax oils is very important when building and strengthening your nutritional foundations.

The amount varies depending on the person. It is good to reiterate: *everyone is different*. The amount and kind of fat that nutritional therapists recommend depends on age, sex, activity level, size, skin condition, brain function, and many other factors.

Typical serving sizes can vary from one teaspoon to two tablespoons under certain conditions. A little bit of fat goes a long way and you will find if you utilize oils in your salad dressings and fats to cook your food, you will be consuming adequate amounts to meet your body's needs.

Nutritional Nugget

Fat is one of the cleanest burning fuel sources for the body. When burned for energy, fat forms carbon dioxide and water, which leave the body by exhalation and urination, making this one very valuable resource for athletes seeking nutritious foods to increase energy and efficiency! I'd take a shot of coconut oil and maple syrup over goopy energy gel packets anytime!

Eating consciously and being aware of how you feel after eating fats or oils will be your best guide. For instance, you may experience mental clarity and satiation when you cook your eggs in coconut oil, but feel heavy and nauseous if you cook eggs in butter. You may feel light and energetic with olive oil and walnut oil on your salads, but avocado oil may not sit well with you. Your body may crave lots of oils and fats in the beginning, and then once you are up to par, your body may tell you to back off and eat less fat.

The most effective way you can customize your own diet is to listen to your body and honor it when it tells you it does not want something. Often one to two bites is all that is needed for you to gauge whether or not your body likes it, or does not want it. Recommended amounts may be convenient, but not everyone has the same needs. If you are new at listening to your body's signals, be patient and alert; know that it will come if you continue to cultivate an alert awareness of how you feel when you eat and tune in to your body and its signals.

Fat Considerations

Keep in mind that when you cook with fats, you are typically cooking for more people than yourself. Many recipes call for a tablespoon of fat, but serve four people.

Many other foods, such as animal proteins, fish, nuts, and seeds, also contain fat, so you don't have to add a lot of fat to these when you cook them.

I use the term quality fat to identify fats and oils that have not been refined, hydrogenated, or gone rancid. The more you eliminate these unhealthy fats and incorporate unrefined quality fats such as coconut oil, walnut oil, olive oil, ghee, butter, palm oils, and yes, even lard, the less you will have to worry about fat, and the more solid your nutritional foundation will be.

You don't need to go out of your way to get fat. A wide variety of vegetables should dominate your diet. Legumes, nuts, and animal proteins are your perfect proteins, to be consumed in moderation. Fat is the golden ingredient that makes it all taste good. Fat just naturally slips onto your plate when you prepare these foods.

Delicious Quality Fats and Ideas for Using Them

The following will give you some great ideas on how to utilize certain fats and oils, which taste better in certain dishes, and how they can be used. I consider this whole section one big nutritional nugget!

Animal Fats

Harmful substances that animals eat end up stored in the fatty tissues of the animal, so always be sure your animal fat comes from organic, local, or grass-fed sources you trust. This caution limits your exposure to these substances when you eat them. *Good Decisions* is intent on restoring animal fat to its rightful place in our diets by showing you that there's no reason to fear fat—and many reasons to embrace it in reasonable amounts.

Nutritional Nugget

Thinking that you have to have three different foods on your plate is a tradition that does not need to be continued today. Weight loss often can be achieved by decreasing the size of the evening meal from three items to two and incorporating a little quality fat for satiation!

Organic Chicken, Duck, and Goose Fat

These animal fats are mouthwateringly delicious and stable for use at medium to high temperatures. Searing a duck breast will render a lovely amount of fat that contributes exquisite flavor to legume, rice, and grain dishes. Duck fat is now available at specialty stores. I often use duck fat to add flavor when I sauté kale, Swiss chard, Brussels sprouts, and broccoli. It is also especially good on root vegetables, such as sweet potatoes, turnips, and parsnips.

Organic chicken, duck, and goose fat are very *Good Decisions*.

Organic Ghee (Clarified Butter)

Ghee is a clarified butter in which the milk solids are removed. For this reason, ghee is stable and a great choice for cooking at high temperatures. Anytime I sear a steak, fish, or chicken and want the crust to be brown and crisp, I reach for ghee. If you are intolerant to butter, try ghee. The milk proteins that people do not tolerate have been removed from it, and it is delicious melted over vegetables. Ghee is delicious when added to breakfast grains, when roasting nuts, and in legume dishes.

Ghee is definitely a *Good Decision.*

Organic Lard

Lard is pork fat. Anytime you cook bacon, reserve the fat for later use to add flavor to roasted potatoes, grains, and legume dishes. Nothing makes a legume taste better than a dab of lard. (Think split pea soup with a nice ham hock, yum!) And breakfast potatoes take on a whole new flavor when cooked in lard!

Organic lard is a *Good Decision.*

Pork Belly and Lima Beans with Thyme Wine Broth

Serves: 8
Total Time: 2 hours and 30 minutes, plus 24 hours soaking time

Ingredients

- 16 ounces dried Lima beans or three 15.5 ounce cans, rinsed and drained
- 2 bay leaves
- 2 medium onions, diced
- 1 leek, coarsely chopped
- 2 cloves minced garlic
- 1 tablespoon olive oil
- 1 tablespoon chopped fresh thyme
- Salt & Pepper
- 1 pinch red pepper flakes
- ½ cup dry white wine
- ½ cup chicken broth
- One 2-pound pork belly, bones out

Directions

1. If using dried beans, soak the beans in warm water for 24 hours. Drain and place into a very large saucepan, add bay leaves, cover with water, and bring to a boil. Remove and discard any froth that floats to the surface with a draining spoon; reduce heat to a simmer and partially cover with a lid. Leave the beans to cook for 45 minutes until almost tender. Drain and set aside.

2. Preheat oven to 425°F. In a large sauté pan, over medium heat, sauté the onions, leek, and garlic in olive oil until tender. Add thyme, salt, pepper, and pepper flakes. Add the beans, white wine, and broth, and bring to a simmer. Using a heavy kitchen knife, slice the piece of pork belly into eight squares. Salt the skin generously. Place the bean mixture into a large casserole dish. Place pork pieces into the beans, making certain that the pork stands above the beans. Bake for 20 minutes until the pork is golden and lightly crisp. Lower the heat to 350°F, and continue cooking for an hour. The pork should be crisp on top. Spoon some of the beans onto a plate and top with pork. Garnish with a sprig of thyme or sliced leek.

Organic Beef and Lamb Tallow

Tallow is safe for cooking and frying. Tallow is 50-55 percent saturated fatty acids, 40 percent monounsaturated fatty acids, and only 3 percent or less polyunsaturated fatty acids. Great for making homemade fries and sweet potato wedges. It also adds flavor and depth to legumes and vegetables and turns an ordinary quinoa stuffing into a rich delicious one!

Organic beef and lamb tallow are both very *Good Decisions*.

Organic Butter

Remember from our chapter on carbohydrates how butter and cream can help the absorption of the vitamins and minerals of grains, vegetables, and legumes? These dishes taste great with a dab of butter. When I use butter, I always think of the many ways it boosts my immune system—AND can be used to create a delightfully mouthwatering

French sauce! Butter is great for sautéing eggs and vegetables. It is also delicious spooned over organic polenta, or even fruit before roasting to add satiation and another level of fulfillment.

Organic butter is considered a very **Good Decision**.

Plant Fats

Pesticides sprayed on plants before they are pressed into fats and oils do end up in the product, so it is best to choose organic whenever possible. This choice limits your exposure to these chemicals when you ingest them.

Organic Coconut Oil

Let's start with the All Star of the vegetable fats category. When I tell my clients that they should replace canola oil with coconut oil, they are visibly alarmed. "Really?" they ask. "But that's a *saturated* fat!" There's that bad word again: **saturated**. It's good to remind ourselves that the information that's been disseminated for the past fifty years isn't always accurate. Not only is it okay to consume saturated fats, but it's advisable.

Coconut oil is an excellent morning decision to help remove the morning fog and give your brain an energetic boost. It can be used in your morning cereal grain, smoothies, and is delicious when used to sauté eggs. Coconut oil lends its exotic flavor well to any Thai or Asian recipe. Think cashew nut chicken, green curry halibut, seven flavor beef, and Thai spicy clams! My mouth is watering; how about yours?

On those not-so-most-of-the-time occasions where you are in the mood to bake and don't want to use Crisco, coconut oil is an excellent baking alternative. It departs a mild coconut flavor to the dish you are cooking and is very versatile. Sometimes I even eat it right off the spoon!

Coconut oil is one of my favorite saturated fats, and one of the most delicious contributors to the nutritional foundations, so let's take a moment and look at just a few of the health benefits of coconut oil.

CHAPTER NINE

Coconut Oil and Brain Health

Dr. Richard Veech of the National Institutes of Health has done research on ketone bodies and their potential for therapeutic uses. His studies show that our body digests medium-chain triglycerides (MCT), found in abundance in *coconut oil,* differently than it digests other fats. Instead of storing all MCTs as fat, the liver converts them directly to ketone bodies, which are then available for use as energy. Ketone bodies are the important byproducts of fatty acids when they are broken down in the liver. Dr. Veech discovered that our cells can use ketone bodies as an alternative fuel when glucose is not available.

Brain cells are more limited than other cells in the type of fuel they can use to function and to stay alive. Normally, brain cells require glucose (sugar), but they can also use ketone bodies. Humans do not normally have ketone bodies circulating and available to the brain unless they have been starving for a couple of days or longer or are consuming a ketogenic (very low carbohydrate) diet, such as The Atkins Diet.

In Alzheimer's disease, brain cells in certain areas of the brain are unable to take in glucose.[12,13] This "insulin resistance of the brain" slowly causes cells to die off, a process that appears to happen ten or more years *before* Alzheimer's symptoms become apparent. Alzheimer's is diagnosed using MRI imaging to look at brain tissue. If these tissues show signs of atrophy (shrunken areas), it supports a clinical diagnosis of Alzheimer's. It appears that persons with Parkinson's disease,[14] Huntington's disease,[15] multiple sclerosis, and ALS[16] have a similar defect in utilizing glucose, but in different areas of the brain or spinal cord.

If these cells had access to ketone bodies, they could potentially stay alive and continue to function. Oral and intravenous administration of MCT (found in coconut oil) produces hyperketonemia, U.S. Patent No. 20080009467-A1 (2008),[17] or circulating ketone bodies, which are then available to the brain for energy. In addition, hyperketonemia results in a substantial (39 percent) increase in cerebral blood flow,[18] and appears to reduce cognitive dysfunction associated with systemic hypoglycemia.[19] This result offers tremendous hope for many battling these conditions.

Mary Newport, MD, a physician in Tampa Bay, Florida, discovered that her husband, Steve, had Alzheimer's disease. Two weeks after Steve started using coconut oil, his condition improved considerably. After several weeks on this regimen, Steve showed dramatic improvement in intellectual, emotional, and physical function. This miraculous change prompted Dr. Newport to write a book, *Alzheimer's Disease: What If There Was a Cure?*

Nutritional Nugget

The thyroid gland is extremely sensitive to heavy metals and unhealthy compounds found in lotions and other beauty products; it takes the biggest hit when we expose ourselves to these items. Between coconut oil and ghee, the fountain of youth and hormonal balance is only an application away! Most people find using these natural fats as lotions does not make their skin break out, but some do, so try it and see whether it is an option for you.

Coconut Oil and Cardiovascular Disease

The largest producer of coconut oil is the Philippines, where coconut and its oil are food staples. Additionally, it's produced in India, Thailand, and other parts of Southeast Asia, the Caribbean islands, and even in south Florida. The Philippines has one of the lowest incidences of cardiovascular disease in the world. Studies have shown that total cholesterol to HDL ratio improves with non-hydrogenated coconut oil. The people in this part of the world also eat fish regularly, providing them with Omega-3 fatty acid, which probably also contributes to the lack of cardiovascular disease.

"Some people have been afraid to consume coconut oil because they think it's bad for the heart. But it's actually very healthy," said Dr. Beverly Teter, a researcher at the University of Maryland and an expert in the area of dietary fat. "Years ago, coconut oil was criticized for raising cholesterol. But scientists have since learned there are two kinds of cholesterol: LDL (the bad kind) and HDL, the good cholesterol, which is the kind that coconut oil raises. So they put out the message that it increased serum cholesterol,"

Teter explained. "But the truth of the matter is, it was helping the profile of the serum cholesterol. That never has been corrected in the public press, and I think that's the reason people have misconceptions about it."[20]

Coconut Oil's Antimicrobial, Antiviral, and Antifungal Properties

Coconut oil also has antimicrobial, antiviral, and antifungal properties. Bacteria and viruses contain a lipid (fat) coat, which wraps their DNA and other cellular materials. When consumed by humans, coconut oil disrupts this lipid membrane, killing the pathogens without damaging the host or harming health-promoting intestinal bacteria. The antimicrobial properties stem from the monoglycerides and free fatty acids (mainly lauric acid and capric acid) in coconut oil. Coconut oil also has strong antifungal properties, both in the gut and when applied topically to the skin.

Eliminating refined carbohydrates and sugar, along with a consistent intake of coconut oil and garlic is one of the best treatment protocols for Candida. The antimicrobial properties of coconut oil can also help fight gas-producing bacteria and decrease gas and bloating.

Doesn't coconut oil sound like a dream come true? Doesn't it make you want to go home and lather yourself up with coconut oil and consume it on a regular basis? Unfortunately, coconut oil is still fighting its way back to the list of healthy fats. It has taken a pretty bad beating, and it may take some time for this All-Star fat to catch on.

Need more reasons to include coconut oil in your diet? Read on.

Skin and Hair

Pure coconut oil is easily absorbed, prevents free radical damage, and can improve the appearance of skin and hair. The synergistic combination of coconut oil and cod liver oil help maintain the right fatty acids in cell membranes, contributing to beautiful skin. Coconut oil can also be used directly on the skin for reduction of wrinkles.

Walk down the beauty aisle of your grocery store and look at all the products we put on our skin, hair, teeth, lips, and face. Read some of the labels to get an idea of the chemicals these products contain that can be absorbed through the skin. Save your money, your skin, and your body by using coconut oil!

Sexual Lubrication

Coconut oil can also be used as a sexual lubricant. I have a jar of coconut oil in my kitchen for cooking at medium temperatures, a bottle in my bathroom to put on my skin after I get out of the shower, and one in the bedroom! Too much information? I have been called the Dr. Ruth of coconut oil because of my passion for all the good this wonderful oil can do.

Remember the antimicrobial, antibacterial, antifungal, and antiviral properties? What better properties could be incorporated into a sexual lubricant? It's also perfect for soothing the tender delicate tissues of the vagina after too much activity or signs of infection. If there is a Candida or bacterial infection, using coconut oil might not make it go away all by itself as that is caused by improper pH and one's internal environment, but it will give a woman much-needed relief.

A word of caution here, though: coconut oil should not be used with latex condoms, as it will degrade them.

Coconut oil is definitely a *Good Decision*.

Mussels in Curry Coconut Broth

Serves: 8 as an appetizer, or 4 as a main course
Total Time: 20 minutes

Ingredients

- ½ cup coconut milk
- ¼ cup thinly sliced peeled fresh ginger
- 2 tablespoons lemon juice
- 2 teaspoons red curry powder
- Dash of salt
- 2 cups organic chicken broth
- 2 pounds mussels, scrubbed and debearded
- ¼ cup chopped fresh organic basil

Directions

1. Combine the first 6 ingredients in a Dutch oven; bring to a boil. Add mussels; cover and cook 5 minutes or until shells open. Remove from heat; discard any unopened shells. Transfer to a serving bowl and garnish with basil. Serve!

Organic Red Palm Oil

This vegetable fat has been used in food preparation for thousands of years. Only recently have scientists begun to explore the hidden health benefits of this oil. Red palm oil contains alpha and beta-carotene, lycopene, vitamin E, and other vital carotenoids that act as powerful antioxidants, immune boosters, anti-aging, and anti-cancer substances. The vitamin E in red palm oil is a unique form of vitamin E that is considered especially beneficial to humans.

In the past few years, studies have revealed several key benefits to using red palm oil:

- It can decrease the rate of arteriosclerosis, a disease in which the arteries harden and typically damage the heart.[21]

- Red palm oil inhibits the growth of cancer cells in the breast.[22]
- Red palm oil reduces the clotting function of blood, which, when combined with drugs designed to dilate blood vessels, may aid in the prevention of strokes and heart attacks.[23]
- Red palm oil helps in the reduction of oxidative stress and blood pressure.[24]
- It improves immune function.[25]

As more research accumulates, scientists are likely to discover even more benefits, and the popularity of this oil will increase.

Red palm oil adds flavor to African, Indian, and some Thai dishes, and it is fantastic in paella, saffron rice, and curries. Surprisingly, red palm oil does not lend as powerful a flavor as you would think, and it is wonderful for use at high temperatures. Because it is red, it may color certain dishes, which can actually lend creativity and flavor to Brazilian, tropical, or even Spanish dishes.

Organic red palm oil is a very **Good Decision**.

Organic Olive Oil

Olive oil contains an abundance of antioxidants and is known for its many health benefits, particularly those linked to slowing the progression of cancer. Mediterranean studies link olive oil with decreased risk of heart disease and, due to its high levels of polyphenols, which have been shown to function as both antioxidants and anti-inflammatory nutrients, olive oil can help with any number of inflammatory conditions, from arthritis to irritable bowel.

Olive oil is delicious when used in salad dressing and when used to sauté vegetables. Organic expeller-pressed, unrefined olive oil is definitely an All-Star oil and a very **Good Decision**.

Expeller-Pressed, Unrefined Organic Avocado Oil

Expeller-pressed, unrefined avocado oil is distinctly green due to its chlorophyll content. Don't be fooled by a clear version of this oil. Avocado oil boosts absorption of carotenoids (free radical scavengers) in your food, according to a study published in the March

2005 issue of the *Journal of Nutrition*.[26] Fat-soluble carotenoids found in many bright-colored vegetables rely on dietary fats for their absorption, but most foods that are high in carotenoids are low in fat.

This low fat makes avocado oil ideal for salad dressings and vegetable dishes to increase nutrient absorption. While this may be true of any oil, it is good to know that by adding a little fat to your vegetables, you will increase your body's ability to absorb the nutrients in those veggies.

People who consume diets rich in carotenoids from fruits and vegetables are healthier and have lower mortality from a number of chronic illnesses.[27] Interestingly, however, a recent meta-analysis of 68 reliable antioxidant supplementation experiments, involving a total of 232,606 individuals, concluded that consuming additional beta-carotene from *supplements* is unlikely to be beneficial and may actually be harmful.[28] A good reason to get your nutrients from food and not supplements.

Avocado oil is delicious in summer recipes such as pan-seared sea bass with citrus avocado sauce; spicy shrimp drizzled with avocado oil pesto, and particularly in avocado vinaigrettes. It can also be used in many different salsas, and pairs well with any dish utilizing cilantro. You can find recipes for these dishes and more at www.gooddecisions.com.

Expeller-pressed, organic, unrefined avocado oil is a very *Good Decision*.

Nut Oils

Nuts are sprayed with pesticides, endosulfan, which is highly toxic to humans and animals, phosmat, atrazine, and other chemicals to prevent mold, rot, or pests. It is therefore preferable to purchase organic nut and seed oils.

Organic Macadamia Nut Oil

Macadamia nut oil adds flavor to many dishes. When expeller-pressed and unrefined, it is a light amber color and has a mild buttery taste; refined macadamia oil is almost transparent. Macadamia oil has an Omega-6 to Omega-3 ratio of 1:1, which makes it an ideal oil to help you keep your Omegas balanced, which lowers your risk of developing chronic diseases such as cancer, cardiovascular disease, and rheumatoid arthritis.

The monounsaturated fats are less prone to oxidation, compared to polyunsaturated fats, which give macadamia oil a stability that other nut oils lack. Roughly 84 percent of the fatty acids in macadamia nut oil are monounsaturated, making it ideal for use at medium cooking temperatures. When it is cold-pressed, it is also a good source of polyphenols and flavanols, in addition to providing cholesterol-lowering plant sterols.

I use macadamia nut oil in salad dressings, on seafood (particularly scallops), and in Hawaiian dishes! Think macadamia nut crusted Mahi Mahi, macadamia nut pesto, and macadamia nut sauce to drizzle over shrimp and fish!

Organic, unrefined, and expeller-pressed macadamia nut oil is a *Good Decision*.

Organic Hazelnut Oil

Hazelnut oil is a good source of Omega-6 fatty acids and also contains beta-sitosterol, a plant sterol that is closely related to cholesterol. Beta-sitosterol comes from plants and has been found to promote prostate health, urinary function, and cardiovascular health. Some claim that it may play a role in preventing hair loss.

Hazelnut oil is a good source of Vitamin E, which is essential for healthy heart muscles and other muscles. Vitamin E is necessary for normal functioning of the reproductive system. Oleic acid, which is found in hazelnut oil, prevents a rise of cholesterol in the blood and serves as a fabulous toner for the skin.

This oil is wonderful for use in salad dressings and drizzled over dishes after cooking to add a rich nutty flavor. It is delicious when used in holiday grain and legume dishes.

Organic, unrefined, and expeller-pressed hazelnut oil is a *Good Decision*.

Mango Macadamia Nut Poppy Seed Salad

Serves: 4

Total Time: 20 minutes

Ingredients

- ½ cup apple cider vinegar
- 2 tablespoons grade B maple syrup
- ½ red onion, coarsely chopped
- 1 tablespoon Dijon mustard
- ¼ teaspoon salt
- ¾ cup macadamia nut oil
- 1 teaspoon poppy seeds
- 4 cups Bibb lettuce
- 1 cup crushed macadamia nuts, toasted

Directions

1. For the dressing, place vinegar, maple syrup, red onion, mustard, and salt into a food processor. Cover, and puree on high until smooth. Reduce blender speed to medium-low; slowly pour in the oil and blend until incorporated and the dressing is creamy. Stir in the poppy seeds with a spoon.

2. To make the salad, place 1 cup of mixed greens per plate. Drizzle with dressing and garnish with crushed macadamia nuts.

Nutritional Nugget

Macadamia nuts have been used in the treatment of sexual phobias and as a sexual tonic. A small amount of macadamia nut oil may be just what the doctor ordered when it comes to boosting sex drive, not to mention that it makes a very tasty salad dressing!

Harvest Salad with
Creamy Maple Walnut Dressing

Serves: 4

Total Time: 25 minutes

Ingredients

- 1 cup whole toasted walnuts, split
- ½ cup apple cider vinegar
- ¼ cup Grade B maple syrup
- 1 teaspoon Dijon mustard
- 1 cup walnut oil
- Salt and pepper to taste
- 4 cups mixed salad greens
- 1 apple, sliced
- ½ red onion, thinly sliced
- ½ cup whole roasted walnuts
- ¼ cup dried cranberries
- 6 ounces crumbled raw milk feta goat cheese

Directions

1. For the dressing, combine ½ cup of toasted walnuts, vinegar, maple syrup, and mustard in a blender. Puree until smooth. With the blender running, slowly drizzle in the walnut oil. Season generously with salt and pepper.

2. To make the salad, combine the greens and apple slices in a large bowl, and add just enough dressing to coat. Serve on individual plates and top with the red onion slices, walnuts, cranberries, and goat cheese. Serve!

Organic Walnut Oil

Walnut oil contains high levels of natural antioxidants, which help reduce the effects of free radicals. It is also very good for the skin because it's a good source of vitamins B1, B2, B3, and E—all of which benefit the skin. It is great in salad dressings, smoothies, and any other recipe that does not use heat. Look for this oil in its cold-pressed, unrefined form. Rich in Omega-3 essential fatty acids, walnut oil can help prevent inflammation-related diseases, such as arthritis, and is considered a very *Good Decision*.

Flaxseed Oil

Flaxseed oil contains the essential fatty acid ***alpha-linolenic acid*** (ALA), which the body converts into *eicosapentaenoic acid* (EPA) and *docosahexaenoic acid* (DHA), the Omega-3 fatty acids found in fish oil. Some researchers think flaxseed oil might have some of the same benefits as fish oil, but the body is not very efficient at converting ALA into EPA and DHA. The benefits of ALA, EPA, and DHA are not necessarily the same. Omega-3 fatty acids, usually from fish oil, have been shown to reduce inflammation and help prevent certain chronic diseases, such as heart disease and arthritis. Studies are mixed about whether flaxseed oil is useful for the same conditions.

If you don't like fish, don't think that you can make up for it by consuming flaxseed oil. But don't avoid it either. Many studies herald the benefits of flaxseed oil. For instance, researchers recruited twenty-nine postmenopausal women who suffered at least fourteen hot flashes each week for at least one month, but who would not take estrogen because of a perceived increased risk of breast cancer. After taking 40 grams (1.4 ounces) of crushed flaxseed each day for six weeks, the frequency of hot flashes decreased 50 percent, and the overall hot flash score decreased an average 57 percent for the twenty-one women who completed the trial.[29] This goes to show that fats play an important role in hormone function. Flaxseed oil is often utilized within the Ayurvedic and Naturopathic communities to treat hot flashes.

Flaxseed oil is also known to help with Sjogren's syndrome, which is dryness of the eyes. It has been shown to reduce the risk of cancer, aid in the growth of healthy hair and nails, and be beneficial for those who suffer from Crohn's disease and colitis. Flax oil is not a stable oil, so it should be handled carefully and not be exposed to heat. When cold-pressed and unrefined, it is a wonderful addition to salads, smoothies, and other dishes that do not utilize heat. As with fish oils, you don't need more than a teaspoon each day. Always keep ground flax seeds and flaxseed oils refrigerated.

Organic, cold-pressed, and unrefined flaxseed oil is considered a *Good Decision.*

Diversify the Fats in Your Diet

It is good to diversify your consumption of fats and avoid eating only one All-Star fat. Each fat and oil gives your body something different. For instance, coconut oil is a dream come true for your brain and immune system; flaxseed oil and cod liver oil are heart-healthy blood thinners. Butter is great for your immune system. Olive oil, known for its antioxidant and anti-cancer properties, has an impressive heart-friendly nutritional profile. It is truly essential to utilize a wide variety of all of these natural fats.

How to Cook with Fats and Oils

As mentioned earlier, fats are a combination of different fatty acids, some saturated, some monounsaturated, and some polyunsaturated. The degree of saturation, along with the antioxidants found within the fat or oil, and the way it has been extracted and processed all play a role in the stability or instability of oil and how high you can safely heat it without the oil degrading or becoming unhealthy. The following guidelines and quick reference table will help you make sense of it all.

Smoke Point

The "smoke point" of fat or oil is a way of measuring the point at which your fat has been overheated and deteriorates chemically. The point is marked by smoke or vapors, and can begin as a fine wisp and end as a house full of smoke if you are not careful. But degradation and decomposition of a fat or oil can begin before it begins to smoke. While smoke is a clear indicator that your fat or oil has deteriorated and should be discarded, how do you know how much an oil has degraded before you begin to see smoke? To determine this, we must first determine what type of dominant fatty acids the particular fat contains in order to determine its stability and whether or not it should be exposed to heat, oxygen, or light.

Temperature Ranges

For your reference, the following are typical temperature ranges chefs use when describing certain temperatures. It is not an exact science and can create some confusion, which is why I use specific temperatures instead of using only these terms. For example, coconut oil and butter can be heated to 350°F, which is just on the border between medium and medium-high temperatures. If I tell you these are okay to heat at medium-high temperatures, they may be used inappropriately at 400°F. However, knowing these terms can be helpful when you are operating your stove and need to determine the temperatures at which you are cooking.

- Low temperatures range between 200°F and 300°F.
- Medium temperatures range between 300°F and 350°F.
- Medium high temperatures range between 350°F and 400°F.
- High temperatures range between 400°F and 485°F.

All-Star Oils for Use in Recipes that Do Not Involve Heat

Unrefined Cold-Pressed Flaxseed Oil and Unrefined, Cold-Pressed Walnut Oil

Consume flaxseed oil and walnut oil in small amounts; as little as one teaspoon per day can have significant impacts. These oils are rich in Omega-3 fatty acids, and they add flavor and nutrients to dishes that do not require heating. These oils are great for use in salad dressings, smoothies, and cold dishes like dips and salsas. These oils can deteriorate easily when heated, have a low smoke point (225°F), and are not suitable for cooking.

Unrefined, Cold-Pressed Sesame Oil

Sesame oil is predominantly polyunsaturated; it is unstable and should be kept refrigerated to prolong shelf life. The packaging should be dark and opaque to prevent oxidation and degradation of the oil. Sesame oil should not be heated.

You may have noticed that sesame oil is used often in Asian cooking to lend its unique flavor to certain dishes. The refined version of this oil is often used at high temperatures for sautéing. Although the antioxidants in this oil are high and can prevent degradation, the polyunsaturated fatty acids are still unstable and should not be heated. If you have a dish that just won't taste the same without sesame oil, let the dish cool a bit; then add the sesame oil at the last moment.

Also, keep in mind that I am talking about cold-pressed, unrefined oils. These oils can be, and are, made stable by refining, degumming, fractionation, and hydrogenation, which produce the products that typically line our grocery shelves. Avoid these refined oils. Unrefined versions of these oils can sometimes be difficult to find. So, when you do find these oils in an unrefined state, enjoy them fully!

All-Star Oils for Cooking at or below 320°F (Low to Medium Temperatures)

When cooking at low to medium temperatures, the fats and oils that contain the moderately stable monounsaturated fatty acids can be used. Because these oils contain monounsaturated fatty acids as their predominant fatty acids, they do not break down as easily and can be used at low to medium temperatures.

Many people use olive oil when cooking at high temperatures. However, high temperatures are not appropriate for olive oil because it is comprised predominantly of monounsaturated fatty acids, which are only moderately stable. The cold/expeller-pressed version of olive oil is even more vulnerable, and the potential for it to deteriorate is even higher. Olive oil is best used only at low to medium temperatures to preserve the healthful qualities and flavor of the oil.

These oils are perfect for use in salad dressings and at lower to medium temperatures. Here are my favorites in this category:

- Unrefined, cold/expeller-pressed olive oil
- Unrefined, cold/expeller-pressed macadamia nut oil
- Unrefined, cold/expeller-pressed avocado oil
- Unrefined, cold/expeller-pressed hazelnut oil

It is always a good idea to be cautious with nut and seed oils and to be alert for rancidity. When you purchase oil that is not refined, you can tell its freshness by the cloudiness and deliciously strong aroma. These four oils are all similar in their fatty acid profile, with substantial monounsaturated fatty acid content as their predominant fatty acids, a moderate amount of saturated fatty acids, and only a small amount (7.4-12 percent) of polyunsaturated fatty acids. Olive oil has the highest percentage of polyunsaturated fatty acids. These oils are best stored in a cool, dark, dry location for longevity. Storing oil above the stove exposes oil to heat and is not a good idea.

Unrefined, Expeller-Pressed Peanut Oil

Peanut oil contains 32 percent polyunsaturated fatty acids, 46 percent monounsaturated fatty acids, and almost 17 percent saturated fatty acids. If you can find this oil in an unrefined, cold/expeller-pressed form, it can be consumed in small amounts. It can be used at low and medium temperatures and, as long as it is handled with care and stored properly, can be used in those dishes that just will not taste the same without it.

Peanut oil is *not* an *All-Star* oil because it contains only Omega-6 fatty acids, and no Omega-3 fatty acids to balance it out, which means it may promote inflammation. Most people use the refined version of peanut oil at very high temperatures, which shows what refinement and processing can do!

All-Star Fats for Cooking Between 320°F and 375°F (Medium to Medium High Temperatures)

Fats that contain saturated fatty acids as their predominant fatty acid are very stable fats. These are usually solid or semi-solid at room temperature and can be used for cooking between medium and medium-high temperatures. Even though these fats contain a fair amount of saturated fatty acids, which are more stable, these fats and oils still contain monounsaturated fatty acids that will break down at high temperatures and form those carcinogenic polymers that will gum up your pans and are unhealthy for your body. Use the following fats only when cooking at medium-to-medium high temperatures or lower.

- Butter (organic only): 350°F and lower
- Coconut oil (unrefined, expeller-pressed): 350°F and lower
- Palm Kernel oil (unrefined, expeller-pressed): 350°F and lower
- Lard (unrefined): 360° and lower
- Chicken, duck, and goose fat (unrefined): 375°F and lower

All-Star Fats for Cooking Between 420°F to 450°F (High Temperatures)

- Beef and lamb tallow (unrefined): 420°F and lower
- Red Palm Oil (unrefined), expeller-pressed: 425°F and lower
- Ghee (clarified butter): 485°F and lower

These saturated fatty acids are the most stable choices when cooking at higher temperatures, and they add wonderful flavor to many dishes. I know what you may be thinking: "Beef and lamb tallow? Really?" Absolutely. These fats have been used for generations and are rich in the vitamins and nutrients our bodies need. They have not been processed or refined and are easy to obtain—not to mention they add delicious flavor to many dishes. Who said eating healthy wouldn't taste good?

Nutritional Nugget

Almost any dish that requires medium to high-heat can be adapted to a medium heat. It may require a little more patience and a longer cooking time, but often the resulting dish will not suffer as a result of cooking it at a lower temperature.

Fat and Oil Quick Reference Table

All-Star Oils for Use in Recipes that Do Not Involve Heat
Unrefined, Cold-Pressed Flax Seed Oil
Unrefined, Cold-Pressed Walnut Oil
Unrefined, Cold-Pressed Sesame Oil

All-Star Oils for Cooking at or below 320°F (Low to Medium Temperatures)
Unrefined, cold/expeller-pressed olive oil
Unrefined, cold/expeller-pressed macadamia nut oil
Unrefined, cold/expeller-pressed avocado oil
Unrefined, cold/expeller-pressed hazelnut oil
Unrefined expeller-pressed peanut oil

All-Star Oils for Cooking between 320°F and 375°F (Medium to Medium High Temperatures)
Butter (organic only): 350°F and lower
Coconut oil (unrefined, expeller-pressed): 350°F and lower
Palm Kernel oil (unrefined, expeller-pressed): 350°F and lower
Lard (unrefined): 360° and lower
Chicken, duck, and goose fat (unrefined): 375°F and lower

All-Star Oils for Cooking between 420°F and 450°F (High Temperatures)
Beef and lamb tallow (unrefined): 420°F and lower
Red Palm Oil (unrefined), expeller-pressed: 425°F and lower
Ghee (clarified butter): 485°F and lower

Oils to Avoid Completely

- Corn oil
- Soybean oil
- Cottonseed oil
- Safflower oil
- Sunflower oil
- Canola oil

Avoid the above oils—and *any* hydrogenated oils. These fats are highly refined and processed, contain pesticides and solvents, and contain few nutrients that contribute toward improved health and wellbeing.

The high processing of these oils allows them to tolerate heat. Corn, soy, canola, and cottonseed oils are some of the biggest genetically-modified crops in the U.S. Organic versions of these oils are difficult to find in cold-pressed, unrefined form. There are many other tasty, nutrient dense choices to choose from, so it's best to stay away from these.

Other Oils

Accessory oils (often found in supplemental form), such as cod liver, fish liver, borage, black currant oil, and evening primrose should NOT be used for cooking. These therapeutic fatty acids are mostly found in nutritional supplements, but there are some free-flowing versions now available. If you plan on using a free-flowing version of one of these oils, keep it cold at all times, store it in an opaque bottle, and take it as a supplement—right off the spoon—as directed by your health care practitioner.

Selection, Storage, Rancidity

The three biggest enemies of fats and oils are:

1. Heat: Always be sure your unstable oils were not processed using heat, and that your oil is stored in the refrigerator or a cool dry location.

2. Light: Store your fat or oil out of direct light. When selecting oil, choose from those in dark brown or green containers, which help protect your oil from light.

3. Oxygen: Always be sure the cap is on tight so the oil is not exposed to oxygen.

Unrefined fats and oils are not our enemies. They contribute significantly to good health and wellbeing. From mental clarity to increased sexual function, there is no reason to avoid these and many reasons to enjoy them in moderate amounts.

The Psychology of Food
Our Beliefs

For decades, we were instructed to "Eat a low-fat diet to lose weight," and obesity still skyrocketed. People then took matters into their own hands and followed a low-carb diet. But it turned out that people weren't losing weight or getting any healthier on that diet either. Whether it was the Atkins, Ornish, or the Zone diet, many people gave these diets their best efforts and lost nothing, or gained what losses they did make back. Over and over, we have followed other people's diets and then beat ourselves up because they didn't work for us. Why?

To answer this question, let's return to our methodology. Let's examine the way we go about making decisions and arriving at what does or does not work for us. There are two ways we can move through life and form our beliefs, which influence our behaviors.

1. We Gain Experience and Then Arrive at a Belief.

This first method is used when we spend time and energy embarking on diets other people have created. We do this to gain evidence, experience, and results from which we derive or arrive at our belief of whether or not the diet works. If we lose weight, then we believe the diet works. This method is fundamental to how we learn. This is the *experimental* method. When we use this method, we draw conclusions and look for evidence or results so we can come up with the belief or create a more accurate belief so we have more confidence in it.

This is a great method and should not be discarded, but it takes up a lot of life's precious time and energy gaining experience, experimenting, and trying different methods to figure out which diet or approach we should take to discover whether or not it will work for us.

But perhaps there is a different approach we could take that would use less time, energy, and mental resources.

2. We Could Set the Belief First, and Then Live by It.

This second method involves *setting the belief first*, then living in accordance with it. Instead of trying a certain diet and trying to prove, disprove, or validate our belief of whether the diet works or not (arriving at a belief), we can set the belief first.

In this method, you decide how you want to live your life relative to food and habits. Then you start living according to those beliefs instead of trying what others have already created. You jump off everyone else's treadmill and create a map of sorts by which you want to live your life. The beliefs that you then come up with act as guides for you as you move through life.

In this second method, life energy is not spent focusing on proving or arriving at the belief, because you have already set it. What you do, then, is just live by it.

Here is an example: I am not going to gather evidence and results to arrive at the belief that honesty is the best policy; I'm just going to decide that is what I believe and live by it.

This method allows each individual to come up with his or her own belief system. Like a company's mission statement, it is not something that needs to be proved; it is used as a guide.

When I was first exposed to this method, I was concerned with how easy it would be for people just to set random, inappropriate beliefs. But it turns out that people are good at using common sense, and my concern was unnecessary.

Practicing Good Decisions

What Are Your Beliefs?

Set aside some time to decide how you want to live your life relative to food and habits.

- Create a mental image of what you look and feel like at your desired weight. What is your skin and energy like? Do you have mental clarity? If you could create a mental image of your best self, what would you look like? How would you feel?

- Next, write down which foods and habits you **believe** will give you the results you desire. Do you get up earlier? Juice more? Cook more? Or choose healthier restaurants to frequent? What does your lifestyle look like? Do you exercise? If not, that's okay; this is your life. Set it up how you want to live it, and write down the habits you believe will give you your desired results.
- Now, start living according to it.

I know what you are thinking. "Really? Nothing can be that easy." Yes it can! Of course you will experience some discomfort, and until your new habits become solid, you may face challenges living according to your beliefs. Be gentle with yourself and remember that you don't have to do it all at once or have it all mapped out, and it doesn't have to be perfect.

While it may seem overly simple, this method can work well, especially now that you have been exposed to several methods that will help you delay gratification, increase your psychological hardiness, and not worry so much about what others think. This is your life; why not live according to your own beliefs?

The recommendations in this book are just that, recommendations. While *Good Decisions… Most of the Time* promotes moving away from sugars, processed foods, chemicals, and moving toward vegetables, legumes, fruits, quality proteins, and fats…*most of the time*, the foods you ultimately choose to incorporate daily are entirely up to you!

Truth and knowledge, processes, principles, and laws indicate that the foods you eat will have an effect. You will feel very differently when you consume a bacon cheeseburger versus salmon and a salad. The question to answer is, "What effect are you looking for?" And "What behaviors do you believe will take you there?" Once these questions have been answered, all that is left to do is begin living your life, in accordance with your beliefs, one step down your hallway at a time.

Chapter Ten

Water and Electrolytes

In this chapter, you will learn about the importance of water and why it is one of the foundations of nutrition. You will learn how it can be used to increase mental clarity, decrease the effects of harmful substances, decrease the appearance of wrinkles, help with weight loss, joint health, and much more. You will learn how to pick up on the signs of dehydration and how to tell whether you are hydrated. We will discuss which types of water are best and whether bottled water is really any better than tap water. And of course, enjoy a few nuggets along the way! We will end with our final homework assignment and the psychology of food.

Hydration

Building the Fifth Nutritional Foundation

In my practice, most of the people I see want to lose weight. They are willing to do "anything" to lose weight—well, anything except give up coffee, soft drinks, wine, beer, and other dehydrating substances. When I advise them to eliminate these substances and increase their intake of water, I see them envisioning life without coffee or sugar. At times, I think they'll stand up and walk out the door! Those who choose to take on this "water challenge" find a vitality they never knew existed. Not only do they lose weight, but they become free from frustrating food compulsions or addictions that have held them hostage for so long. Those who don't take on the water challenge usually remain stuck in a cycle of ill health that only they have created.

As I continue to meet with clients who have stepped up to this challenge, I can quickly see the changes take place. They glow with good health and experience a vitality they never knew existed! Not only is their skin and health markedly improved, but their minds are noticeably sharper. They seem more comfortable physically and emotionally, and they almost shine in their well-nourished skin. I wonder at times whether some people are afraid to experience life. By dulling their senses with coffee, alcohol, and sugar, they subconsciously avoid good health in favor of what they believe to be an easier journey. Unfortunately, the journey of life is anything but easy if your health is compromised. Even worse, the journey can be devastating if your compromised health leads to a deadly disease.

Choosing beverages that *cause* dehydration means choosing *not* to become vibrant, *not* to shine. It means choosing poor health over vitality. Now don't get me wrong; I enjoy an occasional glass of wine or a beer. In small amounts, these beverages have some healthful qualities. The key is to make Good Decisions *most* of the time, and when you do indulge, offset the side effects by drinking plenty of water.

Dehydrating Beverages

- Coffee
- Caffeinated tea
- Soft drinks
- Alcohol
- Fruit juices
- High sugar flavored water

Dehydrating Foods

Sugar

When you eat sugary foods, your kidneys work to excrete the excess sugar in your body through urine. This is great, but along with the sugar, you also lose water. This process, known as osmotic diuresis, causes increased urination due to the presence of certain substances in the fluids filtered by the kidneys. Basically, your body is trying to get rid of the substance, which is perceived by the body as waste, so it flushes it out through your urine, with water. The result is dehydration. This type of dehydration is common among diabetics, who need to urinate frequently to eliminate excess sugar.

Salt

Water "follows" salt, and while after eating salt, you may feel like you are retaining water as your fingers swell up like little pork sausages, this is actually your body trying to get rid of, or dilute, the salt. When you consume salt, the ion concentration in your blood increases, which pulls water out of your cells via osmosis. Your body will then try to eliminate the excess salt through your urine, thereby causing you to lose more water than you retain, dehydrating you at a cellular level.

Tangerine, Thyme, and Fennel Comfort Cooler

Yields: 7 cups
Total Time: 7 minutes, plus 2 hours to chill

Ingredients

- 7 cups water
- 2 tangerines sliced
- ½ cup sliced fresh fennel
- 2-3 sprigs of thyme

Directions

1. In a 2-quart pitcher, combine water, tangerines, fennel, and thyme. Cover and chill at least 2 hours or up to 8 hours. Add ice cubes, a sprig of thyme, and a tangerine slice to each glass. Pour water into glass and serve.

Why Do We Need Water?

Water is necessary for many bodily functions and supports the overall health of your body. I will list a few reasons why water is foundational for anyone wanting to increase energy, improve digestion, lose weight, increase mental clarity, or just eliminate that heavy sluggish feeling. Understanding why the body needs water helps us to understand why drinking enough water is so important and how water can be used to improve health and wellbeing.

Weight Loss

We have hunger pangs and thirst pangs. We often mistake our thirst pangs for hunger, and we often eat when we are merely thirsty. The next time you think you need a snack between meals, drink a glass or two of water and see what happens. If you are simply thirsty, your "hunger" will be sated. This is a good opportunity to practice tuning into your body and its signals.

When we drink plenty of water and decrease beverages that lead to dehydration, our hunger pangs die down. The outcome of reducing our hunger pangs is weight loss. At first, we may gain a few pounds of water weight. This can be discouraging, but those who stick with it will notice a decrease in appetite, which then leads to a decrease in food intake, making water a powerful appetite suppressant.

Many recipes for flavored water incorporate fruit or veggies that you can snack on while you are enjoying the water. For instance, cucumber and orange added to water may make water more enjoyable and provide mini-snacks that you can munch on to reduce hunger pangs further!

Cucumber and Mint Medley

Yields: 7 cups
Total Time: 7 minutes, plus 2 hours to chill

Ingredients

- 7 cups water
- 10 thin slices cucumber
- A few sprigs of mint

Directions

1. In a 2-quart pitcher, combine water, cucumber, and mint leaves. Cover and chill at least 2 hours or up to 8 hours. Add ice cubes, 1 mint leaf, and a cucumber slice to each glass. Pour flavored water into the glass and enjoy!

Nutrient Absorption

We need water for nutrients to be absorbed. Our bodies are estimated to be between 50 and 70 percent water, depending on our age, body composition, and how hydrated we are. Women tend to run closer to the 50-60 percent levels and men 60-65 percent. Babies can be over 75 percent water. Each of us is uniquely different, as is our body composition. For instance, lean muscle tissue contains more water than does fatty tissue.

If we look deeply into the body, we will see that our muscles and tissues are made up of trillions of cells. These cells are composed of 60 to 80 percent water. Water is the body's chief solvent, meaning it is the main substance in which other material is dissolved. Virtually all chemical reactions in the body depend on water and its properties as a solvent. This is one way our bodies use water to break down and use nutrients.

Blood plasma (which is at least 90 percent water) dissolves nutrients, oxygen, and waste carried through the body. When we do not drink enough water, these fluids stagnate, nutrients cannot be delivered optimally to the body, and wastes concentrate in the blood and tissues, which ultimately means that lack of adequate water—dehydration—creates a perfect environment for disease.

Nutritional Nugget

Many people don't like the taste of water and have a hard time "choking" it down. Adding a sweet fruit to flavor the water often changes this and can help people stay hydrated. You can also infuse herbs into water to give it the properties and flavor you desire. For instance, rosemary is known to improve mental clarity; basil improves focus and mental fatigue, and peppermint is a stimulating herb that can enliven the mind and boost energy. All of these are delicious when the flavors are infused into water.

The Brain

The brain is composed mostly of water and fat. The brain actually floats in a water-filled vault that protects it from damage. When events occur that can traumatize the brain, such as motor vehicle accidents or falls, water cushions and protects the brain from slamming against the walls of our skulls. When we don't drink enough water, the brain and spinal cord—having first priority—will take water from other areas of the body in order to continue to function.

Dehydration makes your thinking sluggish. You lose mental sharpness, and as with other parts of our bodies, nutrients cannot be delivered to the brain, and waste products cannot be carried away.

A common complaint I hear from my dehydrated clients is that they experience loss of concentration; they feel "spacey," distracted, and have a hard time focusing. Once they replace coffee, alcohol, and sugar with plenty of water, their sharpness and mental clarity returns every time. Water is definitely needed for clarity of thought.

Herbal Brain Booster

Yields: 7 cups
Total Time: 7 minutes, plus 2 hours to chill

Ingredients

- 7 cups water
- 10 thin slices cucumber
- 4 thin slices lemon
- 4 sprigs fresh mint, slightly crushed
- 2 sprigs fresh rosemary, slightly crushed
- 2 sprigs fresh basil

Directions

1. In a 2-quart pitcher, combine water, cucumber, lemon, mint, rosemary, and basil leaves. Cover and chill at least 2 hours or up to 8 hours. Add ice cubes, a slice of cucumber, and a mint, rosemary, or basil sprig to each glass. Pour water into glass and serve.

Mucous Membranes

Mucous membranes located throughout the body rely on water as their dissolving medium. We need water and good quality fats to provide lubrication so our organs don't rub against each other. Dehydration causes these membranes to become viscous (thick and sticky). Have you ever felt a twinge of pain in your abdomen and wondered, "What was that?" Chances are, you were dehydrated, and some tissues were probably sticking!

Joints

Water is your body's shock absorber. Water cushions and protects our joints as we move. Synovial fluid (the slippery fluid that lubricates joints) is composed mostly of water. Cartilage, a flexible material found in various parts of your body (including between your bones), is made of up to 80 percent water! As mentioned before, when you are dehydrated, your brain takes water from other areas of your body, thus water in muscles and joints is re-directed to give your brain and spinal cord the water it needs. When we don't drink enough water, our joints become dehydrated and fluids stagnate. Cellular wastes are not flushed out, which then causes inflammation and damage to the joint. Without the water in your knee joints, bone would rub on bone and you wouldn't be able to walk. We need water for the intervertebral discs (the cushions between the bones in your spine) to be able to absorb the compression that occurs when you walk, run, or jump.

Dehydration is a substantial factor in joint disease. It makes sense to treat joint problems by drinking a hearty supply of foundational water.

Blood

Blood is 90 percent water. Blood transports various nutrients and substances inside your body, including the vital nutrient *oxygen*. If you become dehydrated, your blood becomes viscous. Oxygen transport is affected, and nutrients and wastes can become concentrated. Drinking sufficient water dilutes the blood, which then prevents cholesterol deposits, discourages plaque build-up, and keeps blood from clotting during the circulation process. Water is a powerful tool in the treatment of heart disease and stroke. Am I crazy for wondering why doctors don't write prescriptions for water?

Again, if we think of an herb to infuse into water to give us the properties we desire, in the case of blood stagnation or poor circulation, we would think of rose petals. Many people don't think of rose as an herb, but it is. Rose petals have anti-inflammatory properties that could help to decrease cholesterol deposits in the arteries. Rose petals are also a blood tonic, which means they help the body produce more blood cells and promote general wellbeing. Rose petals also have antibacterial and antidepressant qualities to them.

Rose Water Tonic

Yields: 7 cups
Total Time: 5 minutes, plus 30 minutes to steep

Ingredients

- 3 cups clean fresh rose petals (grown without pesticides)
- 7 cups water

Directions

1. Place fresh petals in a bowl. Bring water to a boil and pour over rose petals. Let steep for 30 minutes. Strain petals from liquid and serve hot as a tea or store in a glass bottle in the refrigerator to pour over ice cubes just before serving. Add fresh rose petals to each glass as garnish if desired.

Digestion and Constipation

We need large amounts of water to digest what we eat. Just the *thought* of food is enough to make our mouths water. This sensation is the body's way of getting the juices flowing in preparation for a meal. Saliva is 95 to 99 percent water. Under normal conditions, your stomach pours out up to three liters (think three one-liter soft drink bottles!) of gastric juices daily to break your food into small particles so the nutrients can be digested. This process helps ensure that you absorb the nutrients from your food.

After food is broken down, it leaves your stomach and moves into the small intestines, where clear pancreatic juice neutralizes acidic food particles so your small intestines can absorb nutrients. Pancreatic juice consists mainly of water. As the nutrients make their way through your small intestines, additional intestinal juice, which is mostly water, is secreted to help move the nutrients through the small intestines. Indigestible food residues, which are transported in fluid, are then passed into the large intestines. The large intestine absorbs water from what was not digested, and the material that is left after this process is eliminated as "poop."

When you're dehydrated, your large intestine squeezes every last drop of water from these indigestible residues to try to keep your body hydrated. This process makes it difficult to keep these materials soft and moving to be passed as stools. Hence, a dehydrated body is a constipated body. This means water is a powerful laxative! To help treat or prevent constipation, drink two or three glasses of water first thing in the morning instead of coffee, and drink lots of water throughout the day. You may be pleasantly surprised at how quickly water will get things moving!

When you drink enough water to meet your body's needs, you are properly hydrated. Waste materials can be excreted, nutrients can be delivered, and joints can be properly lubricated.

Nutritional Nugget

How many times have you gone to the bathroom and noticed your urine is bright orange or yellow? These colors indicate concentrated levels of wastes in the body. When you take in an adequate amount of water, then oxygen delivery is improved, waste products can be flushed out, and your urine becomes clear!

Without water, waste materials stagnate within us; this creates inflammation, which can damage tissues. Inflammation is *dehydration* at its worst, and it occurs when your body doesn't have enough water to function as it should, which can result in suboptimal cellular health. Suboptimal cellular health results in suboptimal bodily function, which creates the perfect environment for disease.

Muscles

Dehydration plays a major role in muscle tightness, cramps, and fatigue. A dehydrated muscle is not a happy muscle. Remember, your muscles are among the first to be sacrificed when your brain needs more water. Have you ever awakened in the middle of the night screaming because your calf muscle has contracted tightly and feels like it will never let go? Or have you had a toe cramp that feels like you are a puppet and someone is pulling the string attached to your toe? Dehydration can be a major culprit in muscle cramps. So, even if you aren't an athlete, drinking lots of water will enable your muscles to work their best.

Nutritional Nugget

Remember that rose water recipe you learned about earlier? You can make that same recipe, and instead of drinking it, let it cool and splash it on your face for its skin tightening, astringent properties. Rose water is used throughout the world topically for younger looking skin. In fact, Cleopatra is said to have used rose water just before moisturizing with ghee!

Skin

When you're dehydrated, your skin becomes wrinkled and dull. Eliminating dehydrating foods and beverages, and consuming adequate amounts of water will make your skin plump and juicy. You may even notice some wrinkles disappear! It's ironic that we're all looking for a fountain of youth to make us feel better and look younger—and it's right under our noses in the form of water! It is easy to see why water is foundational to good health and vitality.

Symptoms of Dehydration

These are only a few of the symptoms of dehydration. What many people don't know is that fatigue and anxiety are also signs of dehydration. Irritability and depression can be debilitating, but no one ever thinks about reaching for a glass of water to ease these symptoms. Water's importance is not emphasized, and many people don't know that dehydration can impact the body at a very deep level. Cravings and muscle cramps, along with headaches, heartburn, joint pain, back pain, and colitis are other indications dehydration may be present. These symptoms are often treated with drugs when relief can perhaps be only a glass of water away. Ironically, you can be dehydrated and not feel thirsty. So don't wait until you feel thirsty to drink water.

So, we really are "walking water balloons." You've probably heard the saying that the body can go weeks without food, but only days without water. Still, most of us are dehydrated on a daily basis. Dehydration has become epidemic, and water's importance to our health is not emphasized. Water is essential for transporting nutrients in and out of every cell in your body. It carries away the undesirable substances within that last soft drink, pastry, or candy bar.

People often tell me, "If I drink more water, I'll need to go to the bathroom all the time!" In truth, the body will adjust to this new practice. I believe you will find that this is a small price to pay for optimal health, clear thinking, and more energy. The question to ask yourself is, "Am I willing to let waste products stagnate within me and cause health problems rather than drink more water?" It's an easy remedy to flush out these waste products and become healthier.

How Much Water Should I Drink?

Okay, this is what you've been waiting for. Enough about anatomy, right? "Just tell me how much water to drink!" First, the amount of water your body needs can change daily, depending on your physical activity, the weather, and even your current health condition. A good guideline for how much water you should drink is to divide your weight in half. That number, in ounces, is the amount of water to consume each day.

So, if you weigh 140 pounds, you should drink about 70 ounces of water each day. An average glass holds around eight ounces of water, so this is equivalent to 8.75 eight-ounce glasses of water per day.

If you drink a dehydrating beverage or eat a dehydrating food, try to add two glasses of water to compensate for the diuretic effect. So, if you have one eight-ounce cup of coffee, you will need to add 16 ounces of water on top of your 70 ounces for a total of 86 ounces of water for that day.

Your body can't store water; it can only utilize about six ounces every twenty minutes. So, if you weigh 200 pounds and you drink a cup of coffee in the morning, your goal will be to drink 116 ounces of water (100 ounces of water, plus 16 extra ounces to compensate for the coffee). Sipping six ounces every twenty minutes will enable you to drink 18 ounces of water an hour. If you do this, it will take 6.5 hours to reach your goal. It's very doable, especially if you work at a desk all day or carry a water bottle with you as you go about your activities.

If you don't drink any water at all, begin by drinking three glasses of water a day until it becomes easy and natural. Then increase the amount until your urine is clear most of the time, which means that undesirable substances and other byproducts are being eliminated from the body. Many people don't like the taste of water. If this is the case for you, try squeezing a fresh lemon, orange wedge, or other delectable fruit into your water to make it more palatable.

How to Tell Whether You Are Properly Hydrated

Other than observing the color of your urine, another hydration test that some people use is to pinch the skin at the back of the hand and observe how quickly the skin returns to its original position. If it takes more than one or two seconds, you are dehydrated. The thing I do not like about this test is that if it takes one to two seconds for your skin to return to its normal position, you are *seriously* dehydrated. Plus, as we age, the elasticity of our skin decreases, which can affect the accuracy of this test.

My sister will pinch the skin just under her eye and watch how quickly (or slowly) the skin returns to its original position. Again, if it takes one to two seconds for the skin to return to its original position, you are seriously dehydrated! This is a very good example of how dehydration can cause our skin to wrinkle and give it a limp, dull quality—and how drinking water can make some wrinkles go away and give skin a plump, juicy look.

Pineapple, Ginger Elixir

Yields: 8 cups
Total Time: 15 minutes

Ingredients

- 4 cups fresh chopped pineapple
- 4 cups water
- 2 tablespoons minced fresh ginger
- 1 tablespoon raw honey
- 2 tablespoons lemon juice
- 1/8 teaspoon ground allspice
- 4 ½-inch-thick pineapple rings and/or lemon wedges, for garnish

Directions

1. Puree pineapple, water, and ginger in blender until smooth. Strain liquid through fine-meshed strainer into a bowl, stirring with spoon to extract as much as possible. (If you like, you can skip straining for an extra hit of fiber and nutrients.) Discard pulp and return the liquid to the blender. Add honey, lemon juice, and allspice to blender; blend until smooth. Serve over ice and garnish with pineapple rings or lime wedges.

Water Retention and Electrolytes

Some of my clients return to me and say they've been drinking lots of water and are going to the bathroom constantly, but they are still not passing the pinch tests. Most of these clients have difficulty retaining water, which means they are *drinking* water, but not *utilizing* it. In these cases, I find these clients are not getting enough electrolytes (salts and minerals that can conduct energy in the body) in their diets.

Electrolytes are the "spark plugs" of the body and play a large role in how our bodies utilize water. For my clients who have a hard time maintaining proper hydration, a few grains of unrefined sea salt, fresh fruit, and vegetables mashed or infused into the water, and the electrolyte lemonade recipe in Chapter 2 usually takes care of the problem.

It is important to mention the difference between table salt and an unrefined sea salt. Table salt has been bleached, stripped, and often contains synthetic iodine to prevent iodine deficiency. On one hand, this is good because it helps with iodine deficiencies. On the other hand, it is a poorly mineralized salt that's unbalanced and unnatural. Some theories claim that if people have high blood pressure and use only natural unrefined sea salt, it won't raise their blood pressure, but I haven't found any studies that either substantiate or disclaim this claim. I recommend checking with your physician before you embark on a new diet or increase your salt intake.

If you add sea salt to your water or food and find that you are retaining water and feeling bloated, you have taken too much salt. Increase your water intake for the rest of the day and your bloating will diminish. Decrease the amount of salt until you find your balance. Everyone is different. Some clients don't need any salt at all; some need just a few grains; others are athletes and find that putting a healthy pinch of unrefined sea salt in their water is required to meet their needs. Most people don't need to add salt to their water as they get sufficient salt from their diet.

I have found a Celtic Sea Salt with an impressive mineral composition at www.celticseasalt.com. This salt not only contains sodium and chloride, but magnesium, calcium, and potassium as well. Other quality sea salts are available at most grocery stores. Be sure to look for *unrefined* sea salt.

If you exercise and sweat or live in an area with a hot climate, you may need more salt. Salts as electrolytes are valuable because your nerve, heart, and muscle cells use them to maintain voltages across their cell membranes. Just don't overdo the salt. Again, if you are swollen and bloated, you may have consumed too much salt. Drink plenty of water to increase your urine output to get rid of your swelling. Everyone is different, so there isn't a perfect or set amount. It won't take long for you to find your balance.

What Type of Water Is Best?

Many of my clients are concerned about water purity. They want to find the best water they can, and rightly so. At first, I advise them not to worry about the quality of water they are drinking because it's hard enough for them to get back to drinking water! Any water is better than no water. Then, if they want to take it a step further, we talk about water quality.

Tap Water

Also called *municipal water*, tap water in the United States is some of the safest water in the world, but it does have some problems. Many additives, such as fluoride and chlorine, are used to treat municipal water and improve its safety.

Chlorine is produced by sending an electric charge through salt water to break the bonds of sodium and chloride. The free chlorine is then collected and used in many household products such as Clorox bleach. Chlorine doesn't like to be alone; it needs to bond to other elements, and it loves organic substances. Bacteria, parasites, and other bugs found in water are organic, and when chlorine bonds to them, it kills them, thus rendering the water "drinkable." Chlorine does a terrific job at killing bacteria and other harmful microorganisms. It will also attack your hair, skin, and lungs because they are organic material as well. When chlorine reacts with organic material, it forms toxic chemical *disinfection byproducts* (DBPs). These products are also responsible for the potentially harmful effects of chlorinated water.

Flocculants (coagulants), used in treating municipal water, cause pollutants to clump together for more efficient filtering. Traces of these flocculants can end up in your drinking water.

If you live in an agricultural area, then your well or public water supply may be laced with *pesticides or nitrates* from nitrogen fertilizer runoff.

Lead can contaminate water if its source is old pipes and plumbing.

Drugs, such as hormone and birth control pills, acetaminophen (Tylenol®), anticonvulsants, and a host of other contaminants, can be found in tap water. Traditional water treatment systems can't remove these drugs and, unfortunately, they can end up in your tap water when it is not filtered.

But don't be disheartened; water suppliers test tap water regularly and are constantly striving to improve the quality of tap water. They also provide customers with an annual Consumer Confidence Report, or CCR, a water quality report that lists the amount of contaminants in your water, what impact these contaminants might have on your health, and whether government standards have been met. I can tell you that your tap water most likely contains chlorine, fluoride, and traces of byproducts of chlorine disinfection. It may also contain lead and copper from corrosion of household plumbing. These potential hazards can be addressed simply by filtering your water to remove these substances. Any filter is better than no filter, but carbon-based filters seem to work the best.

Nutritional Nugget

The chlorine in water is volatile, meaning it can evaporate. Let a glass of unfiltered tap water sit for thirty minutes and the chlorine will evaporate into the air of your home. This is why water has a different taste after it has been sitting.

When looking for my water quality report, I visited the Environmental Protection Agency's website, but I was unable to pull the report for my area. Instead, I receive a report periodically in the mail. These reports are usually hard to decipher, and it takes patience and a dictionary to sort out what is actually coming out of your tap. However, there is a great resource you can use to discover what's in your drinking water. Visit EWG's website at http://www.ewg.org/tap-water/whats-in-yourwater. Type in your zip code and water provider and you'll get a list of the contaminants found in your water.

Many of these contaminants may be unfamiliar to you, but a few—such as arsenic, lead, chloroform, aluminum, and nitrate—are easy to identify. The EWG website also provides a water-filter search application. Simply enter the contaminant(s) found in your water, and EWG will recommend a filter to best remove it. Using a filter is the cheapest, easiest, most environmentally healthy way to get top quality water. Keep in mind that often the contaminants in your water are at very low levels, usually listed in parts per million (ppm). And while it is important to remove as many of these contaminants as possible, the levels are not high enough to warrant avoiding tap water. Tap water is much healthier than soda pop, fruit juices, or other dehydrating, high-sugar beverages.

I love the transparency of tap water and the ease with which I can find information regarding what is coming out of my tap, and how I can best remove any undesirable substances.

Filtered Water

Water filters remove contaminants and are a great option for cleaning up your tap water. Drinking filtered water is more economical than drinking bottled water. It's better for the environment, too, which is taking a significant hit as garbage dumps are filling with plastic bottles. There are different types of filters that block or absorb various contaminants. As already mentioned, the best filters utilize carbon. These work better than distillation or reverse osmosis because the carbon binds with the contaminants and keeps them from passing into the water you drink. The distillation process misses some contaminants, and reverse osmosis filters larger-molecule contaminants, so any contaminant the same size as the water molecule still gets through.

Carbon filters are not limited by the size or type of contaminant they remove. Carbon does not discriminate; it's a *Good Decision* to utilize carbon in your water filtration system. Charcoal is often the form of carbon utilized in these filtration systems. Charcoal is known for its detoxification abilities; hospital emergency rooms use charcoal as an antidote for poisons, including pharmaceutical toxins. One gram of activated charcoal particles can absorb enough toxins to fill the square footage of four tennis courts. Now, *that's* what I want my water to flow through before it goes into my glass!

You can choose from several different types of filtration systems. When looking for a water filter, look for a product that has been certified by the National Sanitation Foundation (NSF) International, a third-party testing organization for water filtration systems.

Whole-House Water Systems

These are a good way to supply good quality water to your entire house and for preventing gases from evaporating into your home. They are expensive and some use carbon, some do not. Whole house water filtration systems that utilize carbon filters are very *Good Decisions*.

Point of Use Water Systems

These systems are installed where you will use the water (the point of use). They are often found on or under the kitchen sink. Point of use products prevent contaminants, such as lead from pipes, from entering your drinking water. Higher quality units have two stages or two containers, which serve as an indicator of a superior product. Point of use water systems that utilize carbon filters are also very *Good Decisions.*

Shower Water Systems

Here, the filter attaches directly to your showerhead. It may be the most important water filter in the house. As mentioned, chlorine and other compounds in water evaporate. This process happens more so in the shower because hot water speeds up the evaporation process. Without a filter, you will absorb these compounds through your skin and as you breathe. Shower water systems that utilize carbon filters are very *Good Decisions.*

Don't feel that you have to spend hundreds of dollars on the latest and greatest. Water filters are cost-effective because they use no more energy than what's required to propel water through your home plumbing system. They also do not waste water, like reverse osmosis and distillation systems, which can add to your pocketbook over time. Many filtration systems are affordable and do an excellent job of removing contaminants and are very *Good Decisions*.

Distillation

Distillation uses heat and evaporation to separate pure water molecules from contaminants. In this process, water is heated until it boils and begins to evaporate.

Contaminants with a boiling point higher than water stay in the original container, and the evaporated water is collected in a separate container.

Distillation removes most minerals, viruses, bacteria, and any chemicals with a higher boiling point than water. Distillation also eliminates heavy metal materials such as arsenic, lead, and mercury. Because distillation removes bacteria and viruses, some developing nations and areas where the risk of waterborne disease is high use distillation as a water purification method.

Opponents of distillation do not like this method because it results in mineral-free, acidic water. Many believe it's even dangerous because it causes calcium and other essential minerals to be pulled from bones and teeth in order to neutralize the acidity. I have not found any studies to support or discredit this. Others say distilled water is great for cleansing the body because it acts like a magnet and picks up toxins as well as minerals and eliminates them from the body. I have not found any studies to support or discredit this either, only many people's passionate opinions.

From a purity standpoint, distillation does not remove chlorine, chlorine byproducts, or contaminants such as insecticides and herbicides because these have a lower boiling point than water. So, with distillation, some contaminants do remain in the water. Distillation is also wasteful because a good portion of the water is discarded with the contaminants. When distilled water is purchased in a plastic bottle, we still face the problems of dealing with the plastic containers that are discarded after the water is consumed and materials from the plastics migrating into the water itself, rendering it more contaminated than tap water.

Many home distillation systems utilize carbon filters. This is a good combination and results in high-quality, safe tap water.

Reverse Osmosis

Reverse osmosis (RO) uses pressure to force water through a selective, semi-permeable membrane that separates contaminants from the water. Because salt molecules are larger than water molecules, the membrane keeps salt particles—along with contaminants such as lead, asbestos, and sediment—from entering the water. Molecules of some contaminants, such as insecticides and herbicides, are smaller than water molecules, and the semi-permeable membrane cannot keep them from getting into the water.

Opponents of the RO method do not like it because it results in acidic water and, as with the distillation process, it removes minerals from the water. Many RO systems also utilize carbon filters. This is a great combination and results in high-quality, safe water. RO systems are less wasteful than distillation, but they can waste more water than they produce, depending on the system.

If you choose a reverse osmosis system with a carbon filter, you've made a *Good Decision*.

Is Bottled Water Better Than Tap Water?

While the EPA regulates tap water, and provides us with detailed information regarding the content and quality of our tap water, the FDA regulates bottled water and does *not* provide information regarding product safety. Bottled water is rarely tested, and it can be difficult to find information regarding the quality of water in any bottle.

So, how can you know if a product is reliable? Knowing what is (or isn't) in bottled water can be a guessing game. Bottled water does have label guidelines—even though they may not be adequately enforced.

Understanding Bottled Water Labels

According to the FDA, "Bottled drinking water means all water which is sealed in bottles, packages, or other containers and offered for sale for human consumption, including bottled mineral water."[1] Approved sources may be from "spring, artesian well, drilled well, municipal water supply, or any other source, that has been inspected and the water sampled, analyzed, and found to be of a safe and sanitary quality according to applicable laws and regulations of State and local government agencies having jurisdiction."[2] The key words to pay attention to here are "any other source." This means you could bottle water from your tap, have it tested, and if it meets the "safe and sanitary" guidelines, you may sell it! Who tests the water to see whether it meets these guidelines? The company selling the water!

So what does "found to be safe" mean? Again, we look to the FDA to regulate safety standards, and according to the FDA, bottled water may contain, "no added ingredients except that it may contain safe and suitable antimicrobial agents. Fluoride also may be added within the limits set by FDA."

Let's look at the FDA's labeling regulations and see whether we can make sense of the different labels and discover what they really mean.

Artesian Water/Artesian Well Water

The FDA defines artesian water as "Water from a well tapping a confined aquifer in which the water level stands at some height above the top of the aquifer."[3]

This definition basically means water obtained from the ground that is confined under pressure between layers of essentially impermeable underground rock. Artesian water can contain ground contaminants such as arsenic and fertilizer runoff. As mentioned above, antimicrobial agents and fluoride may be added. Some brands that use the "artesian" label are Fiji®, Jana®, Voss®, Nicolet®, and Hawaiian Springs®.

Mineral Water

The FDA defines mineral water as: "Water containing not less than 250 ppm total dissolved solids that originates from a geologically and physically protected underground water source. Mineral water is characterized by constant levels and relative proportions of minerals and trace elements at the source. No minerals may be added to mineral water."[4]

This explanation means that when the water is taken from its source, it must contain certain amounts of minerals and trace elements in order to be labeled "mineral water." No minerals may be added to this product. If the mineral content of the water is below a certain level, the statement "low mineral content" must appear on the label. Conversely, if the mineral content is above a certain level, it must be labeled "high mineral content." S. Pellegrino®, Acqua Panna®, Apollinaris Classic®, and Volvic® are some mineral water brands.

Mineral water can be effervescent (sparkling) or not. Sparkling mineral water is water that, after treatment and possible replacement of carbon dioxide, contains the same amount of carbon dioxide that it had at emergence from the source. Some sources produce a wonderful sparkling water, while others have carbon dioxide added. Antimicrobial agents and fluoride may be added, and ground contaminants may also be found in mineral water.

Purified Water

According to the FDA, purified water is "water that is produced by distillation, deionization, reverse osmosis or other suitable processes and that meets the definition of 'purified water' in the *U.S. Pharmacopeia*, 23rd Revision, Jan. 1, 1995."[5]

This water is most often tap water that has gone through distillation, deionization (demineralization), or reverse osmosis. These types of water may also be called "demineralized water," "deionized water," "distilled water," and "reverse osmosis water."

Sparkling Bottled Water

Sparkling bottled water is defined by the FDA to be "water that, after treatment and possible replacement of carbon dioxide, contains the same amount of carbon dioxide that it had at emergence from the source."[6]

Any bottle can bear this label, and you will not know if it has been carbonated by man or if it is naturally carbonated. Soda water, seltzer water, and tonic water are not considered bottled waters.

In 1990, the FDA ruled that Perrier water's claim to be "naturally sparkling water" was false. According to an article in *The New York Times*,[7] "It is not a naturally sparkling water," said Edward J. McDonnell, director of the FDA's district office in Boston. "It is fabricated from carbon dioxide and water, which are taken out of the ground separately."

Spring Water

The FDA defines spring water as "water derived from an underground formation from which water flows naturally to the surface of the earth at an identified location. Spring water may be collected at the spring or through a bore hole tapping the underground formation feeding the spring, but there are additional requirements for use of a bore hole."[8]

Bottled spring water usually goes through some kind of filtration and ozonation process. Bromate, which has been classified as a carcinogen in laboratory animals, is a byproduct of the ozonation process. The debate continues over whether this disinfection is worth the risk. Spring water can contain antimicrobial agents and may have fluoride added to it as do other bottled waters. It may also contain ground contaminants.

Many people seek out local springs, take their own containers, and fill up directly from the spring. I looked up a spring forty minutes away from my home on www.findaspring.com and found that many people had commented on the quality of the spring's water. While most people loved it, several people wanted to know whether anyone else was experiencing stomach upset and diarrhea after drinking its water. Natural spring water can provide high-quality water. However, if you choose to use water from a local spring, it is a good idea to filter it.

Well Water

According to "The World's Water," a report by the Pacific Institute, "Well water is water from a drilled, bored, or otherwise constructed hole in the ground, which taps into the water of an aquifer."[9] It can contain contaminants and should be filtered.

Municipal Bottled Water

According to Peter Gleick, world-renowned water expert and author of *Bottled and Sold: The Story Behind Our Obsession With Bottled Water,* municipal water (tap water) is used as a source for more than 45 percent of the bottled water sold in the United States.[10] Water bottled from municipal water supplies is often taken from a local municipal water supply at no cost and then sold back to the community for a profit. These waters must be labeled as obtained from municipal supplies. In addition, if municipal water has gone through additional distillation or reverse osmosis, it can be labeled as distilled or purified water.

Natural Water

The word "natural" is allowed for bottled water obtained from springs or wells where the natural minerals and trace elements in the water have not been altered. It says nothing about the level of contaminants in the water.

So it seems that bottled water may not be any better than what comes out of your tap at home, and in some cases, much worse. Let's take a look at who dominates the bottled water industry and see what they're doing.

Nestle Waters North America, part of Nestle SA (NESN.VX, NSRGY), is the largest bottled water company in North America, with $4.2 billion in 2010 sales.[11] Nestle claims to be the global leader in the bottled water industry, with sixty-seven commercial brands at the end of 2010,[12] including Arrowhead®, Poland Spring®, and Deer Park®, plus five imported brands, including San Pellegrino® and Perrier®. Nestle bottles and sells filtered tap water.[13]

PepsiCo N.A. The world's number-two beverage company produces Aquafina®. The source of this water comes from the tap.[14]

Coca-Cola sells Dasani®. In 2007, the company admitted that the source for its Dasani brand of bottled water is tap water that goes through reverse osmosis and ozonization.[15]

These and other bottled water manufacturers use terms such as "pure," "pristine," and "mountain water" on their labels. These words are simply marketing techniques with no meaning or regulation. For instance, Aquafina® has images of snow and mountains on the label, despite the fact that it is bottled using processed municipal water. Dasani® is labeled as "pure, still water" and is purified tap water.

In 1999, the National Resources Defense Council (NRDC) published results of a four-year study in which researchers tested more than 1,000 samples of 103 brands of bottled water. The researchers found, "An estimated 25 percent or more of bottled water is really just tap water in a bottle—sometimes further treated, sometimes not."[16] The question, then, that begs to be asked is, "Why aren't we just filtering our own tap water for the same quality and perhaps higher level of purity for less money?"

Effects of Bottled Water on the Environment and Body

In 2006, 827,000 to 1.3 million tons of plastic PET (*polyethylene terephthalate)* water bottles were produced in the U.S., requiring the energy equivalent of 50 million barrels of oil. Of those bottles, 76.5 percent ended up in landfills.[17] Because plastic water bottles are shielded from sunlight in landfills, they will not decompose for thousands of years.[18] Every year, Americans throw away enough paper and plastic cups, forks, and spoons to circle the equator 300 times.[19]

Bottled water sales reached a historical high of 9.1 billion gallons in 2011.[20] These bottles are a huge contributor to pollution worldwide. Bottled water companies' use of valuable resources is not regulated, and the production of billions of plastic bottles has put a huge strain on the environment.[21,22] "Approximately 17 million barrels of oil (equivalent) were needed to produce the plastic water bottles consumed by Americans in 2006—enough energy to fuel more than one million cars for a year."[23]

"CRI estimates that in 2005, an estimated 144 billion containers were wasted in the United States. Wasted means not recycled: sent to landfills or incinerators, or littered along our country's roads and parks, fields and streams, and rivers and beaches. This includes approximately 54 billion aluminum cans, 52 billion plastic bottles and jugs, 30 billion glass bottles, and about 10 billion pouches, cartons, and drink boxes."[24] When it rains, these plastics are carried to the ocean. There, they accumulate in what is now called the "Great Pacific Garbage Patch" where an accumulation of plastics, chemical sludge, and other debris have been trapped by currents in the North Pacific Ocean. No one knows for certain how big this garbage patch really is. It has been estimated to be as small as the size of Texas, and as large as twice the size of the continental United States. Regardless of the size of this garbage patch, the main point is that there should be no plastics or toxic debris floating around in our oceans at all. These plastics harm wildlife and affect our precious food chain.

This planet is our home; we only have one planet earth. In order for the human race to survive as a species, we need to protect it and treat it like the sacred habitat it is. There are many steps we can all take to increase the health of our planet; here are just a few:

- Recycle as much as you can.
- Buy local products to support your community's ability to sustain itself.
- Buy natural products and avoid products with toxic or harmful substances.
- Avoid plastics, bags, bottles, forks, spoons, cups, etc.
- Take a shorter shower and conserve water.
- Reduce waste; some people strive for zero waste households! How much can you reduce the waste you produce?

When we decrease the level of pollutants in our environment, we decrease the level of pollutants in our food chain. The healthier our planet, the healthier the people who inhabit it.

Health Problems and Plastics

Even the purest water, taken from the deepest mineral-rich water resources, can become a hazard if it's put into a plastic container. Most water bottles are made of *polyethylene terephthalate* (PET). Look at the bottom of the next bottle you purchase; more than likely, you'll find the number "1" in a triangle with PET just below it. PET is used to make microwavable trays and plastic containers for sports drinks, salad dressings, condiments, mouthwash, and peanut butter. Recent reports indicate that the materials used in the production of PET leach into the food and beverages from these containers. For instance, some say contaminants such as phthalate, a synthetic substance used to make plastic bottles more flexible, may cause disruptions of the endocrine (hormonal) system.[25]

Antimony, a substance used in the production of PET, is known to "migrate" into food and drinks.[26] Acetaldehyde is a volatile substance that forms when PET degrades. When acetaldehyde forms, some of it remains dissolved in the walls of the container and then can diffuse into the product.[27][28] Although the FDA deems all this as safe,[29] the risk is large enough for me to recommend glass containers and a good home carbon filtration system.

If you do choose to use plastics, choose products that are labeled with one of the following numbers. These plastics are known not to leach harmful substances:

- High-density polyethylene, labeled as "#2 HDPE"
- Low-density polyethylene, labeled as "#4 LDPE"
- Polypropylene, labeled as "#5 PP"

Always be sure to recycle plastics.

The best way to get delicious, clean drinking water is to find a good filter and enjoy water directly from your faucet. It is easy to know what is coming out of your tap and the best way to filter it. In contrast, bottled waters have the potential to cause harm, are not tested, and you really don't know what is in them. Not to mention they are expensive and creating havoc with our environment. Tap water is easy, affordable, and reduces the pollutant load on our planet. When you need to take water with you, it is best to utilize glass or stainless steel containers. If you are worried about breakage, insulators are easy to find.

While the temptation may be strong to demonize the bottled water industry, we should keep in mind that it is responding to consumer demand. Our obsession with bottled water is interesting, and while marketing may influence what we do, in the end, it is our demand for water in plastic containers that has driven the bottled water industry to produce so much plastic.

Tap water has been portrayed as impure and unhealthy, but when the comparison is done, water in plastic containers poses much more of a health risk and is not nearly as well-regulated or tested as the municipal water supplies. Overall, I would much rather enjoy filtered water from my tap for free than pay a large company to put it in a plastic bottle, which contaminates the water and the planet, to sell it back to me for a profit.

Bottled water is not better than tap water, and it is not considered a *Good Decision.*

Adjusting to Water

Be sure to increase your water intake gradually so your body has time to adjust. If you don't like the taste of water, then add a few slices of cucumber to a pitcher of filtered water in the fridge; a squeeze of lemon or orange also increases the flavor and enjoyment of water.

As you begin to increase your water intake, you might feel worse before you get better. This feeling is common because your body is releasing stored noxious substances into the blood as they make their way out of your body. Acne, bad breath, body odor, nausea, and fatigue can be a result of this detoxification, but do not let them stop you. Increasing your water intake gradually will reduce these symptoms.

The World's Water Supply

In the future, some say, wars will not be fought over oil, but water. Throughout history, water has been the determining factor in whether or not a community survived. Almost, if not all, major rivers around the world have been dammed, rerouted, or tapped to supply water to a thirsty world. In the U.S., we take advantage of the abundant supply of clean water pumped through our faucets every day. We take long showers and let precious water just run down the drain as we brush our teeth. Water is undervalued and unappreciated as the most precious natural resource on the planet. We would be wise as a species to stop, look around, and do what we can to conserve our precious water supply and protect the planet that provides for us.

As you strengthen your nutritional foundations, the fogginess that has been your constant companion will start to clear and your concentration will improve. Your thinking will become quicker and clearer, and your memory will improve. Your skin will take on a new glow, and some wrinkles may even go away. Digestion will improve and you will feel energized and more alive than you ever imagined. Weight loss will be a delightful side effect and hormones will naturally return to balance when you make *Good Decisions… Most of the Time.*

The Psychology of Food
Psychological Hardiness

It is interesting to note that we are the only species on earth that consumes more than we need. If you observe nature, no animal, bug, or bird takes more than it needs. Only when animals are domesticated do they overeat. Food and water throughout the last hundred years have been consumed greedily and our environment polluted recklessly.

In Peter Farb's book, *Man's Rise to Civilization*, he writes about how many ancient tribal cultures believed that the accumulation of private property or food beyond one's needs was considered a mental illness. If we look at America today, mental illness in the form of overconsumption is rampant, so rampant it has become normal. We eat to soothe ourselves, and as a result, more than one-third of U.S. adults (35.7 percent) are obese. That number is on the rise, and while we each have our own unique choices and things we would like to do or achieve, weight loss is one of the most common goals in the U.S. today. Yet it can be one of the most difficult goals to achieve.

The more wealthy and technologically advanced our society becomes, the weaker we become when it comes to emotional, psychological hardiness. Horrible nutrition is the result of immediate gratification and a psychological diet, where we have coddled ourselves with fast food, which is more conducive to devolving than evolving. Today's youth are less able to handle delay of gratification, and from an emotional nutritional view, we are less able to tolerate discomfort—we can't wait.

There are many aspects to the psychology of food, but the primary reason we don't achieve our weight loss goals appears to be because we are not emotionally hardy. Like other mammals, we do not stop once we have had enough. Delaying gratification to achieve weight loss and increase our energy and vitality stirs up a lot of emotions and is a mountain we are not taught to climb. Instead, we have been taught immediate gratification. Our default, knee-jerk reaction is to operate from emotions.

We can choose to become increasingly enslaved by this methodology, or we can become empowered and freed by truth and knowledge. This freedom can only be experienced by mastering the art of delaying gratification for a greater cause, and increasing our awareness of what happens within us.

When delaying gratification, you may struggle at first. Sometimes, you may be able to delay gratification without too much emotional turmoil; other times, a raging battle may occur within you. Either way, the more you practice delaying gratification and paying attention to your thoughts, actions, and what drives your behaviors, the easier it becomes, and the more you will be able to achieve.

Delaying gratification is like an itchy mosquito bite that you can't scratch. But if you ride it out, it becomes less intense and your actions are more in alignment with principles, processes, and laws. Truth and knowledge tell us that if you consume excess sugar, you will gain weight. If you consume too many foods processed with chemicals, you may become sick. This is law. When emotions get involved, we are less able to handle delay of gratification; we cast truth and knowledge aside because we have not been taught to sit through the discomfort of not having what we want.

The *ah-ha* moment comes when you feel the discomfort of delaying gratification, but you are consciously aware that this discomfort will pass. And when it does, you experience the joy of your ability to self-govern. The more you do delay gratification, the easier it is, and the more psychologically hardy you become.

Truth and knowledge are things you can absolutely trust. Emotions make us wacky because emotions vary from moment to moment. How you feel depends on where you go, what you do, and how you perceive events. Too much sugar, potato chips, and processed foods that aren't good for us are things we submit to because they reduce bad feelings and give us the temporary sensation that we have been fulfilled. But what's more important? Increasing awareness and our ability to self-govern, or temporarily soothing ourselves to avoid uncomfortable emotions?

Becoming aware of how your emotions can drive you and practicing delaying gratification indicate that you are operating from intellect and not emotions. This change reflects the highest level of freedom and independence. It is to be truly satiated and fulfilled. If a level of conscious awareness is present, any food challenge can be overcome.

Practicing Good Decisions

Live According to Truth and Knowledge

Making *Good Decisions...Most of the Time* isn't just about making healthy decisions when it comes to food, or tuning into your body to give it what it needs, or even dealing with emotions and improving your ability to self-govern. It is ultimately a philosophy of living in accordance with truth and knowledge when it comes to food and habits.

Truth and knowledge tell us that when we feed the body foods found in nature, prepared as our ancestors prepared them for generations, they will perform phenomenally well for us. When we consume too much sugar or processed foods, our mental clarity begins to fog, we lose energy, and the health of our physical body suffers. While it serves no purpose to demonize certain foods, it does serve a purpose to operate using intellect and know how certain foods affect the body. Then we can make informed decisions—*Good Decisions...Most of the Time*—regarding what foods we want to consume as we journey down our own individual hallways of life.

We are all beautifully different, with different metabolisms, different food sensitivities, different ethnicities, and different beliefs. There is no one diet that works for everyone, but there is an abundant amount of wholesome natural food for all of us to choose from and cook as we desire. Whether you are a fast food junkie, raw foodie, a vegan, or carnivore, there is no right way or wrong way to eat—only truth and knowledge that point us toward foods that contribute to health and wellbeing, and those that do not.

I hope you have enjoyed reading *Good Decisions...Most of the Time* and feel inspired to make healthy changes in your own life. You are invited to join the *Good Decisions* community at www.gooddecisions.com, where you will find an abundant amount of healthy recipes and articles on food and nutrition.

I feel honored to be with you on this journey down your hallway of life, and I sincerely wish you many victories as you learn to delay gratification, tune in to your body, and self-govern according to truth and knowledge. I wish for you all that you wish for yourself, and I hope you enjoy making **Good Decisions...Most of the Time!**

Pay it Forward!

If you found the balanced approach of *Good Decisions* helpful, pay it forward!

- Share this book with one or more friends you feel would really benefit from it.
- Invite them to take on the "No Sugar Challenge" with you. This helps you to become accountable and forms a supportive network, which can give better results.

Thank you for buying the book! I really appreciate your feedback and love hearing what you have to say.

Please leave a helpful review on Amazon.com

Endnotes

Chapter One

1. http://www.uclahealth.org/body.cfm?id=561&action=detail&ref=1897

2. Obesity and overweight. (2013). Retrieved from World Health Organization Media Centre http://www.who.int/mediacentre/factsheets/fs311/en/

3. Child & Family Research Institute (2007, November 21). Too much sugar turns off gene that controls effects of sex steroids. *Science Daily*. Retrieved from http://www.sciencedaily .com/releases/2007/11/071109171610.htm

4. How Science is going sour on sugar. Rapid Response; The Excessive Carbohydrates Intake and the MUST HUMAN SYNDROME. *British Medical Journal*. Retrieved from http://www.bmj.com/content/346/bmj.f307/rr/625981

5. Lyle, M.H. (2006). The reclassification of sugar as a drug. *Lethbridge Undergraduate Research Journal*. (Volume 1, Number 1). Retrieved from http://www.lurj.org/article.php /vol1n1/sugar.xml

6. Yudkin, J., (1957). *The Lancet,* 11:155-62; Yudkin, J., et al, (1986). *Annals of Nutrition and Metabolism*, 30:4:261-66; Yudkin, J., Edelman, J., Hough, L., (1971). Sugar: chemical, biological and nutritional aspects of sucrose. London, United Kingdom: Progressive Customer Publishing.

7. Lopez, A. (1966), *American Journal of Clinical Nutrition*, 18:149-153.

8. Beasley, J.D., M.D., and Swift, J.J., M.A., (1989). The Kellogg report, Annandale-on-Hudson, New York: The Institute of Health Policy and Practice, 132; Yudkin, J. (1972). *Sweet and Dangerous*, New York, NY: David McKay Company.

9. Hoebel, B.G., Rada, P., Avena, N.M. (2008). Evidence for sugar addiction: behavioral and neurochemical effects of intermittent, excessive sugar intake. *Neuroscience and Biobehavioral Review* 32 (1): 20-39. doi:10.1016/j.neubiorev.2007.04.019

10. Risk to oral health and intervention. (n.d.) World Health Organization. Retrieved November 21, 2012 from http://www.who.int/oral_health/action/risks/en/

11. Hoover, D.W., Milich, R. (1994). Effects of sugar ingestion expectancies on mother-child interaction. *Journal of Abnormal Child Psychology*, 22:501-515.

12. Wolraich, M.L., Lindgren, S.D., Stumbo, P.J., Stegink, L.D., Appelbaum, M.I., Kiritsy, M.C. (1994). Effects of diets high in sucrose or aspartame on the behavior and cognitive performance of children. *New England Journal of Medicine*, 330(5):301-307.

13. UAB study links children's diabetes risk to mother's blood sugar during pregnancy. (2010, June 25) Retrieved from University of Alabama News Archive website http://www.uab.edu/newsarchive/78241-uab-study-links-children-s-diabetes-risk-to-mother-s-blood-sugar-during-pregnancy

14. McCollum, E.V. (1957). A history of nutrition: the sequence of ideas in nutritional investigation, Boston, MA: Houghton Mifflin, p. 88.

15. Price, W. A., D.D.S. (2008) *Nutrition and physical degeneration: a comparison of primitive and modern diets and their effects* (8th ed.). Addison, TX: The American Academy of Applied Nutrition.

16. Bartley, J., McGlashan, S. R. (n.d.) Does milk increase mucus production? Retrieved from National Center for Biotechnology Information *PubMed* http://www.ncbi.nlm.nih.gov/pubmed/19932941

17. Zoghbi, S., et al. (2006) beta-Casomorphin-7 regulates the secretion and expression of gastrointestinal mucins through a mu-opioid pathway. *American Journal of Physiology, Gastrointestinal and Liver Physiology*. Retrieved from http://www.ncbi.nlm.nih.gov/pubmed/16357059

1. URI scientist discovers 54 beneficial compounds in pure maple syrup. (2011, March 30). Retrieved from The University of Rhode Island website http://www.uri.edu/news/releases/?id=5758

2. Burroughs, S. (1993). *The Master Cleanser: With Special Needs and Problems.* Burroughs Books, (Revised ed.)

3. Harnessing honey's healing power. Retrieved November 21, 2012, from BBC News website http://news.bbc.co.uk/2/hi/health/3787867.stm

4. Budge, E.A.W. (2010) *The Mummy: A Handbook of Egyptian Funerary Archaeology.* (2nd ed.) Cambridge: Cambridge University Press. (Reprinted New York: Dover Publications)

5. Snowdon, J.A., Cliver, D.O. (Aug 1996). Microorganisms in honey. *International Journal of Food Microbiology* 31 (1–3): 1–26. doi:10.1016/0168-1605(96)00970-1

6. Frequently asked questions. Retrieved November 21, 2012, from The National Honey Board website http://www.honey.com/faq/

7. Effect of cinnamon on postprandial blood glucose, gastric emptying, and satiety in healthy subjects (2007). *The American Journal of Clinical Nutrition*, 85(6):1552-6. Retrieved from National Center for Biotechnology Information website http://www.ncbi.nlm.nih.gov/pubmed/17556692

8. Vanillin health benefits. Retrieved November 21, 2012 from Ray Sahelian, M.D. website http://www.raysahelian.com/vanillin.html

9. Bozin, B., Mimica-Dukic, N., Simin, N., Anackov, G. (2006). Characterization of the volatile composition of essential oils of some lamiaceae spices and the antimicrobial and

antioxidant activities of the entire oils. *Journal of Agricultural and Food Chemistry,* 54 (5): 1822–8. doi:10.1021/jf051922u

10. Chiang L.C., Ng, L.T., Cheng, P.W., Chiang, W., Lin, C.C. (2005). Antiviral activities of extracts and selected pure constituents of Ocimum basilicum. *Clinical and Experimental Pharmacology and Physiology*, 32 (10): 811–6. doi:10.1111/j.1440-1681.2005.04270.x

11. de Almeida I., et al. (2007). Antigiardial activity of Ocimum basilicum essential oil. *Parasitology International,* Res. 101 (2): 443–52. doi:10.1007/s00436-007-0502-2

12. Manosroi, J., Dhumtanom, P., Manosroi, A. (2006). Anti-proliferative activity of essential oil extracted from Thai medicinal plants on KB and P388 cell lines. *Cancer Letters*. 235 (1): 114–20. doi:10.1016/j.canlet.2005.04.021

13. Duke, J.A. (2008) *Alternative and Complementary Therapies.* 14(1): 5-8. doi:10.1089/act.2008.14101.

14. Sahu, A.P., Saxena, A.K. (October 1994). Enhanced translocation of particles from lungs by jaggery. Environmental Health Perspectives (Brogan &#38) 102 (S5): 211–214. doi:10.2307/3432088. JSTOR 3432088. PMC 1567304. PMID 7882934. Retrieved 2007-05-20.

15. American Physiological Society (2008, October 19). Fructose sets table for weight gain without warning. *ScienceDaily*. Retrieved October 13, 2013, from http://www.sciencedaily.com /releases/2008/10/081016074701.htm; University of Cincinnati Academic Health Center. Research may provide new links between soft drinks and weight gain. Retrieved from http://healthnews.uc.edu /news/?/825/;
Bray, G.A., Nielsen, S.J., Popkin, B.M. (2004). Consumption of high-fructose corn syrup in beverages may play a role in the epidemic of obesity. *The American Journal of Clinical Nutrition.* 79(4):537–543. Retrieved from http://www.ajcn.org/cgi/content/full/79/4/537

16. Huang, J. (2006, March 10). The bitter truth about fructose. Annotate (NYU Journalism Institute forum). Retrieved from http://journalism.nyu.edu/publishing/archives/annotate/blog/14-56270

17. Extraction of stevia. Retrieved from the International Stevia Council website http://www.internationalsteviacouncil.org/index.php?id=152

18. Stevia. Retrieved from the Memorial Sloan Kettering Cancer Center *Integrative Medicine* mskcc.org: adverse reactions

19. Draft guidance for industry: ingredients declared as evaporated cane juice. (2009, October 7). U.S. Food and Drug Administration *Federal Register.* Retrieved January 11, 2010, https://www.federalregister.gov/articles/search?conditions%5Bterm%5D =evaporated+cane+juice&commit=Go

20. Environmental Health Perspectives (2006, February 13). Artificial sweetener causes cancer in rats at levels currently approved for humans, new study suggests. *ScienceDaily.* Retrieved October 13, 2013, from http://www.sciencedaily.com/releases/2006/02/060213093019.htm

21. Englun-Ogge, L. et al. (September 2012). Association between intake of artificially sweetened and sugar-sweetened beverages and preterm delivery: a large prospective cohort study. Retrieved January 22, 2013 from *American Journal of Clinical Nutrition* 96: 552-559; doi:10.3945/ajcn.111.031567

22. Swithers, S., Davidson, T. (June 29, 2004). Artificial sweetener may disrupt body's ability to count calories. Retrieved January 22, 2013, from *Purdue News.* http://www.purdue.edu/uns/html4ever/2004/040629.Swithers.research.html

23. Yang, Q. (June 2010) Gain weight by "going diet"? Artificial sweeteners and the neurobiology of sugar cravings. *Yale Journal of Biology and Medicine*; 83(2): 101–108. Retrieved January 22, 2013, from http://www.ncbi.nlm.nih.gov/pmc /articles/PMC2892765

Chapter Three

1. Bode, L. (2009). Human milk oligosaccharides: prebiotics and beyond. Retrieved from *Nutrition Reviews* 67 (2): S183–91. doi:10.1111/j.1753 -4887.2009.00239.x.

2. Sulfur Dioxide Fact Sheet. (January 2001). Idaho Department of Health and Welfare. Retrieved from http://healthandwelfare.idaho.gov/portals/0/Health /MoreInformation/13HealthEffectsofSulfurDioxide.pdf

3. Lomaroff, A. reviewing Ridaura, V.K. et al. Science 2013 Sep 6. Le Chatelier E et al. Nature 2013 Aug 29. Cotillard, A. et al. Nature 2013 Aug 29. More Data Incriminating Gut Bacteria in Obesity, Dyslipidemia, and Insulin Resistance. Retrieved from *New England Journal Of Medicine* NEJM http://www.jwatch.org /na32276/2013/10/10/more-data-incriminating-gut-bacteria-obesity-dyslipidemia

4. Suszkiw, J. Phytochemical profilers investigate potato benefits. Retrieved from United States Department of Agriculture http://www.ars.usda.gov/is/AR/archive /sep07/potato0907.htm

5. Beliveau, R. and Gingras, D. (2006) *Foods to Fight Cancer*. New York: McClelland & Stewart Ltd.

6. Bohn, L., Meyer, A.S., Rasmussen, S.K. (June 15, 2010). Dietary roles of phytate and phytase in human nutrition: a review. *Food Chemistry*, V. 120, No. 4, pp. 945-959. Phytate: Impact on environment and human nutrition. A challenge of molecular breading. *Journal of Zhejiang University*. Science. Vol. 9, pp. 165-91.

7. Hurrell, R.F., Reddy, M.B., Juillerat, M.A., Cook, J.D. (May 2003) Degradation of phytic acid in cereal porridges improves iron absorption by human subjects,

American Journal of Clinical Nutrition, Vol. 77, No. 5, 1213-1219 Retrieved from http://www.ajcn.org/cgi/content/full/77/5/1213

8. Frontela C., Scarino, M.L., Ferruzza, S., Ros, G., Martínez, C. (April 28, 2009) Effect on dephytinization on bioavailability of iron, calcium and zinc from infant cereals assessed in the Caco-2 cell model, Department of Food Science and Nutrition, Faculty of Veterinary Science and Food Science and Technology, Murcia University, Murcia, Spain. Retrieved from http://www.ncbi.nlm.nih.gov /pubmed/19399930

9. Nagel, R. Living With Phytic Acid. Retrieved from http://www.westonaprice.org /food-features/living-with-phytic-acid

Chapter Four

1. National Research Council (U.S.). Food Protection Committee (1973). Toxicants occurring naturally in foods. National Academy of Sciences. pp. 363–371.

2. Phytochemicals.info at http://www.phytochemicals.info/phytochemicals/phytic-acid.php

3. Iqbal, T.H., Lewis, K.O., and Cooper, B.T. (September 1994) Phytase activity in the human and rat small intestine. *Gut.* 35(9):1233-1236.

4. Reddy, N.R., Sathe, S.K., Salunkhe, D.K. (1989) Phytates in cereals and legumes. Boca Raton, FL: CRC Press.

5. Reddy, N.R., Sathe, S.K., Salunkhe, D.K. *Food Phytates* (2001), Boca Rotan, FL: CRC Press.

6. Vucenik, I., Shamsuddin, A.M. (November 2003) Cancer inhibition by Inositol hexaphosphate (IP6) and Inositol: from laboratory to clinic. *The Journal of Nutrition* 133 (11 Suppl 1); Jenab, M. and Thompson, L. U. (August 21, 2000).

Phytic acid in wheat bran affects colon morphology, cell differentiation, and apoptosis. *Carcinogenesis* (8):1547–52.

7. Cebrian, D., Tapia, A., Real, A., Morcillo, M.A. (2007) Inositol hexaphosphate: a potential chelating agent for uranium. *Radiation Protection Dosimetry* 127(1-4):477–9.

8. Retrieved from http://www.phytochemicals.info/phytochemicals/phytic-acid.php

9. Sandberg, A.S. and Svanberg, U. (1991), Phytate hydrolysis by phytase in cereals; Effects on in vitro estimation of iron availability. *Journal of Food Science*, 56: 1330–1333. DOI: 10.1111/j.1365-2621.1991.tb04765.x

10. Wilbald, L., Svanberg, U. (1993),Lactic-fermented cereal gruels with improved *in vitro* protein digestibility, Vol. 44, No. 1 , pp. 29-36; DOI: 10.3109/09637489309017420

11. Prom-U-Thai, C.; Huang, L.; Glahn, R.P., Welch, R.M., Fukai, S., Rerkasem, B. (2006). Iron (Fe) bioavailability and the distribution of anti-Fe nutrition biochemicals in the unpolished, polished grain and bran fraction of five rice genotypes. Journal of the Science of Food and Agriculture 86 (8): 1209–15. doi:10.1002/jsfa.2471.

12. Famularo, G., De Simone, C., Pandey, V., Sahu, A.R, Minisola, G. (2005). Probiotic lactobacilli: an innovative tool to correct the malabsorption syndrome of vegetarians? Med. Hypotheses 65 (6): 1132–5. DOI:10.1016/j.mehy.2004.09.030.

13. Peers, F. G. (1953) Phytase of wheat. *The Biochemical Journal* 53(1):102-110.

14. Reddy, N.R., Sathe, S.K. (Eds.). (2001) *Food Phytates*, Boca Raton, FL: CRC Press.

15. Reddy, N.R., Sathe, S.K. (Eds.). (2001) *Food Phytates*, Boca Raton, FL: CRC Press.

16. Malleshi, N.G. (1986) Nutritive value of malted millet flours. Springer Publisher.

Chapter Five

1. Ric Bessin, Bt-CORN: WHAT IT IS AND HOW IT WORKS retrieved from University of Kentucky College of Agriculture website http://www2.ca.uky.edu /entomology/entfacts/ef130.asp

2. Netherwood, et al. "Assessing the survival of transgenic plant DNA in the human gastrointestinal tract," *Nature Biotechnology* 22 (2004):2 NCBI Retrieved on December 10, 2013 from http://www.ncbi.nlm.nih.gov/pubmed/14730317

3. N. Tomlinson of UK MAFF's Joint Food Safety and Standards Group 4, December 1998 letter to the U.S. FDA, commenting on its draft document, "Guidance for Industry: Use of Antibiotic Resistance Marker Genes in Transgenic Plants."

4. Carrie Swadener, "Bacillus thuringiensis (B.t.)," *Journal of Pesticide Reform* Vol. 14, no. 3 (Fall 1994).

5. Yearly food sensitivity assessment of York Laboratory, as reported in Mark Townsend, "Why soya is a hidden destroyer," *Daily Express*, March 12, 1999. Retrieved from http://www.mindfully.org/GE/Increase-Soy-Allergies.htm

6. Doug Gurian-Sherman, Genetic engineering—a crop of hyperbole retrieved from http://www.utsandiego.com/uniontrib/20080618/news_lz1e18gurian.html

Chapter Six

1. *Endocrine-Disrupting Chemicals: From Basic Research to Clinical Practice.* Humana Press; 8 June 2007. (Contemporary Endocrinology). ISBN 978-1588298300.

2. The Globe and Mail Website retrieved from http://www.theglobeandmail.com /life/health/new-health/paul-taylor/bpa-being-absorbed-from-canned-food-study /article2248262/

3. U.S. Department of Health & Human Services. Bisphenol A (BPA) Information for Parents; 15 January 2010 [cited 15 January 2010].

4. National Institute of Health website retrieved from http://ods.od.nih.gov /factsheets/Selenium-HealthProfessional/

5. The World's Healthiest Foods website retrieved from http://www.whfoods.com /genpage.php?dbid=95&tname=nutrient

Chapter Seven

1. National Organic Program | Agricultural Marketing Service | U.S. Department of Agriculture. (2013). Organic livestock requirements. Retrieved from http://www .ams.usda.gov/AMSv1.0/getfile?dDocName=STELPRDC5102526

2. United States Department of Agriculture, Agricultural Marketing Service 7 CFR Part 205. (2007). *Federal Register,* Vol. 72, No. 199, 58469. Retrieved from http:// www.ams.usda.gov/AMSv1.0/getfile?dDocName=STELPRDC5066629

3. United States Department of Agriculture, Agricultural Marketing Service (2007). United States standards for livestock and meat marketing claims, grass (forage) fed claim for ruminant livestock and the meat products derived from such livestock. *Federal Register*, Vol. 72, No. 199, 58631. Retrieved from http://www .ams.usda.gov/AMSv1.0/getfile?dDocName=STELPRDC5063842

4. Humane Farm Animal Care. Retrieved from http://www.certifiedhumane.org /index.php?page=standards

5. Humane Farm Animal Care. Retrieved from http://www.certifiedhumane.org /index.php?page=standards

6. Certified humane. Humane Farm Animal Care. Retrieved from http://www.certifiedhumane.org

7. Science based standards. American Humane Association. Retrieved from http://www.humaneheartland.org/our-standards

8. Animal Welfare Approved. Standards. Retrieved from http://www.animalwelfareapproved.org/standards/

9. Demeter Association, Inc. Mission. Retrieved from http://demeter-usa.org/about-demeter/

10. Demeter Association, Inc. Demeter biodynamic® farm and processing standards. Retrieved from http://demeter-usa.org/learn-more/biodynamic-farm-standard.asp

11. Demeter Association, Inc. Retrieved from http://demeter-usa.org/learn-more/animal-welfare.asp

12. European Commission Directorate-General XXIV Consumer Policy and Consumer Health Protection Directorate B - Scientific Health Opinions Unit B3 - Management of scientific committees II. (1999). Opinion of the scientific committee on veterinary measures relating to public health: assessment of potential risks to human health from hormone residues in bovine meat and meat products. Retrieved from http://ec.europa.eu/food/fs/sc/scv/out21_en.pdf

13. European Commission Directorate-General XXIV Consumer Policy and Consumer Health Protection Directorate B - Scientific Health Opinions Unit B3 - Management of scientific committees II. (1999). Opinion of the scientific committee on veterinary measures relating to public health: assessment of potential risks to human health from hormone residues in bovine meat and meat products. Retrieved from http://ec.europa.eu/food/fs/sc/scv/out21_en.pdf

14. Biro, F.M., et al. (2010). Pubertal assessment method and baseline characteristics in a mixed longitudinal study of girls. Retrieved from

http://pediatrics.aappublications.org/content/early/2010/08/09/peds.2009-3079. abstract

15. Latham, J.R., Wilson, A.K., Steinbrecher, R.A. (2006). The mutational consequences of plant transformation. *The Journal of Biomedicine and Biotechnology*, Vol. 2006, 1-7, doi:10.1155/JBB/2006/25376; Wilson, A.K., Latham, J.R., Steinbrecher, R.A. (December 2006). Transformation-induced mutations in transgenic plants: analysis and biosafety implications. *Biotechnology and Genetic Engineering Reviews*, Vol. 23. Retrieved from http://www.econexus.info/sites/econexus/files/ENx-BGER_vol23_2006.pdf

16. National Geographic Fukushima Fallout Not Affecting US Caught Fish. Retrieved from http://newswatch.nationalgeographic.com/2013/09/11/fukushima-fallout -not-affecting-u-s-caught-fish/

17. Bioremediation and tolerance of humans to heavy metals through microbial processes: a potential role for probiotics? Monachese, M., Burton, J.P., Reid, G. Retrieved from http://www.ncbi.nlm.nih.gov/pubmed/22798364

18. Food and Drug Administration. (2004). What you need to know about mercury in fish and shellfish. Retrieved from http://www.fda.gov/food/resourcesforyou /consumers/ucm110591.htm

19. Natural Resource Defense Council. (n.d.) Learn about mercury and its effects. Retrieved from http://www.nrdc.org/health/effects/mercury/effects.asp

20. Natural Resource Defense Council. (n.d.) Learn about mercury and its effects. Retrieved from http://www.nrdc.org/health/effects/mercury/effects.asp

21. Hites, R.A., Foran, J.A., Carpenter, D.O., Hamilton, M.C., Knuth, B.A., Schwager, S.J. (2004). Global assessment of organic contaminants in farmed salmon. *Science*, Vol. 303, No. 5655, 226-229. doi: 10.1126/science.1091447

22. United States Environmental Protection Agency, Office of Water, EPA 823-B-00-008. (2000). Guidance for assessing chemical contaminant data for use in fish

advisories: volume 2 risk assessment and fish consumption limits. Third edition. Retrieved from http://water.epa.gov/scitech/swguidance/fishshellfish /techguidance/risk/upload/2009_04_23_fish_advice_volume2_v2cover.pdf

23. Daniel, K.T. (2005). *The whole soy story: the dark side of America's favorite health food.* Warsaw, Indiana: NewTrends Publishing, Inc.

24. Commercial processed food may have endocrine-disrupting potential: soy-based ingredients making the difference. Omoruyi, I.M., Kabiersch, G., Pohjanvirta, R. Retrieved from http://www.ncbi.nlm.nih.gov/pubmed/23886479

25. Byrnes, S. (1999). The myths of vegetarianism. *The Ecologist*, Vol. 29, No. 4. Retrieved from http://www.theecologist.info/page14.html

26. Byrnes, S. (1999). The myths of vegetarianism. *The Ecologist*, Vol. 29, No. 4. Retrieved from http://www.theecologist.info/page14.html

Chapter Eight

1. U.S. National Library of Medicine/National Institutes of Health. (2003). Framingham study greatly overestimates the absolute coronary risk assigned to individuals in the United Kingdom. *PubMed.gov.* Retrieved from http://www.ncbi .nlm.nih.gov/pubmed/14644971

2. Sassi, F., Devaux, M. (2012). Obesity update 2012. Retrieved from Organization for Economic Co-operation and Development website://www.oecd.org/health/49716427. pdf

3. Matzinger, D., Degen, L., Drewe, J., Meuli, J. Duebendorfer, R., Ruckstuhl, N., D'Amato, M., Rovati, L., and Beglinger, C. (May, 2000). The role of long chain fatty acids in regulating food intake and cholecystokinin release in humans. Gut, 46(5): 688-693. doi:10.1136/gut.46.5.689

4. "You Can Control Your Cholesterol: A Guide to Low-Cholesterol Living." Merck & Co. Inc. Retrieved 2009-03-14.

5. Terés, S., Barceló-Coblijn, G., Benet, M.; Alvarez, R., Bressani, R., Halver, J.E., Escribá, P.V.(September 2008). Oleic acid content is responsible for the reduction in blood pressure induced by olive oil. *Proceedings of the National Academy of Sciences of the United States of America* 105 (37): 13811-6. doi:10.1073/pnas.0807500105

6. Kris-Etherton, P., Eckel, R.H., Howard, B.V., St. Jeor, S., Bazzare, T.L. (2001). AHA science advisory: Lyon diet heart study. *Circulation* 103:1823. Retrieved from American Heart Association http://circ.ahajournals.org /content/103/13/1823.full

7. Dewailly, E., Blanchet, C., Lemieux, S., Sauvé, L., Gingras, S., Ayotte, P., Holub, B.J.. (October, 2001) N-3 fatty acids and cardiovascular disease risk factors among the Inuit of Nunavik. *The American Journal of Clinical Nutrition*, 74(4):464-473. Retrieved from http://www.ncbi.nlm.nih.gov/pubmed/11566644

8. Iso, H. et al. (January 17, 2001). Intake of fish and omega-3 fatty acids and risk of stroke in women. The *Journal of the American Medical Association*, 285(3):304-312. Retrieved from http://jama.jamanetwork.com/article .aspx?articleid=193470

9. Mozaffarian, D., Pischon, T., Hankinson, S.E., Fifai, N., Joshipura, K., Willett, W.C., Rimm, E.B. (April, 2004). Dietary intake of trans fatty acids and systemic inflammation in women. *The American Journal of Clinical Nutrition*. 79(4), 606-12. Retrieved from http://www.ncbi.nlm.nih.gov/pubmed/15051604

10. Mann, D. (n.d.). Trans fats: the science and the risks. Retrieved from http://www .webmd.com/diet/features/trans-fats-science-and-risks

11. Harvard School of Public Health. (n.d.). Fats and cholesterol: out with the bad, in with the good. *The Nutrition Source.* Retrieved from http://www.hsph.harvard.edu/nutritionsource/what-should-you-eat/fats-full-story/index.html

12. Hu, F.B., van Dam, R.M., Liu, S. (July, 2001). "Diet and risk of type II diabetes: the role of types of fat and carbohydrate." Diabetologia 44 (7): 805-817. doi:10.1007/s001250100547

13. Health Canada and the Heart and Stroke Foundation of Canada Trans Fat Task Force (June, 2006). TRANSforming the food supply (Appendix 9iii). Retrieved from http://www.hc-sc.gc.ca/fn-an/nutrition/gras-trans-fats/tf-ge/tf-gt_rep-rap-eng.php

14. Gosline, A. (June 12, 2006). Why fast foods are bad, even in moderation. New Scientist. Retrieved http://www.newscientist.com/article/dn9318#.UnXbY43n_IU

15. Chavarro, J.E., Rich-Edwards, J.W., Rosner, B.A., and Willett, W.C. (January 2007). Dietary fatty acid intakes and the risk of ovulatory infertility. The American Journal of Clinical Nutrition, 85 (1): 231-237. Retrieved from http://ajcn.nutrition.org/content/85/1/231.abstract

16. Roan, S. (January 28, 2011). Food with bad fats linked to depression, study finds. Sydney Morning Herald. Sydney, Australia. Retrieved from http://www.smh.com.au/lifestyle/diet-and-fitness/food-with-bad-fats-linked-to-depression-study-finds-20110127-1a6vy.html

17. Food and Nutrition Board, Institute of Medicine of the National Academies. (2002/2005). Dietary reference intakes for energy, carbohydrates, fiber, fatty acids, cholesterol, protein and amino acids. Retrieved from http://www.nal.usda.gov/fnic/DRI//DRI_Energy/energy_full_report.pdf

18. Unified Agenda 0910-AC50. (2011). Food labeling: trans fatty acids in nutrition labeling; consumer research to consider nutrient content and health claims and

possible footnote or disclosure statements. *Federal Register,* Vol. 68, No. 133. Retrieved from http://federalregister.gov/r/0910-AC50

19. Retrieved from Stop Trans Fats website: http://www.stop-trans-fat.com/walter -willett.html

20. Retrieved from Stop Trans Fats website: http://www.stop-trans-fat.com/walter -willett.html

21. Retrieved from Ban Trans Fats website: http://bantransfats.com/theoreocase. html

22. Enig, M. Know Your Fats: The Complete Primer for Understanding the Nutrition of Fats, Oils and Cholesterol. Bethesda Press (2000)

23. Whigham, L.D., Watras, A.C., Schoeller, D.A. (January, 2007). Efficacy of conjugated linoleic acid for reducing fat mass: a meta-analysis in humans. *The American Journal of Clinical Nutrition.* 85 (5): 1203-11. Retrieved from http://www.ncbi.nlm.nih.gov/pubmed/17490954

24. Clement, L.P., Scimeca, J.A., Thompson, H.J. (August 1, 1994). Conjugated linoleic acid. A powerful anti-carcinogen from animal fat sources. Cancer 74 (3): 1050-4. doi:10.1002/1097-0142(19940801)74:3+<1050::AID-CNCR2820741512>3.0.CO;2-I.

25. Dhiman, T.R., Anand, G.R., Satter, L.D., Pariza, M.W. (2005). Factors affecting conjugated linoleic acid content in milk and meat. *Critical Reviews in Food Science and Nutrition,* 45(6):463-82. Taylor & Francis Online. Retrieved http://www.ncbi.nlm.nih.gov/pubmed/16183568

26. American Heart Association (Producer). (September 6, 2013). What your cholesterol levels mean. (Online Video) Retrieved from http://www.americanheart.org/presenter.jhtml?identifier=183#Triglyceride

27. Dopamine: Why It's So Hard to "Just Say No." Recovering from addiction is about healing mind, body and life. August 19, 2010. Smithstein, S. Retrieved from http://www.psychologytoday.com/blog/what-the-wild-things-are/201008/dopamine-why-its-so-hard-just-say-no

Chapter Nine

1. Veech, R.L. (2004). The therapeutic implications of ketone bodies: the effects of ketone bodies in pathological conditions: ketosis, ketogenic diet, redox states, insulin resistance, and mitochondrial metabolism. *Prostaglandins, Leukotrienes, and Essential Fatty Acids*, 70, 309-319.

2. Newport, M.T. *Alzheimer's Disease: What If There Was a Cure?* Basic Health Publications (2011).

3. Hooper, L., et al. (2004). Omega 3 fatty acids for prevention and treatment of cardiovascular disease. *Cochrane Database of Systematic Reviews*, CD003177. Retrieved from http://www.ncbi.nlm.nih.gov/pubmed/15495044

4. Balk, E.M., Lichtenstein, A.H., Chung, M., Kupelnick, B., Chew, P., Lau, J. (2006). Effects of omega-3 fatty acids on serum markers of cardiovascular disease risk: A systematic review. *Atherosclerosis*, 189(1):19-30. Retrieved from http://www.ncbi.nlm.nih.gov/pubmed/16530201

5. Hartweg, J., Farmer, A.J., Holman, R.R., Neil, A. (2009). Potential impact of omega-3 treatment on cardiovascular disease in type 2 diabetes. *Current Opinion in Lipidology*, (1):30-8. Retrieved from http://www.ncbi.nlm.nih.gov/pubmed/19133409

6. Berbert, A.A., Kondo, C.R., Almendra, C.L., Matsuo, T., Dichi, I. (2005). Supplementation of fish oil and olive oil in patients with rheumatoid arthritis. *Nutrition*, 21:131-6. Retrieved from http://www.ncbi.nlm.nih.gov/pubmed/15723739

7. Bahadori, B., Uitz, E., Thonhofer, R., Trummer, M., Pestemer-Lach, I., McCarty, M., Krejs, G.J. (2010). Omega-3 Fatty acids infusions as adjuvant therapy in rheumatoid arthritis. *Journal of Parenteral and Enteral Nutrition*, 34(2):151-5. Retrieved from http://www.ncbi.nlm.nih.gov/pubmed/20375422

8. Goldberg, R.J., Katz, J. (2007). A meta-analysis of the analgesic effects of omega-3 polyunsaturated fatty acid supplementation for inflammatory joint pain. *Pain*, 129(1-2):210-23. Retrieved from http://www.ncbi.nlm.nih.gov /pubmed/17335973

9. Dopheide, J.A., Pliszka, S.R. (2009). Attention-deficit-hyperactivity disorder: an update. *Pharmacotherapy*, 29(6):656-79. Retrieved from http://www.ncbi.nlm.nih. gov/pubmed/19476419

10. Aben, A., Danckaerts, M. (2010). Omega-3 and omega-6 fatty acids in the treatment of children and adolescents with ADHD. *Tijdschrift voor psychiatrie (Journal of Psychiatry)*, 52(2):89-97. Retrieved from http://www.ncbi.nlm.nih.gov /pubmed/19476419

11. Itomura, M., Hamazaki, K., Sawazaki, S., Kobayashi, M., Terasawa, K., Watanabe, S., Hamazaki, T. (2005). The effect of fish oil on physical aggression in schoolchildren—a randomized, double-blind, placebo-controlled trial. *Journal of Nutritional Biochemistry*, 16:163-71. Retrieved from http://www.ncbi.nlm.nih. gov/pubmed/15741051

12. Piert, M., Koeppe, R.A., Giordani, B., Berent, S., Kuhl, D.E. (1996). Diminished glucose transport and phosphorylation in Alzheimer's disease determined by dynamic FDG-PET. *The Journal of Nuclear Medicine*, Vol. 37 No. 2, 201-208. Retrieved from http://europepmc.org/abstract/MED/8667045/reload=0;jsessionid =Z9cPcZKjdvJoCbWPKXhR.50

13. Kim, E.J., et al. (2005) Glucose metabolism in early onset versus late onset Alzheimer's disease: an SPM analysis of 120 patients, *Brain*, Vol. 128, 1790-1801. Retrieved from http://www.ncbi.nlm.nih.gov/pubmed/15888536

14. Peppard, R.F., et al. (1992). Cerebral glucose metabolism in Parkinson's disease with and without dementia, *Archives of Neurology*, Vol. 49, No. 12. Retrieved from http://www.ncbi.nlm.nih.gov/pubmed/1449406

15. Kuwert, T., Lange, H.W., Langen, K.J., Herzog, H., Aulich, A., Feinendegen, L.E. (1990). Cortical and subcortical glucose consumption measured by PET in patients with Huntington's disease, *Brain*, Vol. 113, part 5, 1405-23. Retrieved from http://www.ncbi.nlm.nih.gov/pubmed/2147116

16. Guo, Z., Kindy, M.S., Kruman, I., Mattson, M.P. (2000) ALS-linked Cu/Zn-SOD mutation impairs cerebral synaptic glucose and glutamate transport and exacerbates ischemic brain injury, *Journal of Cerebral Blood Flow Metabolism*, Vol. 20, No. 3, 463-8. Retrieved from http://www.nature.com/jcbfm/journal/v20/n3/abs/9590900a.html

17. Henderson, S.T. (2008). Combinations of medium chain triglycerides and therapeutic agents for the treatment and prevention of Alzheimer's disease and other diseases resulting from reduced neuronal metabolism, U.S. Patent No. 20080009467-A1. Washington, D.C. Patent and Trademark Office.

18. Hasselbalch, S.G., Madsen, P.L., Hageman, L.P., Olsen, K.S., Justesen, N., Holm, S., Paulson, O.B. (1996) Changes in cerebral blood flow and carbohydrate metabolism during acute hyperketonemia. *American Journal of Physiology,* Vol. 270, E746-51. Retrieved from http://www.ncbi.nlm.nih.gov/pubmed/8967461

19. Veneman, T., Mitrakou, A., Mokan, M., Cryer, P., Gerich, J. (1994). Effect of hyperketonemia and hyperlacticacidemia on symptoms, cognitive dysfunction, and counterregulatory hormone responses during hypoglycemia in normal humans. *Diabetes,* 43:1311-7. Retrieved from http://www.ncbi.nlm.nih.gov/pubmed/7926305

20. CBNTV News. (2012). Coconut oil touted as Alzheimer's remedy. Retrieved from the Christian Broadcasting Network website http://www.cbn.com/tv/1472017228001

21. Red palm oil: nutritional, physiological and therapeutic roles in improving human wellbeing and quality of life. Oguntibeju, O.O., Esterhuyse, A.J., Truter, E.J. (2009). *British Journal of Biomedical Science,* 66(4):216-22. website http://www.ncbi.nlm.nih.gov/pubmed/20095133 accessed November 7, 2012

22. Sylvester, P.W., Kaddoumi, A., Nazzal, S., El Sayed, K.A. (2010). The value of tocotrienols in the prevention and treatment of cancer. *Journal of the American College of Nutrition*, Vol. 29, No. 3 Supplement 1 324S-333S. Retrieved from http://www.researchgate.net/journal/0731-5724_Journal_of_the_American_College _of_Nutrition

23. Oguntibeju, O.O., Esterhuyse, A.J., Truter, E.J. (2009). Red palm oil: nutritional, physiological and therapeutic roles in improving human wellbeing and quality of life. *British Journal of Biomedical Science*, 66(4):216-22. Retrieved from http://www.ncbi.nlm.nih.gov/pubmed/20095133

24. Oguntibeju, O.O., Esterhuyse, A.J., Truter, E.J. (2009). Red palm oil: nutritional, physiological and therapeutic roles in improving human wellbeing and quality of life. *British Journal of Biomedical Science*, 66(4):216-22. Retrieved from http://www.ncbi.nlm.nih.gov/pubmed/20095133

25. Oguntibeju, O.O., Esterhuyse, A.J., Truter, E.J. (2009). Red palm oil: nutritional, physiological and therapeutic roles in improving human wellbeing and quality of life. *British Journal of Biomedical Science*, 66(4):216-22. Retrieved from http://www.ncbi.nlm.nih.gov/pubmed/20095133

26. Unlu, Nuray Z. et al. Carotenoid Absorption from Salad and Salsa by Humans Is Enhanced by the Addition of Avocado or Avocado Oil. *Journal of Nutrition*, retrieved from http://jn.nutrition.org/content/135/3/431.full?sid=e79cee19-58ac -413b-93cf-07790cb15018

27. Diplock, A.T., Charleux, J.L., Crozier-Willi, G., Kok, F.J., Rice-Evans, C., Roberfroid, M., Stahl, W., Viña-Ribes, J. (1998). Functional food science and defence against reactive oxidative species. *British Journal of Nutrition* 1, 80, Suppl. 1, S77–S112. Retrieved from http://www.ncbi.nlm.nih.gov /pubmed/9849355

28. Bjelakovic G., et al. (2007). "Mortality in randomized trials of antioxidant supplements for primary and secondary prevention: systematic review and meta-analysis." *JAMA* 297 (8): 842–57. Retrieved from http://jama.jamanetwork.com/article.aspx?articleid=205797

29. Pruthi, S., Thompson, S.L., Novotny, P.J., Barton, D.L., Kottschade, L.A., Tan, A.D., Sloan, J.A., Loprinzi, C.L. (2007). Pilot evaluation of flaxseed for the management of hot flashes. *Journal of the Society for Integrative Oncology*, 5(3):106-12. Retrieved from http://www.ncbi.nlm.nih.gov/pubmed/17761129

Chapter Ten

1. Code of Federal Regulations Title 21, Vol. 2. (2013). Food and drugs; chapter 1–food and drug administration, department of health and human services, subchapter B: food for human consumption, part 129: processing and bottling of bottled drinking water. Retrieved from U.S. Food and Drug Administration website at http://www.accessdata.fda.gov/scripts/cdrh/cfdocs/cfCFR/CFRSearch.cfm?fr=129.3

2. Code of Federal Regulations Title 21, Vol. 2. (2013). Food and drugs; chapter 1–food and drug administration, department of health and human services, subchapter B: food for human consumption, part 129: processing and bottling of bottled drinking water. Retrieved from the U.S. Food and Drug Administration website at http://www.accessdata.fda.gov/scripts/cdrh/cfdocs/cfCFR/CFRSearch.cfm?fr=129.3

3. Code of Federal Regulations Title 21, Vol. 2. (2013). Food and drugs; chapter 1–food and drug administration, department of health and human services, subchapter B: food for human consumption, part 129: processing and bottling of bottled drinking water. Retrieved from the U.S. Food and Drug Administration website at http://www.accessdata.fda.gov/scripts/cdrh/cfdocs/cfCFR/CFRSearch.cfm?fr=165.110&SearchTerm=bottled%20water

4. Code of Federal Regulations Title 21, Vol. 2 (2013): Food and drugs; chapter 1–food and drug administration, department of health and human services, subchapter B: food for human consumption, part 129: processing and bottling of bottled drinking water. Retrieved from the U.S. Food and Drug Administration website at http://www .accessdata.fda.gov/scripts/cdrh/cfdocs/cfCFR/CFRSearch.cfm?fr=129.3

5. Code of Federal Regulations Title 21, Vol. 2 (2013): Food and drugs; chapter 1–food and drug administration, department of health and human services, subchapter B: food for human consumption, part 129: processing and bottling of bottled drinking water. Retrieved from U.S. Food and Drug Administration website http://www.accessdata.fda .gov/scripts/cdrh/cfdocs/cfCFR/CFRSearch.cfm?fr=129.3

6. Code of Federal Regulations Title 21, Vol. 2 (2013): Food and drugs; chapter 1–food and drug administration, department of health and human services, subchapter B: food for human consumption, part 129: processing and bottling of bottled drinking water. Retrieved from U.S. Food and Drug Administration website http://www.accessdata.fda .gov/scripts/cdrh/cfdocs/cfCFR/CFRSearch.cfm?fr=129.3

7. Meier, B. (1990, April 19). Perrier to bow to F.D.A. and change label. *The New York Times.* Retrieved from http://www.nytimes.com/1990/04/19/business/company-news -perrier-to-bow-to-fda-and-change-label.html

8. Code of Federal Regulations Title 21, Vol. 2 (2013): Food and drugs; chapter 1–food and drug administration, department of health and human services, subchapter B: food for human consumption, part 129: processing and bottling of bottled drinking water. Retrieved from U.S. Food and Drug Administration website http://www.accessdata.fda .gov/scripts/cdrh/cfdocs/cfCFR/CFRSearch.cfm?fr=129.3

9. Gleick, P.H. (2004). From the world's water, the biennial report on freshwater resources: 2004-2005. Washington, D.C.: Island Press.

10. Lebwohl, B. (2010, August). Peter Gleick with more reasons to stop drinking bottled water. Retrieved from the Fast Company website at http://www.fastcompany.com/1678595/peter-gleick-with-more-reasons-to-stop-drinking-bottled-water

11. Ziobro, P. (2011, May 24). Nestle raises bottled water prices nearly 10%. *The Wall Street Journal.* Retrieved from http://www.marketwatch.com/story/nestle-raises-bottled-water-prices-nearly-10-2011-05-24

12. Creating shared value report. (2012). Retrieved from the Nestle Waters North America website at http://www.nestle-watersna.com/en/csv/corporate-citizenship-report

13. McDonald, D. (2008, November 11). Nestle bottles, sells filtered Framingham tap water. *The Metrowest Daily News.* Retrieved from the *Metrowest Daily News* website at http://www.metrowestdailynews.com/news/x947780042/Nestle-bottles-sells-filtered-Framingham-tap-water?photo=0

14. Reuters. (2007, July 27). Aquafina labels to spell out source—tap water. Retrieved from the CNN website at http://www.cnn.com/2007/HEALTH/07/27/pepsico.aquafina.reut/

15. Soft drink is purified tap. (2004, March 1). Retrieved from the BBC News website at http://news.bbc.co.uk/2/hi/uk_news/3523303.stm

16. Olson, E.D. (2013). *Bottled Water: Pure Drink or Pure Hype?* Retrieved from the National Resources Defense Council website at http://www.nrdc.org/water/drinking/bw/chap3.asp

17. U.S. Government Accountability Office Report to Congressional Requesters. (2009, June). Bottled water: FDA safety and consumer protections are often less stringent than comparable EPA protections for tap water. Retrieved from http://www.gao.gov/new.items/d09610.pdf

18. U.S. Environmental Protection Agency. (n.d.). Statistics on the management of used and end-of-life electronics. Retrieved from http://www.epa.gov/epawaste/conserve/materials/ecycling/manage.htm

19. Wills, A. (2010). Recycling to-go plastics. Retrieved from the Earth911 website at http://earth911.com/news/2010/06/21/recycling-to-go-plastics/

20. Press release: Reinvigorated bottled water bounces back from recessionary years. Retrieved from the Beverage Marketing Corp. website at http://beveragemarketing.com/news/viewnews.asp?newsID=220

21. Potera, C. (2002). The price of bottled water. *Environmental Health Perspectives*, 110 (2). Retrieved from http://www.ncbi.nlm.nih.gov/pmc/articles/PMC1240751/

22. Shermer, M. (2003). Bottled twaddle. *Scientific American*, 289 (1). Retrieved from http://www.scientificamerican.com/article.cfm?id=bottled-twaddle

23. Fact Sheet Bottled Water and Energy Fact Sheet: Getting to 17 Million Barrels. Retrieved from the Pacific Institute website at http://www.pacinst.org/publication/bottled-water-fact-sheet/

24. Gitlitz, J., Franklin, P. (2007). Water, water everywhere: The growth of non-carbonated beverages in the United States. Retrieved from the Container Recycling Institute website at http://www.container-recycling.org/assets/pdfs/reports/2007-waterwater.pdf

25. Sax, L. (2010). Polyethylene Terephthalate may yield endocrine disruptors. *Environmental Health Perspective* 118:445-448. Retrieved from http://ehp.niehs.nih.gov/0901253/

26. Tukur, A., Sharp, L., Stern, B., Tizaoui, C., Benkreira, H. (2012). PET bottle use patterns and antimony migration into bottled water and soft drinks: the case of British and Nigerian bottles. *Journal of Environmental Monitoring*, 14(4): 1237-47. Retrieved from http://www.ncbi.nlm.nih.gov/pubmed/22402759

27. Dabrowska, A., Borcz, A., Nawrocki, J. (2003). Aldehyde contamination of mineral water stored in PET bottles. *Food Additives and Contaminants*, Vol. 20, No. 12, pp. 1170-77. Retrieved from http://www.tandfonline.com/doi/citedby/10.1080/02652030310001620441#tabModule

28. Westerhoff, P., Prapaipong, P., Shock, E., Hillaireau, A. (2008). Antimony leaching from polyethylene terephthalate (PET) plastic used for bottled drinking water. *Water Research*, 42(3):551-6. Retrieved from https://www.ncbi.nlm.nih.gov/pubmed/17707454

29. CFR - Code of Federal Regulations Title 21. Food and Drugs, Chapter I, Part 165 - Beverages, Subpart B - Requirements for Specific Standardized Beverages, Sec. 165.110 Bottled water. Retrieved from U.S. Department of Health and Human Services website at http://www.accessdata.fda.gov/scripts/cdrh/cfdocs/cfcfr/CFRSearch. cfm?fr=165.110

Resources & Recommended Reading

Resources and Recommended Reading Chapter 1

Practicing the Power of Now: Essential Teachings, Meditations and Exercises from the Power of Now by Eckhart Tolle, New World Library. (September 2001)

The Biology of Belief: Unleashing the Power of Consciousness, Matter and Miracles by Bruce H. Lipton, Hay House. (2007)

Nourishing Traditions: The Cookbook that Challenges Politically Correct Nutrition and the Diet Dictocrats by Sally Fallon and Mary Enig, Newtrends Publishing, Inc. (Second Edition, 2003)

Nutrition and Physical Degeneration by Weston A. Price, D.D.S, Price-Pottenger Nutrition Foundation. (Eighth Edition, 2008)

Resources and Recommended Reading Chapter 2

Empty Pleasures: The Story of Artificial Sweeteners from Saccharin to Splenda by Carolyn de la Pena, The University of North Carolina Press. (2010)

The Bitter Truth About Artificial Sweeteners by Dennis W. Remington, MD, and Barbara W. Higa, RD, Vitality House International. (First Edition, 1987)

United States Food and Drug Administration website: www.fda.gov

Prescription for Nutritional Healing by James and Phyllis Balch, Avery Trade. (Fifth revision, updated edition, 2010).

Resources and Recommended Reading Chapter 3

The Environmental Working Group website: http://www.ewg.org

Resources and Recommended Reading Chapter 4

Essentials of Food Science by Vickie A. Vaclavik and Elizabeth W. Christian, Springer Science + Business Media. (2008)

Sprouts, The Miracle Food by Steve Meyerowitz, Sproutman Publications. (1999)

Reducing Phytic Acid in Your Food: A Visual Analysis of the Research on Home Kitchen Remedies for Phytic Acid by Amanda Rose, Ph.D. White paper. http://www.rebuildmarket .com/phytic-acid/

Mountain Rose Herbs website: www.mountainroseherbs.com

Living Nutz website: http://www.livingnutz.com

Resources and Recommended Reading Chapter 5

Institute for Responsible Technology website: http://www.responsibletechnology.org

Environmental Working Group website: http://www.ewg.org

Blue Mountain Organics website: http://www.bluemountainorganics.com

Sprout People website: http://sproutpeople.org

Resources and Recommended Reading Chapter 7

American Humane Association, 1400 16th Street NW, Suite 360, Washington, D.C. 20036

Animal Welfare Approved, 1007 Queen Street, Alexandria, VA 22314

Electronic Code of Federal Regulations, www.ecfr.gov

Food Processing Handbook edited by James Brennan. Published by Wiley-VCH; Two-Volume Set Edition (Second Edition, December 19, 2011)

Humane Farm Animal Care Organization, P.O. Box 727, Herndon, VA 20172

The Natural Resource Defense Council (NRDC), www.nrdc.org

SELF Nutrition Data, www.nutritiondata.self.com

The Whole Soy Story: The Dark Side of America's Favorite Health Food by Kaayla T. Daniel, Ph.D. Publisher: NewTrends Publishing, Inc., (First Edition, March 10, 2005)

The World's Healthiest Foods: Essential Guide for the Healthiest Way of Eating by George Mateljan. Publisher: World's Healthiest Foods (First Edition, July 18, 2006)

United States Food and Drug Administration (USDA), www.fda.gov

USDA Nutrient Database for Standard Reference, Release 19

World Society for the Protection of Animals, http://www.wspa-international.org

Resources and Recommended Reading Chapter 8

Bailey's Industrial Oil and Fat Products, Volumes 1-6. Fereidoon Shahidi, Editor. John Wiley & Sons. (Sixth Edition, 2005)

Principles of Food Chemistry by John DeMan. Springer-Verlag Publishers (Third Edition, 1999)

The Lipid Handbook by F.D. Gunstone, John L. Harwood, Fred B. Padley. Chapman & Hall Publishers (1986)

Know Your Fats: The Complete Primer for Understanding the Nutrition of Fats, Oils and Cholesterol by Mary Enig, PhD. Bethesda Press (2000)

The Cholesterol Conspiracy by Ladd McNamara, M.D., OrthoMolecular Medicine, Inc. Publishers (2006)

The Cholesterol Controversy by Edward Robert Pinckney, Cathey Pinckney. Sherbourne Press (1973)

Fats That Heal, Fats That Kill by Udo Erasmus, Alive Books (1993)

Resources and Recommended Reading Chapter 10

The World's Water, The Biennial Report on Freshwater Resources: 2004-2005. Island Press © 2004 Pacific Institute, www.worldwater.org Peter H. Gleick

United States Code of Federal Regulations 21, Bottled Water Web (2003)

Binnie, Chris, Kimber, Martin, & Smethurst, George. *Basic Water Treatment*. London: Thomas Telford Ltd. (Third edition, 2002).

Vigneswaran, S. & Visvanathan, C. *Water Treatment Processes: Simple Options*. Boca Raton, Florida: CRC Press (1995).

Nutritional Therapy Association, Inc. PO Box 354, Olympia, WA 98507

Celtic Sea Salt at www.celticseasalt.com

Bottled and Sold: The Story Behind Our Obsession with Bottled Water by Peter Gleick. Island Press (First Edition, 2011)

Water the Ultimate Cure by Steve Meyerowitz. Book Publishing Company (2000)

A Consumer's Dictionary of Food Additives: Descriptions in Plain English of More Than 12,000 Ingredients Both Harmful and Desirable Found in Foods by Ruth Winter. Random House LLC. (Seventh Edition, 2009)

Books by F. Batmanghelidj, MD:

Your Body's Many Cries for Water
Water: the Shocking Truth that Can Save Your Life
Water: For Health, for Healing, for Life: You're Not Sick, You're Thirsty!
ABC of Asthma, Allergies & Lupus: Eradicate Asthma—Now!
How to Deal with Back Pain and Rheumatoid Joint Pain
Water Cures; Drugs Kill: How Water Cured Incurable Diseases
Obesity Cancer Depression: Their Common Cause & Natural Cure

Index

Bold numbers indicate recipes.

Recipes Index

GOOD DECISIONS ... *Most of the Time*

Notes

Notes